THE PRESS UWI BIOGRAPHY SERIES

Douglas Hall, *Editor*

The Press University of the West Indies invites the submission of work to be considered for publication in this biography series. We recognize the need to record the lives and achievements of people of the Caribbean, but we would not exclude biographical account of expatriates who have lived and worked long and hard with us to our mutual advantage.

The series will not be limited to accounts of those who, by whatever means, have achieved wide acclaim or notoriety. Far more numerous than the famous are the many individuals who by stern and skillful performance in the fields, the workshops, the marketplaces, and in the service of their compatriots have contributed much but remain unrecognized. This series also accounts for them, and is dedicated to the solid contributions of the unsung.

1   A Man Divided: Michael Garfield Smith
Jamaican Poet and Anthropologist 1921–1993
DOUGLAS HALL

2   Law, Justice and Empire
The Colonial Career of John Gorrie 1829–1892
BRIDGET M. BRERETON

3   White Rebel
The Life and Times of TT Lewis
GARY LEWIS

4   Demerara Doctor
Confessions and Reminiscences of a Self-taught Physician
GEORGE GIGLIOLI

Atholl Edwin Seymour ("TT") Lewis in 1946

WHITE REBEL

The Life and Times of TT Lewis

Gary Lewis

THE PRESS UNIVERSITY OF THE WEST INDIES
Barbados • Jamaica • Trinidad and Tobago

The Press University of the West Indies
1A Aqueduct Flats Mona
Kingston 7 Jamaica W I

© 1999 by Gary Lewis
All rights reserved. Published 1999
Printed in Canada
ISBN 976-640-043-1

03 02 01 00 99   5 4 3 2 1

CATALOGUING IN PUBLICATION DATA

Lewis, Gary
    White rebel : the life and times of TT Lewis /
    Gary Lewis.

    p. cm. (The Press UWI Biography Series)

    ISBN 976-640-043-1
    1. Lewis, Atholl Edwin Seymour. 2. Barbados – Politics
    and government. 3. Barbados – Biography. 4. Politicians
    – Barbados – Biography. I. Title.
    F2041.83.L4W55 1999   972.981 dc 20

Set in 10.5/13.75 Garamond x 27 picas
Book and cover design by Karen L. Collins

Cover illustration: Rex Dixon, "Joker", 1989
Acrylic on canvas – 25" x 20" (63.5 x 50.8 cm)
Collection – the artist

Back cover photograph:
Photograph of TT and supporters following the
announcement of the 1946 election results –
reprinted courtesy of Sonya Lawrence

WHITE REBEL

The Life and Times of TT Lewis

Gary Lewis

THE PRESS UNIVERSITY OF THE WEST INDIES
Barbados • Jamaica • Trinidad and Tobago

The Press University of the West Indies
1A Aqueduct Flats Mona
Kingston 7 Jamaica W I

© 1999 by Gary Lewis
All rights reserved. Published 1999
Printed in Canada
ISBN 976-640-043-1

03 02 01 00 99   5 4 3 2 1

CATALOGUING IN PUBLICATION DATA

Lewis, Gary
   White rebel : the life and times of TT Lewis /
Gary Lewis.

   p. cm. (The Press UWI Biography Series)

   ISBN 976-640-043-1
   1. Lewis, Atholl Edwin Seymour. 2. Barbados – Politics
and government. 3. Barbados – Biography. 4. Politicians
– Barbados – Biography. I. Title.
   F2041.83.L4W55 1999   972.981 dc 20

Set in 10.5/13.75 Garamond x 27 picas
Book and cover design by Karen L. Collins

Cover illustration: Rex Dixon, "Joker", 1989
Acrylic on canvas – 25" x 20" (63.5 x 50.8 cm)
Collection – the artist

Back cover photograph:
Photograph of TT and supporters following the
announcement of the 1946 election results –
reprinted courtesy of Sonya Lawrence

CONTENTS

List of Photographs	*vii*
List of Tables and Charts	*x*
Foreword	*xi*
Preface	*xiii*
Acknowledgments	*xiv*
List of Abbreviations	*xv*
Brief Notes on the Interviewees Quoted	*xvi*
Introduction: The Search for TT Lewis	*xx*

CHAPTER ONE
Origins — *1*

CHAPTER TWO
The Formative Years — *24*

CHAPTER THREE
In the Freemasonic Brotherhood — *43*

CHAPTER FOUR
The Early Years in Politics — *57*

CHAPTER FIVE
With the Congress Party — *87*

CHAPTER SIX
The Clerks' Union — *110*

CHAPTER SEVEN
Prelude to the Storm — *122*

CONTENTS

CHAPTER EIGHT
The Lewis Demonstration   *136*

CHAPTER NINE
Later Years with the Barbados Labour Party   *149*

CHAPTER TEN
Life and Death with the
Democratic Labour Party   *168*

CHAPTER ELEVEN
TT Lewis: An Assessment   *183*

APPENDIXES

APPENDIX ONE
Barbados: Geographical Location   *192*

APPENDIX TWO
The City of Bridgetown (1948):
Tramping Ground of TT Lewis   *193*

APPENDIX THREE
Barbadian Constitutional Structure   *194*

APPENDIX FOUR
Barbados Election Results   *197*

APPENDIX FIVE
The Changed Colour Composition of the House   *203*

APPENDIX SIX
Family Names of the Barbadian White Elite in the 1920s   *204*

BIBLIOGRAPHY   *206*

INDEX   *208*

LIST OF PHOTOGRAPHS

All charts, diagrams and other graphics produced in this book were prepared by the author. All photographs unless otherwise specified were taken by the author.

The reason for depicting many of the interviewees in a "before" and "after" photographic sequence is to give the reader a sense of linkage to the past. By using a current visual impression of the speaker and juxtaposing it with a comparable image of that same individual during the period under discussion, readers should more easily be able to project themselves back into the days when TT Lewis lived.

Photograph	Page No.	Photograph	Page No.
A.E.S. ("TT") Lewis in 1946 (courtesy of Sonya Lawrence)	ii	Lewis with Frank Collymore (courtesy of Ellice Collymore)	26
Ellice Collymore (1935) (courtesy of Ellice Collymore)	2	Stage actor (courtesy of Ellice Collymore)	27
Ellice Collymore (1992)	2	Lewis with water polo team (courtesy of Ellice Collymore)	28
Airy Hill plantation yard	3	Lewis with Pickwick Cricket Club (courtesy of Pickwick Cricket Club)	30
Evelyn "Bunghee" Edghill (1940s) (courtesy of Robin Edghill)	10	Lewis with St Ann's Cricket Club (courtesy of Hammond Burke)	31
Edghill with sons (1995)	11		
TT Lewis aged 13 (courtesy of Sonya Lawrence)	14	Scene from the 1937 riots (courtesy of Richard Goddard)	33
Office boy (courtesy of Sonya Lawrence)	16	Barbados Volunteer Force members (courtesy of Barbados Department of Archives)	34
New recruit (courtesy of Sonya Lawrence)	17	The Barbados Literary and Debating Society news clipping (courtesy of *Barbados Advocate*)	36
Lewis in his early twenties (courtesy of Sonya Lawrence)	19	Lewis with the Perryman twins (courtesy of Ellice Collymore)	37
Lewis with Donald Wiles (courtesy of Ellice Collymore)	24	Constance Younglao (1992)	38
Lewis with tennis players (courtesy of Ellice Collymore)	25	Marrying Marge Perryman (1937) (courtesy of Ellice Collymore)	39

Photograph	Page No.	Photograph	Page No.
Wedding photograph (1937) (courtesy of Ellice Collymore)	40	Sir Grattan Bushe (courtesy of Barbados National Trust)	99
Survivor: Donald Wiles (1993)	40	Assisting in the 1946 election count (courtesy of *Barbados Advocate*)	101
Lewis and Marge with Sonya (1938) (courtesy of Ellice Collymore)	41	BLP supporters in the 1946 election (courtesy of *Barbados Advocate*)	102
Major Rudolph Daniel (1992)	49	Grantley Adams (1940s) (courtesy of *Barbados Annual Review*)	102
Detail of Victoria Lodge Master's Roll (1936)	51	Lewis winning the 1946 election (courtesy of Sonya Lawrence)	103
Victoria Lodge (1995)	52		
N.G.D. Atwell (1995)	53	Barbados Clerks' Union (1945) (courtesy of Chris St John)	111
H.A. Vaughn (1930s) (courtesy of *Barbados Annual Review*)	59	Irwin Burke (1992)	112
BEA campaign advertisement (courtesy of *Barbados Advocate*)	61	Vincent St John (courtesy of *Barbados Annual Review*)	112
E.L. "Jimmy" Cozier (1940s) (courtesy of *Barbados Annual Review*)	62	Charlie Thomas (courtesy of *Barbados Annual Review*)	112
E.L. "Jimmy" Cozier (1980s) (courtesy of *Barbados Advocate*)	62	Frank Walcott (1940s) (courtesy of *Barbados Annual Review*)	113
Herbert Dowding (1946) (courtesy of Herbert Dowding)	63	Frank Walcott (1993)	113
Herbert Dowding (1995)	63	Hammond Burke (1942) (courtesy of Hammond Burke)	114
Slum tenement in 1940s Bridgetown (West India Royal Commission Report, July 1945, HMSO, London)	68	Hammond Burke (1992)	114
		Christie Smith (1940s) (courtesy of *Barbados Annual Review*)	116
Cecil Hutchinson (1992)	68	Christie Smith (late 1980s) (courtesy of *Barbados Advocate*)	116
Owen T. Allder (1940s) (courtesy of *Barbados Annual Review*)	69	Ronnie Hughes (1940s) (courtesy of Ronnie Hughes)	119
Owen T. Allder (1992)	69	Ronnie Hughes (1993)	119
J.T.C. Ramsay (1940s) (courtesy of *Barbados Annual Review*)	70	J.P. Coats, Clarke and Co. threadworks (courtesy of Coats Ltd, UK)	127
Barbadians with Royal Air Force during World War II (courtesy of *Barbados Annual Review*)	76	Shirland Medford (1992)	129
Trevor Gale (1940s) (courtesy of *Barbados Annual Review*)	81	Staff of the Central Agency (1946) (courtesy of Sonya Lawrence)	130
Trevor Gale (1992)	81	Andrew Christine (1992)	133
Wynter Crawford (1930s) (courtesy of *Barbados Annual Review*)	88	Big Torch Light Demonstration news clipping (courtesy of *Barbados Advocate*)	137
Wynter Crawford (1980s) (courtesy of *Barbados Advocate*)	88	Lewis and Adams during the march (courtesy of Sonya Lawrence)	138
A.E.S. ("TT") Lewis (1946) (courtesy of Sonya Lawrence)	97	Marchers on Hincks Street (courtesy of Sonya Lawrence)	138
E.D. Mottley (1940s) (courtesy of *Barbados Annual Review*)	97	Marchers (with Allder quote) (courtesy of *Sunday Guardian*, Trinidad)	139

List of Photographs

Photograph	Page No.
Marchers (with Burke quote) (courtesy of Sonya Lawrence)	140
Laurence Small (1945) (courtesy of Chris St John)	141
Father Laurence Small (1992)	141
Marchers (with Marshall quote) (courtesy of *Barbados Advocate*)	142
Freddie Miller (1940s) (courtesy of *Barbados Annual Review*)	143
Lewis, Adams and Walcott during the march (courtesy of Sir Alexander Hoyos)	144
H.N. "Turk" Rogers (1993)	148
E.K. Walcott (1930s) (courtesy of *Barbados Annual Review*)	151
House of Assembly members (ca. 1948–51) (courtesy of Sonya Lawrence)	154
Alexander Hoyos (1940s) (courtesy of *Barbados Annual Review*)	156
Sir Alexander Hoyos (1993)	156
Ronald Mapp (1940s) (courtesy of *Barbados Annual Review*)	162
Sir Ronald Mapp (1992)	162
Barbados' first cabinet (1954) (courtesy of *Barbados Annual Review*)	163
J. Cameron Tudor (1940s) (courtesy of *Barbados Annual Review*)	164
Sir James Tudor (1992)	164
Lewis with bicycle (with Brancker quote) (courtesy of Sonya Lawrence)	166
Frederick Smith (1950s) (courtesy of *Barbados Annual Review*)	169
Sir Frederick Smith (1995)	169
Lewis sick in bed (with Burke quote) (courtesy of Sonya Lawrence)	170
Errol Barrow (1950s) (courtesy of *Barbados Annual Review*)	172
Lewis with daughters (mid 1950s) (courtesy of Sonya Lawrence)	178
Sonya and Diana (1993)	179
Last photograph of Lewis (courtesy of Sonya Lawrence)	180
Lewis' headstone (with Weatherhead quote) (taken by Sonya Lawrence)	181
John Wickham (1992)	184
Tony Hinds (1940s) (courtesy of Tony Hinds)	185
Tony Hinds (1995)	185
Hugh Springer (1940s) (courtesy of *Barbados Annual Review*)	185
Sir Hugh Springer (1992)	185

LIST OF TABLES AND CHARTS

Freemasonic Lodges in Barbados	47
1942 Election: Strange Faces in the Assembly	71
1944 Election: The Swing Towards Labour	90
1946 Election: Bushe and the First Labour Government	100
1948 Election: BLP Ascendancy	125
Purview of a Travelling Salesman	132
1951 Election: Universal Adult Suffrage Arrives	158
1956 Election: Emergence of the DLP	171

FOREWORD

Biography can be seen as a durable bridge between scholarship and the popular audience because its comprehensive look at one actor can enhance comprehension of the complexities of the particular period of which he or she is a part. In Barbados (and the Anglophone Caribbean) where an indigenous popular literature barely predates political independence and where the popular audience needs every stimulus for its subsistence, publication of biography (and autobiography) is especially important. Biographies of the giants of the political and professional scene (of individuals such as Norman and Michael Manley, Grantley and Tom Adams, Alexander Bustamante, Eric Williams, Errol Barrow, Arthur Lewis, H.O.B. Wooding, et al.), apart from purveying easily accessible information, offer opportunities for a vicarious participation in great events and provide the substance for the creation of role models. Biographies of less prominent men and women carry significance as well: these may operate as more fully open windows on the historical action because the power of the personalities and the range of activities that they describe are unlikely to dwarf the reconstruction. Biography, therefore, can comfortably take historical reconstruction beyond the doctoral dissertation and the monograph into the realm of popular education.

White Rebel is in this context important for a number of reasons. First, it is a contribution to the recent political history of Barbados. The three decades from the 1930s to the 1950s were the most turbulent and socially productive in the postslavery experience of the island. They witnessed the campaign for political inclusion fought through popular skirmishes and industrial action, experimentation with socialist ideology, protoparty political organization, mass political mobilization, and muted nationalist assertion. *White Rebel* offers a perspective on all this, and fills out the record in some important particulars. It is the best guide to the electoral history of the period because it provides the detailed information on electoral contests that cannot be found in the work of F.A. Hoyos and Patrick Emmanuel. It concisely describes the rise and fall of various political groupings, and charts the migrations of many politicians to and from political parties. Most important, *White Rebel* brings on stage a variety of main and bit players who, pressed into service to provide recollections to fill out the slender archival record, do furnish important sidelights on the career of "TT" Lewis and at the same time, sometimes unwittingly, call attention to their own activities.

The second important characteristic of *White Rebel* is the portrait of Barbadian society that it presents. It may not be too wild an exaggeration to suggest that, both at the level of folk wisdom and informed commentary, the factor of race has confused the perception of the social structure of Barbados. Put simply, the impression seems to exist that the pervasiveness of notions of white supremacy has resulted in an attenuated social structure. Whites and nonwhites, it is alleged, do not constitute the same social classes: nonwhites are clearly stratified; but differentiation in wealth, education and professional standing among whites is merely a temporary condition because white solidarity ensures upward mobility for *all* whites. In this scenario, the poorest whites, the so-called "Redlegs" of the sea-coasts, are, like gypsies, aberrations, not always meriting social categorization. *White Rebel* confronts these simplistic notions and, by documenting stratification inside the white segment of society, fully reveals the complexities in the Barbadian social structure. In this regard, Gary Lewis, by demonstrating that class analysis can be applied to Barbados, makes a contribution to Caribbean social history. He joins Karl Watson and Howard Johnson in restarting work on what had become a social group somewhat neglected by historians.

The third important aspect of *White Rebel* is the depiction of its subject inside a particular social context. This is a story of that rarity in politics, a man of principle. But what is particularly fascinating about the story is that the man of principle is a *white* politician, socialist in orientation, who lives his life and practises his politics in full accord with his ideological convictions. His life – private life, political and professional career – therefore constitutes a tragedy because its content, representing a major contradiction in Barbadian society, imposed an extreme and perpetual vulnerability. "TT" Lewis was characterized as a traitor and restricted in gainful employment by those to whom he was tied by racial ancestry; but he was never always certain of his reception among those whom he saw as his natural allies, to whom he was drawn by ideological conviction and active social conscience. *White Rebel* is therefore valuable social history because it highlights those obdurate issues that must surround the conversion of racially bifurcated communities into genuinely multiracial societies.

Woodville K. Marshall, Pro Vice Chancellor
Professor of History, University of the West Indies, Cave Hill, Barbados
January 1999

PREFACE

The compilation of *White Rebel* took place over a period of four years (1991–95). The amount of full-time effort required was well over an entire year. The interviews were conducted, naturally, in Barbados. The compilation and writing was done in Barbados, Scotland, Austria and Pakistan – places I happened to be working or spending time during those four years. Since *White Rebel* was very much under construction during the arrival of each of our three children, you could say that it accompanied them into this world. The patter of little feet and the seemingly endless cycle of feeding, crying and nappy changing that robbed me of sleep and concentration, hopefully also allowed me to bring to the book my own sense of what is real in life and what matters. Readers will therefore appreciate why, for their understanding, tolerance and support, I choose to dedicate this book to my three little girls Ria, Phoebe and Sarah and to their patient, long-suffering and devoted mother, Elizabeth.

December 1995

ACKNOWLEDGMENTS

My most sincere thanks to those who helped with their advice and support. In Barbados: Ronnie Hughes, Ralph Jemmott and Henry Fraser. Juana Franklin of the Barbados Registry. Christine Matthews (Chief Archivist) and David Williams (Archivist) at the Barbados Department of Archives. Edwin Ifill (retired Deputy Director), June Ward (former acting Deputy Director) and the Staff of the Barbados National Library Service (better known as the Barbados Reference Library). Andrew Williams and the Library Staff at the *Barbados Daily Nation* newspaper. Ray Winstone of the Barbados Census Office. Carlisle Best at the Reference Library of the University of the West Indies (Cave Hill). In Jamaica: Karen Collins for her care and attention to detail in working with me to produce the desired look and finish, Pansy Benn for running with this project through to actual production. In Austria: Wolfgang Schiefer, Kourosh Entekhabi and Thomas Pietschmann. In Pakistan: Chris van der Burgh.

The names of all interviewees are listed below. Their patience and the lively detail with which they recounted to me their memories of Barbados past is greatly appreciated: Owen Allder, Warren Alleyne, Geoffrey Armstrong, N.D.G Atwell, Seymour Beckles, Stanley Blanchette, J.E.T. Bourne, Theodore Brancker, Ursuila Brathwaite, Carlton Burke, Hammond Burke, Irwin Burke, Peter Campbell, Louie Carrington, Robert Cecil, J.W. Chandler, Sybil Chenery, Andrew Christine, John Cole, Ellice Collymore, Maggie Cozier, Wynter Crawford, H.N. Daniel, Sybil Davis, Keeling Davis, Jack Dear, Herbert Dowding, Evelyn Edghill, Velery Evelyn, Euchard Fitzpatrick, Elsie Foster, Mike Foster, Trevor Gale, Tony Gale, Marjorie Haynes, Perlita Hinds, Tony Hinds, Gladstone Holder, Alexander Hoyos, Ronnie Hughes, Cecil Hutchinson, Lionel Hutchinson, Penelope Hynam, Betty Jones, Bob King, Joe King, Sonya Lawrence, Douglas Lynch, Ronald Mapp, Vernon Marshall, Shirland Medford, H.N. Niblock, Alfred Pragnell, Laurence Quintyne, Aubrey Roberts, Dolly Roett, Turk Rogers, Peter Ross, Diana Sanchez, Rosita Scott, Bucky Seale, Lisle Sealy, Laurence Small, Christie Smith, Frederick Smith, Kathleen Smitten, Hugh Springer, Mickey Stoute, Edwy Talma, Charlie Taylor, James Tudor, Frank Walcott, Michael Walcott, June Ward, Wayne Ward, Karl Watson, Edna Weatherhead, Noel Weatherhead, Pedro Welch, John Wickham, Donald Wiles, Dudley Wiles, Constance Younglao.

Naturally, any errors of judgement, reasoning or accuracy contained in this book should be laid squarely at the door of the author.

ABBREVIATIONS

BCU	Barbados Clerks' Union
BEA	Barbados Elector's Association
BLP	Barbados Labour Party
BNP	Barbados National Party
BPL	Barbados Progressive League
BS&T	Barbados Shipping and Trading
BVF	Barbados Volunteer Force
BWU	Barbados Workers' Union
DLP	Democratic Labour Party
HMSO	Her Majesty's Stationery Office
MBE	Member of the British Empire
MCP	Member of Colonial Parliament
MP	Member of Parliament
OBE	Order of the British Empire
PCP	Progressive Conservative Party
UK	United Kingdom (Great Britain)
UN	United Nations
UNDP	United Nations Development Programme
UNESCO	United Nations Educational, Scientific and Cultural Organization
UWI	University of the West Indies
YMCA	Young Men's Christian Association
YMPC	Young Men's Progressive Club

BRIEF NOTES ON THE INTERVIEWEES QUOTED

Although scores of interviews were conducted for this book – certainly well over 100 – much of what was recorded in the notes was used solely for the purpose of cross-checking and validation. Less than 5 percent of the resultant text made its way into the pages of this book. Quotations are therefore used to add authenticity, colour and descriptive detail to the points being made. To aid the reader in recognizing and understanding the particular standpoint of the speaker, the following summary biographical notes may be of use. Bracketed dates represent the status as of July 1995.

Owen T. Allder (1909–94) Businessman and parliamentarian of eight years. Started political life as an independent candidate and later became a Member of Colonial Parliament (MCP) for the Barbados Labour Party (BLP) in St John in 1951. Interviewed September 1991 and March 1992. Photograph p. 69.

N.G.D. "Gotch" Atwell (1934–) Businessman, Freemason and writer on Freemasonry in Barbados. Interviewed September 1991 and July 1995. Photograph p. 53.

Seymour Beckles (1916–93) Former Vestry officer and political acquaintance of Lewis. Interviewed November 1991.

J.E.T. "Jonny" Bourne (1906–) Former executive of Cable and Wireless. Freemason. Employed with the Western Telegraph Co and Imperial and International Communications which later became Cable and Wireless. Social acquaintance of Lewis and comrade-in-arms in the Barbados Volunteer Force. Interviewed September 1991.

Sir Theodore Brancker (1909–) Representative of the House of Assembly for St Lucy for 34 years first as an Independent, then as a representative of the Congress and afterwards Democratic Labour Party (DLP). Interviewed October 1991.

Hammond Burke (1914–92) Bridgetown clerk in the firm that is known today as Manning Wilkinson & Challenor Ltd. Member of the Barbados Clerks' Union (BCU). Sporting acquain-

Brief Notes on the Interviewees Quoted

tance (St Ann's Cricket Club) and neighbour of Lewis. Interviewed July 1992. Photographs pp. 31 and 114.

Irwin Burke (1916–) Former Bridgetown clerk. Member of the BCU. Sporting acquaintance (St Ann's Cricket Club) and neighbour of Lewis. Interviewed July 1992 and January 1993. Photograph p. 112.

Robert Cecil (1923–) Resident of Kensington New Road area. Former Chief Engineer of the Barbados Cotton Factory. Social acquaintance of Lewis and his brother in the 1930s and 1940s. Interviewed September 1991.

J.W. Chandler (1921–) Ex-planter of Todds Estate, St John. Interviewed November 1991.

Andrew Christine (1906–93) Former Scottish/Canadian manager of the Central Agency (1940–46). Interviewed February 1992. Photograph p. 133.

Ellice Collymore (1922–) Wife of Frank Collymore. Social acquaintance and neighbour of Lewis in 1940s and 1950s. Interviewed September 1991 and April 1992. Photograph p. 2.

E.L. "Jimmy" Cozier (1912–90) Political associate of Lewis. Freemason. Former Editor-in-Chief of the *Barbados Advocate* and columnist "ELC". [Though not interviewed by the author, Cozier is often referred to and quoted. He thus merits mention.] Photograph p. 62.

Wynter Crawford (1910–93) Prominent politician and leader of the Congress Party in the 1940s and 1950s. Thereafter member of parliament (MP) for the DLP (1956–66). Editor of the defunct *Barbados Observer* newspaper. Interviewed September 1991 and February 1992. Photograph p. 88.

Rudolph Daniel (1922–93) Freemason, former staff member of the Barbados Regiment and ex-Permanent Secretary, *inter alia*, of the Ministry of Education. Interviewed October 1991, June 1992 and July 1992. Photograph p. 49.

Herbert Dowding, MBE, OBE (1913–) Second Lieutenant of the Barbados Battalion, South Caribbean Force during the Second World War. Later independent politician (1946–51) and then representative of the Progressive Conservative Party (1956–61). Businessman. Interviewed July 1992. Photograph p. 63.

Evelyn "Bunghee" Edghill (1923–95) Former bookkeeper and overseer on 11 plantations in the parishes of St John, St George and St Philip. Owner of Ellesmere plantation in St George. Interviewed July 1995. Photograph pp. 10 and 11.

Elsie Foster (1918–) Resident of the Kensington New Road and Fontabelle areas of Bridgetown. Social acquaintance of Lewis. Interviewed September 1991.

Mike Foster (1915–) Friend and sporting acquaintance of Lewis through St Ann's Cricket Club. Uniquely known to have represented Barbados in six sporting disciplines (cricket, football, water polo, boxing, yachting and golf). Interviewed September 1991.

Trevor Gale (1921–) Former Editor and Publisher of the *Barbados Advocate*. Social acquaintance of Lewis. Interviewed September 1991 and October 1992. Photograph p. 81.

Tony Hinds (1918–) Former Editorial Librarian of the *Barbados Advocate* and staff member of the *Barbados Illustrated News* and *Barbados Herald*. Sporting and social acquaintance of Lewis. Interviewed September 1991 and April 1993. Photograph p. 185.

Gladstone Holder (1921–) Columnist and former Government Information Officer. Interviewed October 1991.

Sir Alexander Hoyos (1912–) Writer of several books on Barbadian history. Confidante of Premier/Prime Minister Grantley Adams and political associate of Lewis. Interviewed October 1991, May 1992 and March 1993. Photograph p. 156.

Ronnie Hughes (1924–) Teacher, historical researcher and writer on Barbadian history. Interviewed October 1991, August 1992, March 1993 and July 1995. Photograph p. 119.

Cecil Hutchinson (1918–) Office worker in Bridgetown and eventual Manager of ECAF operations in Barbados. Interviewed August and October 1991. Photograph p. 68

A.R.E. "Bob" King (1920–) Former Bridgetown businessman. Interviewed December 1991.

Sonya Lawrence (1938–) First daughter of TT Lewis. Actively involved in business and community activities since her return to Barbados in 1967 specifically with Secretarial Services Ltd. from 1971 to 1990. Prior to this she resided in Dominica, St Lucia, Antigua and Trinidad. Photographs pp. 41, 178 and 179.

Sir Ronald Mapp (1920–95) Former BLP member of parliament for St Thomas (1946–61). Interviewed October 1991. Photographs pp. 154, 162 and 163.

G. Vernon Marshall (1922–) Bridgetown businessman. Social acquaintance of Lewis. Interviewed October 1991.

Shirland "Hawk" Medford (1910–94) Former messenger at the Central Agency and ex-bartender at Wanderers Cricket Club. Interviewed July 1992. Photographs pp. 129 and 130.

Aubrey Roberts (1920–) Bridgetown businessman, social acquaintance of Lewis and Freemason (Albion Lodge). Interviewed September 1991.

H.N. "Turk" Rogers (1925–) Bridgetown businessman. Employee at the Central Agency under Lewis and subsequently employer of Lewis from 1954–59. Interviewed September 1991 and April 1993. Photograph p. 148.

Laurence Small (1923–) Anglican minister. Founding member of the BCU. Former member of the Barbados Workers' Union (BWU) and marcher in the 1949 Lewis demonstration. Interviewed August 1992 and July 1995. Photographs pp. 111 and 141.

Christie Smith (1911–93) Former Bridgetown clerk employed by DaCosta & Co Ltd. Founder member and Secretary of the defunct BCU. Interviewed September 1991. Photographs pp. 111 and 116.

Brief Notes on the Interviewees Quoted

Sir Frederick Smith (1924–) Member of the BLP and founder member of the DLP. Former Second Lieutenant in the Barbados Battalion of the South Caribbean Force during the Second World War. Attorney-at-law. Barbadian Magistrate. Interviewed July 1995. Photograph p. 169.

Kathleen Smitten (1910–) Social acquaintance of Lewis from the 1940s. One-time official in the Barbados Clerks' Union. Interviewed October 1991.

Sir Hugh Springer (1913–94) General Secretary of the Barbados Progressive League (BPL) and BWU. Member of parliament in the 1940s, University Registrar and eventual Governor-General of Barbados. Interviewed September 1991 and October 1992. Photograph p. 185.

Sir James Cameron Tudor (1918–95) Founder member of the DLP. Member of Parliament in the 1950s and 1960s. School teacher. Freemason. Political associate of Lewis. Interviewed October 1992. Photograph p. 164.

Sir Frank Walcott (1917–) Political independent in the 1940s, BLP representative in the 1950s and DLP representative in the 1950s and 1960s. General Secretary of the BWU (1949–91). Interviewed February 1993. Photographs pp. 113, 140, 144 and 154.

Noel Weatherhead (1907–95) Bridgetown businessman and Freemason (Victoria Lodge). Interviewed September 1991.

John Wickham (1923–) Columnist and political commentator. Son and biographer of legendary Barbadian journalist Clennel Wickham. Interviewed November 1991 and July 1995. Photograph p. 184.

Sir Donald Wiles (1912–) Social acquaintance of Lewis. Former Permanent Secretary to the Premier. Former Administrator of Montserrat. Interviewed September 1991 and October 1992. Photographs pp. 24 and 40.

Constance Younglao, née Perryman (1917–) Sister-in-law of Lewis. Interviewed September 1991 and April 1993. Photographs pp. 37 and 38.

INTRODUCTION

The Search for TT Lewis

I first met Atholl Edwin Seymour (alias TT) Lewis in March 1981. By then he had been dead nearly 22 years. His face and some potted details of his life greeted me from the pages of two Barbadian newspaper clippings which my mother had posted to my university address in Canada. Prior to that date I had never heard of the man. But from what I read of his movements and views, they struck me as being particularly uncharacteristic of a white man in colonial Barbados. I was intrigued and determined to learn more.

If you wanted to measure the importance of the changes brought about during the political life of Lewis and his contemporaries you could compare the situation in Barbados at the time of Lewis' entry into politics with a picture of the political landscape which he left behind. The snapshot is illuminating. Lewis entered the island's lawmaking chamber at a time when the number of people who had the right to vote for representatives in the House of Assembly was less than 4 percent of the entire population. Looked at from another angle, there were only a handful of nonwhites as legislators in a society where over 90 percent was nonwhite. The plantocratic economy was dominant and its owners controlled the island's destiny.

When Lewis died, the British imperial recessional was about to produce an independent Barbados. By then, real executive power was in the hands of a homegrown group of nonwhite Barbadians. Sugar had lost its singularly important status. The economy had become more diversified and thus more viable. Crucially, full adult franchise was an accomplished and accepted fact. The changes at all levels were stupendous. No period in the history of the island contains a larger number of political events of comparable importance. This book sets out

Introduction: The Search for TT Lewis

to show that Lewis' role in many of the events that defined this transformation was considerable.

A capsule version of Lewis' political life would read as follows. At some point before entering the House he became a member of the conservative Elector's Association, but appeared uncomfortable in their midst and left them to contest his first election which he fought and won as an independent in 1942. He subsequently joined Wynter Crawford's radical Congress Party before the 1944 election and contested both this and the 1946 election for Congress. He left Congress in 1947, joined the BLP and won the 1948 election with them. Then came the immensely important 1951 election, the first ever to be fought under universal adult suffrage. Lewis again won a victory with the BLP. Early on in the new five-year term he split with BLP's legendary leader Grantley Adams and joined the newly formed DLP just in time for the 1956 election. This time, he failed to retain his seat, but stayed with the DLP until his deteriorating health led to his death three years later at the relatively early age of 54.

One of the most fascinating aspects of the effort to trace Lewis' impact on Barbadian development is that it allows the observer to move back and forth across the contours of island life during its period of political awakening, an epoch that stretches from the Barbados riots (1937) almost to the arrival of political independence (1966). What happened between these years captures what is arguably the most important period in the island's political development. These years also coincide almost exactly with the dates of Lewis' political activism (1942–59).

During this period nothing evokes so well the exhilarating and yet tragic place Lewis holds in the annals of local folklore as the phenomenal march staged on his behalf by a population deeply aware of the sacrifice he was making in his fight for justice and social improvement.

Reading about and listening to the views which Lewis and his colleagues were propounding and the policies they were proposing, I found it hard to imagine a time when such ideas – reasonable and self-evidently worthwhile as they seem – should even require a struggle to ensure their adoption as laws of the land. The fact that Barbados has stood out as a model of constitutional democratic government in a postwar period when a greater part of the globe was labouring under the rule of one or other form of tyrannical political regime, is, I think, a testimony to the vigilance and vigour with which Barbadian politicians of the time played that game – and stayed within the rules prescribed for all, thereby enabling genuine constitutional democracy to become the predominant characteristic of Barbadian politics.

The Story Behind the Story

It is curious how this detective story began its long trek towards the printer's press. On finding out who Lewis was, I became fascinated by the fact that a blood relative – Lewis was my paternal grandfather's brother – played such an active role in the politics of a period when the islanders were fashioning the Barbados of today. Thereafter, I remember asking questions about the man whenever I came across someone who seemed to be able to place him in their recollections of days gone by. My inquiries, such as they were at this stage, were superficial and certainly disorganized.

Once my career had returned me to Barbados in 1987 after an absence of seven years, I resumed my search for Lewis. In 1991, the story had become mesmerizing enough to prompt me to consider writing down all I was learning. How was it possible that no one had tried to investigate the story behind this man – this perplexing product of colonial Barbadian society?

Everything can be done better in hindsight. But I sometimes reflect that it is a great pity that I hadn't conducted the interviews and research earlier. Doing this immediately upon returning to Barbados in 1987 would have proven more rewarding simply because many more people familiar with Lewis' days would then still have been alive. This is a dwindling band. Several have died since the bulk of the interviews were conducted during the two-year period of 1991–93.

One of my aims in recounting Lewis' story was to allow the reader to "sit in" on the scores of interviews I conducted. As a rule, the book lets elderly citizens, who remembered Lewis in their own way, do the talking for me. Wherever possible, I tried to follow up meticulously every lead offered, but I have no doubt missed many people who would have liked an opportunity to be heard speaking on Lewis. No doubt I would have enjoyed talking to those whom I inadvertently overlooked as much as to those I did manage to interview. Without exception, I found the efforts expended in searching out the truth about Lewis to have been richly rewarding. The varied anecdotal windows offered by my interviewees permitted me to glimpse traces of a world that has already disappeared within the space of a few generations.

I suppose that this book can best be described as a biography. It is certainly an attempt to gather together the scattered bits and pieces of a man's life from a newspaper snippet here, a half-remembered remark there. I confess to having had very little to go on at the outset. In terms of access to family sources, not only was I born three years after Lewis' death and therefore never met him face-to-face, but there is hardly any interface between Lewis' immediate relations and the

Introduction: The Search for TT Lewis

family group in which I move. Interestingly, none of my immediate family remembers much about Lewis or about what he is supposed to have done. I offer this comment not as a criticism, but merely as an observation on how rapidly the passage of time erodes our collective memory about the people who have powerfully shaped our history.

The first lesson I learnt in the search for Lewis is that our history is evaporating in front of our very eyes. The fact that when I began interviewing and writing there were no readily available photographs of Lewis and yet within the space of one month I had amassed at least 50 period photographs shows how much of our history resides outside the normal sources. It is living on the bookshelves and in the closets of our elderly population. And in their minds.

There is another point which readers might wish to consider. Most of the comments about Lewis were reasonably positive. So, as a relative of his, I found I had to keep asking myself whether the interviewees were just being polite or whether they were expressing genuine feelings. After all, here was a man who had apparently offended a great many people during his lifetime. It is for this reason that I very much appreciated and respected the honesty of those few who were prepared to tell me that their view of Lewis had not changed in 40 years: for them he would remain a reckless heretic who had threatened their way of life.

At the same time, I sometimes detected in the accounts relayed by some interviewees – through what they claimed Lewis had said or thought – a projection of their own beliefs which Lewis himself may never have shared. The sort of: "Oh TT would have felt this or that . . ." comment. Conclusion: as individuals reflect on past events, they often throw a more positive light on their role in history than the actual events themselves might justify.

COMPILATION TECHNIQUES AND SOURCES

It is said that biographies tend to fall into one of two categories. First, come the academic works which rely almost exclusively on primary, written source material such as can be found in collections of personal letters, in libraries and archives. Then come the journalistic biographies which rely mainly on interviews. Only occasionally does a biographer combine the academic and the reportorial approaches. Readers may judge for themselves whether I have succeeded in my attempt to do so. While I try to give due regard to the documentary evidence which exists, the testimony of voices from the period is given equally weighty treatment. I firmly believe that the combined approach helps avoid any tendency towards revisionism. If willing raconteurs were able to convey a verifiable account of the contribution or hindrance Lewis made to developments in Barbados at this time, they are given ample space to provide their evidence in the book.

Next to nothing exists in the public domain on Lewis. Glimpses of who the man was are available to the reading public only through a few odd sentences in certain Barbadian history books and a single five-page chapter in local historian F.A. Hoyos' autobiography. The picture was worse at the family level. Early on in the research, I located what was left of Lewis' worldly possessions remaining in the custody of the family. A small brown envelope about a quarter of an inch thick stared up at me. I extracted the contents: a copy of the regulations of the Barbados Volunteer Force; fewer than ten photographs; the text of a comedy sketch in which Lewis participated as a young man; on the back of an envelope, some notes written in Lewis' hand concerning the system of local government; a letter from the clerk of the House of Assembly extending condolences to his wife on the occasion of his death. If I wanted to find out more about the man I would have to rely heavily on oral history.

But as Leo Tolstoy points out in *War and Peace*, there are as many truths about a battle, after it, as there are participants in it. Any given event will mean one thing to one person and something else to another. In this way, the truth gets fragmented the instant it is experienced and the moment it becomes memory.

When a writer records a speech on tape or puts it down immediately after an interview from full notes there is a feeling that the truth of that moment has been captured. Nevertheless, when later weaving it into his story, there is an almost irresistible temptation to rework the text for use in what then purports to be a factual account. For most writers the enticement to "improve" is too great and the end result is that the "truth" of the work is compromised even further than it was already bound to be.

Thus, the risks inherent in the oral interview technique are inevitably compounded in the subsequent process of attempting to write history. In his milestone work on the nature of historical inquiry, E.H. Carr makes the following observation: "It used to be said that the facts speak for themselves. This, of course, is untrue. The facts speak only when the historian calls on them: it is he who decides to which facts to give the floor and in what order or context . . . The historian is . . . selective."[1]

Acknowledging these handicaps to the writing of an objective account of the life and times of Lewis, my approach has been to resist these impulses as much as humanly possible while remaining faithful to the views of the interviewees. I nevertheless make every effort to avoid subjecting the reader to dead end

Introduction: The Search for TT Lewis

sentences and thoughts left hanging in the air simply because of shifts in the cut and thrust of the interview. My own modest hope is therefore that by grouping a sufficiently large number of varied voices in an organized and coherent manner, the resulting sound will authenticate the core issues expressed in this book.

If the past is a foreign country, every interview was a journey to this foreign land, to another time where rules appeared harsh and absolute and where people behaved very differently.

The mechanics went as follows. Most of the 100-plus interviews were conducted face-to-face. But a large number were also done over the phone. Interestingly, I found that people generally responded much more openly over the phone than they did when I spoke to them in person – where all I was armed with was a pencil and notepad. It was once suggested to me to use a tape recorder, but I resisted, arguing that first of all, a recorder is far more intimidating than a pencil and paper. And secondly, it would never have been possible to interview the vast number of people I did, if I had to set aside three to four hours a night for transcribing one hour's recordings while holding down a full time job and helping my wife raise three small children. From my notes I could pick out the main themes and take verbatim the choice quotes which best represented the speaker's thoughts.

Now to the written evidence. It is an axiom of historical research, though one not necessarily heeded by all who claim to be historians, that if you want to examine a period, you must first immerse yourself totally in the mind set of that period. Newspapers always represent a rich source of ambient popular thought and a general flavour of the time. Considerable assistance was provided to me in this regard by the Reference Unit of the Central Library as regards newspaper clippings. The second major written source on which this book depends is the debates of the House of Assembly recorded in Hansard. Fortunately, the Barbados Department of Archives runs a tight and organized ship and most information needed on the debates was readily available there.

Talking about Lewis involved discussing politics. And it is impossible to talk about politics in Barbados without at some point bringing up the subject of race. Yet, so much of our historical literature is infuriatingly evasive on the question of race. Although race is an integral part of the Barbadian psyche, and can be discussed today in an open and noninflammatory way, much of Barbadian history and historiography succumbs to a preference for using veiled language and euphemism to avoid saying what informed citizens would say to like-minded peers in the privacy of their verandahs. The fact that racism exists, and is practised by both whites and blacks, does not mean that democratic and open

Key Dates in Lewis' Life

- 1905 — Born
- 1920 — Joins Central Agency Ltd.
- 1937 — Marries Marge Perryman
- 1942 — Wins first electoral term (Independent)
- 1944 — Wins second term (Congress Party)
- 1946 — Wins third term (Congress Party)
- 1948 — Wins fourth term (Barbados Labour Party)
- 1949 — Massive demonstrations following his dismissal from Central Agency Ltd.
- 1951 — Wins fifth term (Barbados Labour Party)
- 1952 — Is denounced by Grantley Adams
- 1955 — Splits with Barbados Labour Party
- 1956 — Loses seat (Democratic Labour Party)
- 1959 — Dies

practices, properly used, cannot help to overcome it or at least contain its most extreme atavistic tendencies.

The noted British historian and sociologist G.K. Lewis (no relation) rightly contends in his *magnum opus* on Caribbean societies, that our people have a fine detective instinct for the recognition of genetic traces of racial intermixing.[2] This is particularly true of Barbadians of all colours, even if the statement no longer generally carries with it the stifling and oppressive categorizations which predated the 1970s. Readers will note that in the appendixes I have made an effort to provide a picture of what the Barbadian political structure looked like at the time of Lewis. Particularly tricky was the effort to give numerical representation to the evident and palpable changing colour composition of the House of Assembly in the period under review. I lament the fact that given the availability of the information, our own historians appear to have shied away from this highly revealing and historically important analysis. Risking criticism on the grounds of political incorrectness, I have tried to identify and group members of the House of Assembly between 1942 and 1956 into the broad categories of white and black/mixed, with the help of those alive who were acquainted with these people. The results offer a visually descriptive account of the tremendous destructive impact of franchise reform on the political grip of the white political elite in the space of a few short years.

NOTES

1. E.H. Carr, *What is History?*, Penguin, London, 1961, 10–11.
2. G.K. Lewis, *The Growth of the Modern West Indies*, Modern Reader Paperbacks, New York, 1968, 77.

CHAPTER ONE

Origins

CHILD OF A PLANTATION BOOKKEEPER

It is incredible how so little can be known about the whereabouts and early upbringing of a man born in Barbados in this century.

Most of the mystery surrounding Lewis' origins seems to spring from his own attitude of not wanting to talk about them. Contemporaries report that his approach was always to stay silent on such matters or to dismiss them as irrelevancies. He once disclosed to an associate that his early years resembled "the short and simple annals of the poor".[1] The reasons why he chose not to discuss his roots must also remain a mystery. Some of the interviewees speculated that he may have been ashamed to disclose his modest upbringing. But his later espousal of the cause of the underprivileged makes this unlikely. More probable as a cause of the silence is the apparent split with his immediate family which was reported to have taken place during his teenage years. But more of this later.

Of the documentary evidence that exists, here are the facts. Lewis was born on 10 December 1905, one of a set of twins. The twin sister, Zena Elise Geraldine Lewis, lived for only ten months. The birth certificate gives his father's residence as Drax Hall.[2], but Lewis' baptismal certificate states Pool plantation. His father was Henry ("Harry") Seymour Lewis; his mother, Emily Ethel Elise Lewis. Lewis' birth certificate describes his father as a "bookkeeper" at Drax Hall in St George. His father is also known to have worked at nearby Pool plantation in St John in a similar capacity.

> ### WHY THE SOBRIQUET "TT"?
>
> Lewis' birth certificate gives his official names as Atholl Edwin Seymour Lewis, however to everyone he was known as TT. No one knows for certain how he got his nickname.
>
>
>
> Ellice Collymore (1935)
>
> Perhaps the most plausible explanation goes as follows:
>
>
>
> Ellice Collymore (1992)
>
> *TT got his nickname from a loveable clown called "TT" whom his friends thought he resembled. The clown worked for a circus – possibly an American circus – which visited Queen's Park in the decade of 1910–20.*
>
> (Ellice Collymore)

The link between Drax Hall and Pool plantations on Lewis' birth and baptismal certificates is curious. In 1905 both Drax Hall and Pool were managed by the same firm of Bridgetown solicitors, even though they were owned by different absentee proprietors – in the case of Drax Hall, by the Drax family and in the case of Pool, by the Trollope family. This would more than likely explain the shift in Harry Lewis' location from Drax Hall to Pool at the time of the different events. As a bookkeeper, he would have moved between those plantations doing the same type of work probably on more than one occasion. It is known that plantation management would deploy overseer and bookkeeping staff among the estates they controlled. In the absence of additional information on the subject, this would seem to explain the different addresses given on the two documents, although it is also possible that he moved or was reassigned from Drax Hall to Pool between the birth and baptism of his son.

Although he was born on Drax Hall estate, Lewis' mother is unlikely to have delivered Lewis among the main buildings. Birth and baptismal documents, plus the author's investigation, would suggest that Lewis' birthplace was a dwelling located within easy walking or riding distance of both Drax Hall (2.8 km) and Pool (1.2 km) plantations. The main clue to the actual birth place is the location given on the birth certificate for Lewis' twin which was written at a later date. This states the abode of Harry Lewis as "Airy Hill". It is reasonable to suppose that the estate managers would have allowed Harry Lewis and his family to be housed here in the ramshackle overseer's quarters and would have then directed him to work on either of the two estates from this location, as occasion necessitated.

Airy Hill Plantation yard: much-renovated version of the dwelling (left) in which Lewis is assumed to have been born.

If this speculation is accurate, then the building where Lewis was probably born still stands, hidden off the main road to Bridgetown, and currently in a much renovated form. Here is how someone who knew the house in the 1920s describes it:

> The house you see there [at Airy Hill] today is a greatly improved version of the original. The original house was made of rubble stone. It had hardly any foundation at all . . . It was a really miserable little place with only two bedrooms. There was a sort of tiny verandah five foot wide – in which you could not sit and face your company. The whole thing could best be described as more or less an upstairs flat, with the lower part as a place where yamsellers would work during the day selling their wares. There was also a store room below . . . (J.W. Chandler)

Aside from that single categorizable symbol of social status – "bookkeeper" – little is known about Harry Lewis. In the tightly controlled and rigidly run world of turn-of-the-century Barbados, Lewis' father was grouped among the 99 percent of the population which was not entitled to vote. Under the Representation of the People Act (1901) all men who received $240 or more in income annually or who possessed a freehold title with respect to land producing profits of not less than $24 annually were entitled to vote. With the property qualification, a registered voter could vote for two members in any constituency where he owned property.[3] The Barbados Electoral Register for 1905 does not contain the name Harry Lewis.[4]

Of Lewis' immediate family grouping, living memory suggests that besides his parents and his twin sister there were three other siblings: Hal (the eldest), and two younger children, Eyre (the author's grandfather) and Ruby, all of whom eventually predeceased their mother, Ethel.

Lewis' earliest days would have been spent in the rural parishes of St John, St Joseph and St George. He was baptized in St Augustine's Church in the latter parish and was known to have had fond memories of the Horse Hill area of St Joseph, especially of the St Joseph's Boys School in that area. Lewis is also known to have sustained a close and easy relationship with the residents of Pool plantation to the end of his life.[5]

Whether he was dismissed from his job or was simply looking for another avenue to provide for his family of four (the fifth child would be born in Bridgetown), Harry Lewis took his wife and small family to live in Kensington New Road in Bridgetown around 1909. In leaving the plantation to seek work in Bridgetown, he did what many lower income whites were doing at the time. The economic expansion of the island's capital was creating opportunities for lower income whites who reckoned that their skin colour would give them an edge over blacks and coloureds in the search for junior level office jobs in merchant houses and small stores. As a result, in the second decade of this century, whites accounted for nearly 20 percent of the Bridgetown population while comprising less than 10 percent nationwide.

It is not known whether Harry Lewis actually attempted to secure a lowly white collar job in Bridgetown. In the end he never shook off his rural roots and is remembered plying the streets of Bridgetown as a "cow swapper" carrying the distinctive knot of old rope in his hand which served to denote his status as an intermediary in the buying and selling of live animals – normally one or two at a time. At some point thereafter, again according to family memory, Harry Lewis decided to escape the penury of Barbados and migrate to the United States hoping to make his fortune there. In emigrating, he would have formed part of what was then something of an exodus of lower income whites from Barbados to the United States in search of better job opportunities. He never returned. The reason why cannot be ascertained. Family memory recalls that he promised to send home remittances for his family – a promise he is said to have kept until his death some time in the mid 1920s.

BARBADIAN SOCIETY AT THE TURN OF THE TWENTIETH CENTURY

To better understand what the term "bookkeeper" conveys about Harry Lewis and his social standing in this era, we need to look a little deeper into Barbadian society at the turn of the century.

Origins

At the time of Lewis' birth in 1905, Barbados was a densely populated, plantation based, export oriented, island colony of the British Empire. Sugar had been king for two and a half centuries. During that time the cultivation of sugar cane and the export of sugar and its byproducts (molasses and rum) had come to govern the political, economic and social processes at work in the island. Given the centrality of agriculture, land ownership meant everything, for it entitled a person to derive wealth from the soil in a country where almost every nook and cranny was cultivated.

Looked at in purely financial terms, the incredibly lucrative nature of sugar production in the 1600s and 1700s had drawn in both Europeans and Africans for the development of the economy. Europeans seeking profit or adventure or both arrived in the form of British lower nobility as well as less privileged farmers. Other whites – political prisoners and common criminals – were transshipped to serve out their sentences as indentured labourers on the island. As the demands of the sugar economy grew apace, Africans were brought over in ever increasing numbers on the Atlantic slave ships to work on the plantations. An immediate hierarchy based on skin colour and derived racial prejudices was established and perpetuated itself in the years that followed. Thus, the principal determinants of one's position in society were the ownership of land and skin colour.

Unlike most of the other British colonies in the Eastern Caribbean where the number of whites was minuscule compared with that of blacks, Barbados had retained a relatively high percentage of whites since the early days of settlement. According to the 1891 census, nearly 10 percent of the island's population was white. Though whites as a group had established and maintained a system of social control based on land ownership and racial prejudice, it was only a small number of this 10 percent – the white plantocratic elite – which actually ran the colony. The majority of the whites on the island were to be found lower down the white community's class ladder clinging on to this or that particular rung.

Also clinging down below was the coloured or mixed race group. Accounting for just over 20 percent of the population in the same census, the coloureds typically exhibited a psychological insecurity that exceeded that of lower income whites, owing simply to the fact that they clearly belonged to neither the black nor the white group. In stark terms they shunned the former and were themselves shunned by the latter. They tended to hold positions of low level clerical or supervisorial authority and were to be found disproportionately within the Bridgetown city limits where the harshness of the plantation's racial stratification touched their lives less. In the streets of the capital, nearly half of all Barbadian coloureds flourished as teachers, clerks, shopkeepers, artisans and small

> ## Money
>
> Due to its geographical location, Barbados was a British colony with extensive trading links to North America. As a result, while its accounts were maintained in pounds sterling, most of its commercial houses used a dollars and cents system denominated in West Indian currency units. A dual system of currency accounting thus developed from the early 19th century ending in the 1960s with most islanders being perfectly numerate in both West Indian dollars and pounds sterling. A fixed exchange rate underpinned the system. Since this book attempts to faithfully reflect both sets of monetary values as used in original documentary sources without standardizing the unit of account, the above box is intended as an aid to readers unfamiliar with the links between the two sets of currencies.
>
> | Sterling | Dollars |
> |---|---|
> | £1 | $4.80 |
> | S5 | $1.20 |
> | S4+4¢ | $1.00 |
> | S1 | 24¢ |
>
> Key: Pounds (£), Shillings (S), Dollars ($), Cents (¢).

landholders. Many had even acquired enough property to make it into the political limelight.

The black community's subordinate position in society had changed little since slave emancipation in 1838. At emancipation, the white planter elite monopolized nearly all of Barbados' lands. The smallness of the island (430 square kilometres) coupled with the absence of unoccupied public lands (or "Crown lands") for the newly emancipated black population to migrate to (in contrast to the situation in the geographically larger British Caribbean colonies) meant that the planter elite could continue to command the island's destiny through its control of the land and the laws which protected their position of dominance.

With no sources of subsistence or income other than plantation work, newly freed black Barbadians were forced back onto tiny, rented, estate controlled subsistence plots called "tenantries". The arrangement went as follows. In exchange for a small plot of land (usually "rabland" unsuited for sugar cane cultivation) which they were allowed to rent, members of the black working class were obliged to pay part of their rent through the provision of labour usually on that specific estate. Their meagre wage would routinely fluctuate in response to market trends and could be cut – sometimes by as much as 50 percent – if there was a fall in the international price of sugar.

Barbados was also unlike most of the other British Caribbean colonies in that the large majority of its 200-odd estates were run by resident owner-planters.[6] The low level of absenteeism among the white Barbadian elite had forged an intense sense of belonging to and ownership of the island. Crucially, this included the planter-dominated political process. The Barbadian legislature, comprising the 9-member Legislative Council and the 24-member House of Assembly,[7] had enjoyed a degree of semi-autonomy from Britain stretching back to the days when local whites had fought pitched battles with Oliver Cromwell's parliamentary forces in the mid 1600s to resist political encroachment from London. Barbadian lawmakers' perception of their having a special status of semi-independence from the Crown had also enabled them to resist Britain's reasonably consistent efforts to exert a benign influence over the manner in which the island's impoverished majority was treated. The local assembly was thus able to recover from having been forced to pass the emancipation order in 1834 by subsequently passing a series self-serving post-emancipation measures aimed at restricting the movement of blacks through a located labour system which persisted into the 1930s. The local legislature's most egregious recent encounter with Britain had occurred in the early 1880s when the Colonial Office tried but failed to curb the Barbadian legislature's power through an administrative tethering of Barbados to the Windward Islands in a confederation.

During the period under which the system of located labour persisted, the threat of ejection from the plantation tenantries gave the white planter elite immense power over persons who had been technically freed from slavery. Starting in 1840 with the so-called Contract Act, a number of measures were introduced to ensure that the planters would retain control over the labour force. The Contract Act declared, for example, that Barbadians employed in any "occupation in which the emancipated population of this island were usually employed while in a state of slavery, or as apprenticed labourers" were obliged to have a verbal or written contract of employment in the island. Breach of this arrangement would not only risk forfeiture of the employee's job, but also of his or her place to live; it would likely incur a fine as well as imprisonment (possibly with hard labour) for up to fourteen days. Subsequent acts in 1883, 1891, 1897 and 1932 added refinements to this system – generally lessening the punitive weight of the legislation until it was repealed, ironically, just prior to the 1937 riots.

This fierce defence of self-rule and self-sufficiency, did not, however, translate easily into a sense of obligation towards the island's wage labourers – either black or white. Legendary black Barbadian journalist Clennel Wickham described the attitudes of the white assembly in the early twentieth century as follows: "There is no sense of duty to the individuals of the island as a whole. There is no sense of responsibility for broad and reasonable treatment. There is merely a sense of class." The restricted voting system based on franchise reinforced this system by according electoral worth only to those of a certain elevated social status.

Around the time of Lewis' birth at the turn of the century, the mass of black Barbadians – then comprising nearly 70 percent of the island population – were predominately plantation based and poor. Most continued to live in portable "chattel houses" situated on small rented garden plots comprising less than half an acre. The portability of their houses reflected their precarious status. The plots were grouped into tenantries on the rural estates where it was highly probable that their occupants' forefathers had worked since the end of slavery. They tended to till and work the plot of land after a day's labour on the estate. Some blacks, it is true, did manage to acquire enough land to sustain themselves without recourse to plantation work. But by the turn of the century this would not have amounted to more than a fraction of the black population.

While it is true that changes in the system of education following emancipation had by 1900 started to produce a growing educated black intelligentsia which was rising socially over the vast remainder of black Barbadians, the perspective of this group generally tended to be wedded to white establishment opinion. Its views were at best progressive, not radical. Expanded access to education would not by itself prove to be sufficient to disrupt the way Barbadian society worked. The fundamental conservatism of Barbadian society remained undented until the 1937 riots.

One tremendous liberating influence for thousands of black Barbadians starting in the first decade of the 1900s was the inrush of what was then termed "Panama Money". For the ten years following 1905, that segment of the black working class which had emigrated to work on the Panama Canal sent back unprecedented amounts of cash to their family members in the island. The effect of this on the plantation system was momentous in that it enabled landless blacks to purchase land and thereby fulfil the dream which most of them entertained: to own a small plot of land.[8]

In general, however, class divisions within the black community were fewer than they were within the white. Social advances would tend to come their way as a group in the aftermath of the riots in 1937 largely because, owing to their essential class solidarity, they were able to project themselves – through the labour party and trade union movement that had come to represent them – as an imperturbable challenge to the existing white oligarchy.

Origins

Stratification in White Barbados

Despite what appears to be a commonplace view to the contrary, white society in the early part of this century was profoundly fragmented, dividing itself roughly into four segments which can be categorized as follows. At the top was the white planter elite. This group was comprised of approximately 30 elite families which owned almost 80 percent of the land.[9] Its members were easily recognizable for the social and political influence they wielded through monopolization of one precious commodity: land. Most were not well educated. If male, such persons tended to occupy seats in the House of Assembly or the Legislative Council and through their financial influence exercised great control over the limited number of electors in any given parish.

Just below the landed elite one finds the white middle class. This group was comprised principally of Bridgetown merchants who, by this period, were increasingly controlling commerce through the choke point of the capital city and would soon challenge the interests of the landed oligarchy.[10] But it also included smaller planters, plantation managers, professional men (doctors and attorneys) middle level colonial administrators (police officials, for example) and, interestingly, the upper tier of the local Anglican Church which played a considerable role in the running of local government under the Vestry system.

Next to last came the lower income whites. Such people rarely possessed either property or land and did not earn enough to entitle them to vote under the restricted franchise of the day. They tended to work as plantation overseers and bookkeepers, Bridgetown clerks, craftsmen, wheelwrights and blacksmiths both in Bridgetown and on the plantations. It is to this class of Barbadian white that Lewis and his father belonged.

At the bottom of the pile stood a group of whites who were totally marginalized in society, the so-called "poor whites" (also known as "Redlegs" or "poor backra jonnies"). This class of white tended to live in small villages along the island's east coast from as far north as Boscobel in St Peter down to Foul Bay in St Philip. Most were concentrated in St John and eked out a living as fishermen, estate workers or beggars. It is known that the plantations of Colleton and Clifton Hall in St John had, for example, labour gangs comprised of poor whites who harvested sugar cane alongside black gangs as late as the year 1920. The members of such gangs would typically come from the same extended family group and would live on the marginal lands found "under the cliff" to the east of these plantations.

Daily Routine of an Overseer / Bookkeeper

The story of Evelyn "Bunghee" Edghill (1913–95) an elderly white ex-overseer who worked at eleven different plantations in Barbados between 1927–50 is instructive and is worth quoting at length. He was not familiar with Lewis but knew the latter by name. According to Edghill:

"An overseer or bookkeeper wasn't treated better than an ordinary labourer by the manager. Hard practices went on up until about the 1950s. When I started to work in 1927 I was 14 years old. As an assistant bookkeeper I made 10 shillings a week. I really could never express myself too good to take phone messages for the manager and such like, but I could read and write and add and subtract. So they put me to weigh canes . . .

"In 1930 I went to Cliff plantation for a little higher promotion and would also work in the boiler house. They chased me away from [elderly Barbadian term for 'I left'] there and went to work as an overseer at another plantation. This job involved seeing that the stock (goats, sheep, cows and mules) were fed on mornings.

"We got up before dawn and by 7 am after the stock were fed I got on my horse and supervised the work of the drivers.* All the drivers were black and I can tell you that some could manage the estates better than the managers themselves.

"When you came on, they would know the ropes and tell you about the do's and don'ts. You might be surprised to find out that the overseers did not have a lot of authority over the drivers. Drivers took down the information on when each worker used to arrive for work and leave and gave this to the overseer or bookkeeper who would then pass it on to the manager . . .

"Bunghee" Edghill (1940s)

"Each plantation had a number of fields which we planted. And each had a name. The field next to the plantation yard would be called 'yardfield number one', or 'yardfield number two' and so on. The yard near to where the labourers lived was called the 'nigger yard'. Almost every plantation in the island at the time had a 'nigger yard' . . .

"The overseer's quarters was an all-bachelor thing. We got fed by the plantation manager's wife. I remember when I was working at Ruby plantation in 1934–38, I would get $27 a month and the manager took out $15 from this for feeding me . . .

"The riots [in 1937] really changed things up. After the riots, we went from a 9 hour day to working 8 hours. But that still meant that you had to be in that damned saddle for 8 hours a day. You got one hour for lunch and came off at 4 p.m. And don't think there was any security for retired overseers. If the manager felt like it he would give you a little $10 a month or so, but it was up to him . . .

". . . Eventually the fellows [overseers] tried to get a union going. This was 1945. We felt we weren't being treated good. Couldn't get more than a day or so off a month. The quarters were poor and cockroach infested and so on. But, man, when the talk got out that we were forming a union they [the managers and owners] started looking for the ringleaders. They fired three overseers and the rest of us took note. I nearly got fired too. The union was eventually formed, but the reason why it never worked was that the bigger overseers never joined it. The mistake we made was that we never joined the Barbados Workers' Union."

> *Author: Wouldn't the overseers have had problems joining up with a mainly black trade union?*
>
> "True. Many did not want to do it. They were the ones who came from better families and would have seen it as a step down. But I would have done it. Man, the trouble was that jobs were so damn scarce back then that we were frightened to do anything at all..."
>
> *Author: If life was difficult for the overseers, how was it for the workers themselves?*
>
> "Boy, life for us was hell. But the labourers saw hell too. They only got about 12 cents a day – a shilling a day at the most. So whereas I could afford six biscuits and a tin of sardines for lunch, they could not."
>
>
>
> Edghill with sons Robin (left) and Norman (1995)
>
> *Author: As a single man isolated on the plantation, how did you "organize"?*
>
> "Man, if you had a worthwhile looking girl in the gang you would ask her a question. Or, if not, you would have girls in the district who did not work in the field and you would make friends with them. You would get a little something that way."
>
> *[Author's note: drivers were superintendents who actually gave orders to the gangs directly. Gangs of labourers on large estates numbered roughly 20 persons. Smaller estates would have correspondingly smaller gangs.]*

The elite whites treated all other whites like dirt. The established white families victimized the poorer whites (plantation overseers and Bridgetown clerks and so on) badly, but not as badly as they did the blacks... So the point is worth stating that it has always been easier for the poor whites to rise in the social order than the poor blacks. While these whites are not of the old plantocratic or middle class families, you cannot compare them to the children of black plantation labourers. (Ronnie Hughes)

Lower income whites did in fact enjoy a certain access to lower level supervisory work on the plantation based on their ability to cash in on skin colour. Most were taken on as overseers, bookkeepers or assistant bookkeepers. As noted above, by the turn of the century a disproportionate number of whites and mixed race Barbadians were migrating from the plantations to find work in Bridgetown, since the latter offered more scope for upward social mobility and an end to the perpetuation of their comparatively inferior status in the field. The white elite maintained and reinforced these class distinctions by restricting access to land and commerce as well as through the subtleties of social behaviour and nuance.

Elite attitudes establishing social stratification were deeply resented by those lower down the white social ladder. And yet these same lower income whites would, without any apparent sense of self-contradiction, reinforce intra-white class consciousness by rejecting in turn those perceived to be beneath them. This attitude naturally intensified when lower income whites had to deal with blacks with whom both they and poor whites were on an economic par.

Thus the impression that Barbadian whites at this time were one monolithic class is inaccurate. There were clear gradations within the white group even though "whiteness" was a unifying force around which most (even lower income and "poor") whites coalesced against black encroachment. The peculiarly ambivalent status of the lower income white – which is of particular relevance in gauging the social pressures and perspectives that would have borne down upon someone in Lewis' position – is best seen through the story of the Bridgetown clerks whose unhappy tale is recounted in chapter 6.

Plantation Bookkeepers and Overseers

TT Lewis' father, Harry Lewis, is known to have worked as a bookkeeper at Drax Hall and Pool plantations during the early part of this century. The social hierarchy on the plantation went roughly as follows. At the top stood the plantation owner. This person tended to be a local white: often an official in the local vestry or parish administration. He could also be a police official and was more than likely a member of the militia. Given the low level of absentee ownership in Barbados, many of the plantation owners ran their own estates.

If the plantations were absentee owned, as was the case for both Drax Hall, then the island's second largest plantation, and Pool, a much smaller concern,[11] the plantations were run by a local firm of Bridgetown solicitors who recruited a manager to do the job. Managers were responsible for coordinating the estate's field operations and for reporting back to the solicitors regarding daily financial decisions.

Depending on the size of the plantation, the manager would employ one or more white overseers who constituted the next step down on the social ladder.[12] Among this group there would be gradations of rank with the junior overseers being referred to as "bookkeepers". On large estates, there was often a position for assistant bookkeeper. The job of bookkeeper was, among other things, to maintain handwritten journals of all the estate data and, through the drivers, keep track of workers' hours. Bookkeepers were normally expected to rise in time to the level of full overseers.

Beyond this point, however, additional upward social mobility proved more difficult. But it was not impossible. The story of an overseer located at Sedgepond plantation in St Andrew who left a grudging manager to take his monthly day of leave in Bridgetown, and who then returned to confront the fuming manager with the news that while in town he had bought the estate and that his first act as new owner would be to fire the same imperious manager, caused a major stir more because of its rarity than anything else.

As a measure of how split the white population appeared even fifty years ago, there was reference to the existence of an "Overseer Class" during the inaugural meeting of the Overseer's Association on 25 March 1945. Like the BWU and the BCU which had been formed earlier, this association was organized to improve the lot of the overseers and to present a stronger bargaining position when dealing with the manager-owner elite. Unfortunately, like the Clerks' Union, it was riven with internal discord owing to divided loyalties among its members.

Except for his possession of the means to coerce black workers on the plantation, the life of the white overseer or bookkeeper was also one of subservient contract labour. It is possibly this perception of inferior social status which made lower income whites notorious for the bitter race hatred they showed towards similarly inferior blacks to whom they lived in closer proximity and over whom they sought to maintain power and control. Working class blacks would never be perceived as posing the same sort of social threat to the white elite and middle class. As a consequence, the latter's disdain for the mass of blacks took on a more paternalistic character.

In an interesting comparison to the restrictive effects of the located labour system on the black population, the plantation overseer was obliged to spend the entire month on the plantation with only one day off. There was virtually no contact with the outside world. There was certainly no social contact with the manager or owner who often lived on the other side of the plantation yard. Overseers were generally refused permission to use the telephone when these came to be installed during the first quarter of the century in the owner-manager's residence.

The overseer's quarters did not possess electricity or running water. Contemporaries recall that when the overseer wished to take a bath, the plantation watchman would typically carry a bucket of water from the horse trough to a remote location in the plantation yard and dowse the overseer, leaving a bar of soap at his side. Once finished, the overseer would call to the watchman who would return with another bucket and dowse him again to remove the soap.

An overseer's life was seen as one for a single man. Consequently, married men were only rarely hired for the job. (In this regard, Harry Lewis would have been quite an exception.) The only other white woman on the plantation was the manager's wife with whom any form of social contact was strictly forbidden.

Occasion for conversation would most likely relate to the eating of daily meals which were prepared by the manager's wife and ferried over to the overseer's quarters. For these meals the overseer typically paid half of his monthly earnings. White overseers were thus inclined to develop liaisons with black and coloured females who worked in the labouring gangs. Such unions were commonplace and did not generate the sort of social condescension which might otherwise have arisen in a non-plantation setting. The children of such liaisons often found themselves in the fortunate position of enjoying a special status on the estate.

In Kensington New Road

Lewis aged 13

In the period 1920–40, Kensington New Road served as a sort of perpendicular connecting lane between the then wealthy Fontabelle district with the poorer Baxter's Road area. It is a fascinating social laboratory of the time. One's location along this predominantly "white" road designated the social status of the family. One resident from the area at the time recalls that during his early life, TT Lewis occupied a rented room in a house on Kensington New Road. It was located close to the Baxter's Road end. Living memory recorded during the interviews reveals that people who lived in Kensington New Road were considered by the affluent residents of Fontabelle main road to be one step down. It went roughly like this:

At the time, the social scene in Fontabelle and Kensington New Road area was quite complex. On the Fontabelle side of Kensington New Road there were the established families: the Herberts, the Bancrofts, the Hoads, the Badleys and the Wests. The lower class whites lived towards the Baxters Road and New Orleans end where the tenantries were located. (Elsie Foster)

[Lewis] was motivated by his experiences in life and by his low position in society – both he and his brother [Eyre]. Kensington New Road – there were a lot of poor whites down there. Not Fontabelle, but Kensington New Road. These sorts of people were generally clerks while the richer types lived in Fontabelle. (Owen T. Allder)

It is difficult to tell with any certainty what effect Harry Lewis' departure for the USA had on the family unit, but it seems to have produced some strain. Little or nothing is known about Lewis or his brothers and surviving sister at this time. Lewis' mother, remembered fleetingly by a pre-teenage author as a tiny frail woman, was described by others as kind, but superstitious and manipulable. It is likely that holding together a small family on the basis of an overseas remittance which eventually ended when Harry Lewis died, would have been a heavy strain. Things may have fallen apart. Members of a family which lived in the Kensington New Road area in that era said that they recalled seeing Lewis running around the area as a little boy in patches "like a little ragamuffin". According to another source: "TT used to go down to our family house to visit on Sunday afternoons. Apparently TT didn't have any family that he would visit. He visited us also for Christmas dinner." (Robert Cecil)

> ONE KENSINGTON NEW ROAD CHARACTER
>
> On 21 September 1991, the author sauntered along Kensington New Road to see whether there were still any elderly residents who could recall Lewis. In one rum shop, one of the patrons (an elderly black lady not yet fully inebriated) said she remembered Lewis as the "Martian man". At first, the owner and another old man thought it was the rum talking: what did she mean, "Martian man"? They attempted to restrain her colourful language by telling her to sit down and shut up. No doubt they had heard it all before. Then it dawned what she meant: not "Martian man" but "marching man" – i.e. the man in the march. This confirmation rapidly put the wind back in her sails, and re-established her credibility as a repository of information on Kensington New Road, Lakes Folly and New Orleans. Hidden among the several expletives used in conveying her impressions of the man, was the central point of why she still remembered him: "Lewis was the only white man to march for a black cause", she said. Actually, this description is a reversal of what happened during the Lewis demonstration in 1949, but remains an indication of how Lewis is still perceived by the elderly black residents of the area.

Whatever the reason, Lewis left home when he was about ten years old and got odd jobs around the place. He spent a lot of time with the Cecil family then living in the Brandons and Holborn area of the city located near to Kensington New Road. They may have semi-adopted him as the reasonably well-off Chenery family would later do. "When TT came to know 'Colly' [Frank Collymore], the latter remarked that it was as if TT had had no previous life. It seemed that all his previous life had been wiped clean. He maintained no contact with what I assumed must have been his former circle of family and friends." (Trevor Gale)

It is known that Lewis had no great liking for his younger brother Eyre, for whom, because of their similar appearance, Lewis was often mistaken. Lewis and

Eyre would pointedly avoid greeting and speaking to each other in public. As regards the tense relations with his brother, it was speculated that Lewis loathed Eyre because he considered the latter to be a layabout and resented his mother for encouraging this favoured son in his idleness. All interviewees confirmed that Lewis consistently refused to talk on the subject and that what they managed to ferret out came from other sources.

No one really knew what was the cause of the great schism between TT and his family, but I had heard that there was a girl – TT's twin and that she had died – the cause of which may have been blamed on TT. If this is true, it is possible that TT never forgave his mother for blaming him. But you really can't say, it's all speculation. (Constance Younglao)

I never succeeded, even by the most roundabout approach, to discover his origin or ancestry. He simply did not concern himself with such matters. The one thing I knew is that he seemed suddenly to appear on the scene, taking the most avid interest in all the literary, cultural and debating circles of his time . . . He had never attained a high level of formal education, yet he soon stood out as a striking figure not only for his personal integrity but his intellectual power. (F.A. Hoyos in *The Quiet Revolutionary*[13])

Evidence from a photograph dated 1918–20 discovered among Lewis' few surviving possessions, confirms that he was employed by a Bridgetown firm of debt collectors called "W.H. Bryan & Co.", located on Roebuck Street. The firm appears to have been staffed by approximately ten persons of whom Lewis was the youngest: he would probably have worked as a general office helper. During this period, young, lower income whites were to be found working all around

Office boy: between the ages of 13–15 Lewis (back row "X") worked as a general office helper in W.H. Bryan, a Roebuck Street firm of debt collectors.

Bridgetown, mainly as junior clerks or cash boys in the retail stores. One interviewee recalled them as "half-starved, little sallow-faced white boys working for a few shillings a week".

This is likely to have been the only job Lewis held before joining the Central Agency, the firm with which he was to spend the bulk of his working life. Records from the time of his dismissal from the Central Agency date his arrival there in 1920, just before his fifteenth birthday. One interviewee, an elderly lady living in secluded nostalgic splendour in the midst of bustling Bridgetown in the 1990s, and speaking on condition that she not be named, informed the author that around that time one of her older relatives who worked at the Central Agency apparently took young Lewis under his wing for a short spell. She said that in doing so, her family was attempting to give Lewis a leg up in life. A junior level job was thus arranged for the young Lewis at the Central Agency.

Despite several forthright efforts to get to the bottom of the great schism that appears to have ruptured Lewis' relationship with his family, the author was unable to uncover the secret. But something quite momentous appears to have taken place in the family during Lewis' teenage years. Family memory tossed out a number of possible explanations, none of which were entirely convincing. Since his mother never spoke of it either, whatever had happened died with her in 1971. "Somehow, TT came to feel that his mother had been cruel to him. Some terrible thing had happened in the family when TT was young." (Ellice Collymore)

New recruit: in 1920, Lewis (foreground with papers) joined Central Agency Ltd, the Barbadian wholly-owned retail agents for the Scottish cotton and thread giant J.P. Coats, Clark and Co. He would work for this firm for 28 years.

Nonetheless, Lewis and his mother Ethel appear, with the passage of time, to have reconciled their differences. In later years he is supposed to have visited her regularly, and their exchanges were reportedly cordial. She is remembered as taking pride in the fact that her son, despite his alleged radicalism, had become a prominent and respected member of the Barbados House of Assembly.

Schooling the Father of Free Secondary Education

In 1958, the DLP ran a large newspaper advertisement carrying brief résumés of their four candidates for the upcoming elections to the Federal Assembly of the West Indies (see chapter 10). While the text capsules on three of the candidates – Errol Barrow, Edwy Talma and J.C. Tudor – conveyed detailed descriptions of their academic and scholastic achievements, the entry for TT Lewis was spare. It said nothing about where or whether he had gone to school. It stated simply: "The first bona fide employee to be elected to the Barbados House."

This is how one of those three candidates recalls his first encounter with the man:

I was introduced to TT Lewis by Theodore (now Sir Theodore) Brancker upon my return to Barbados from Oxford at the end of 1945. It was Boxing Day. I particularly remember being amazed at the vastness of his knowledge and the precision with which he arranged his arguments. Having just returned from Oxford, I more than likely thought too much of myself and was somewhat snobbishly impressed that someone in Barbados was able to engage me intellectually. *I would say that within 15 minutes of having met TT, I felt that I had come across the most informed mind that I had yet met.* (Sir James Tudor)

It is impossible to trace any records of Lewis having attended school. The author's father recalled: "In those days you would be told that if you went to school it would make your head soft and that it wasn't good for you . . ." Logic suggests that if Lewis had been fortunate enough to have attended school, he would have most likely gone to St Mary's, near the Bridgetown church that bears the same name. The school is known to have opened in the early part of the nineteenth century as a place of education for the children of coloureds and was located near to where he and his mother resided. However, because St Mary's existing school records do not predate the 1930s, by which time Lewis would have long since left, it is impossible to determine whether Lewis attended. In any case he would not have stayed in school much beyond the age of ten.

What is known is that Lewis was largely self taught. Several of the interviewees indicated that he had spent a lot of time educating himself. Probably when he was in his early twenties, but certainly after he joined the Central Agency, Lewis started to learn the practice of bookkeeping. One interviewee recalled that Lewis took bookkeeping lessons from her father in their Roebuck Street home some time in the 1920s.

Lewis in his early twenties

In terms of vocational options open to whites of his social origins, Lewis' choices were rather limited. He could have remained a clerk or he could attempt to improve his marketability by becoming more fully numerate: hence the bookkeeping studies. Nonetheless, it is an interesting reflection on the limited social mobility of the time that Lewis ironically fell into a similar employment path to the one his father had held at Drax Hall and Pool plantations and had emigrated from Barbados to escape: that of a bookkeeper.

A Reflection on the Notion of Class

The most disappointing aspect of trying to understand what motivates people to form themselves into classes is that the concept of class consciousness is more often described than explained. Even if there is little general agreement on what constitutes a proper definition of the term "class", political analysts usually come to the conclusion that class consciousness has a profound impact on politics. Some people measure class simply by what they can observe using such yardsticks as social status, wealth, income, prestige and family lineage. Others – Marxists for example – go further claiming, in a nutshell, that the economic environment casts men into particular roles and that these roles govern men's behaviour and thought.

But this deterministic approach ceases to hold water past the point where you can demonstrate that individuals in similar economic circumstances (and hence class positions) react completely differently in response to the same events. How, for example, can this perspective explain the work of the (albeit few) liberal elite Barbadian whites who tried to ameliorate the oppressive social conditions besetting lower income blacks and whites?

The other problem with this line of argument is that it depersonalizes the issue of natural justice and attributes blame for wrongdoing to "the system" and not to individuals. One could argue that the white Barbadian elite was only following the path of its own predetermined reactionary role in the history of the class struggle and that elite whites can therefore not be judged as individuals. By the same token, snobbish members of the black middle class Spartan Cricket Club in the 1930s (see chapter 2) would incur no blame for their rejection of other blacks deemed to be of lower social worth. The overall conclusion might be that given the opportunity to turn the tables, the same oppressed individuals would have acted no differently from their oppressors.

This leads logically to the question of whether one can judge the individual outside of his or her own historical context – quite clearly not. But natural human elements of sympathy and a search for social justice do exist – the sorts of attributes that make people instinctively aware of what is right or wrong in what they happen to be doing.

If natural justice is neither culture-relative nor time-bound, then for oppression to disappear, reformist attitudes must have a means to be translated into political reality. Hence the question of how the pressure for social justice is handled by the existing political power structure. What avenues exist for the expression of discontent? In this century, many societies have either witnessed retarded social progress or have been utterly destroyed because their political machinery was not structured in such a way as to permit contending points of view to be aired and reasoned argument for social improvement to prevail. We have repeatedly witnessed situations where civic identities formed within a state are not strong enough to counteract other group allegiances based, for example, on race, language, religion or ethnicity. In the 1990s, countries such as Bosnia, Rwanda and Afghanistan are but the worst examples of this tendency. In such a context, the answer to the question "Who will protect me?" becomes "My own people." There is a rush to seek refuge in the partial human solidarities of race, class, religion or ethnicity and this undercuts the possibility of building multi-ethnic societies.

And yet, and in this same century, mature, culturally diverse states have existed, simultaneously and loudly demonstrating that these partial solidarities may prove relatively insignificant if the institutions of state are strong enough and free enough to ensure that the citizen can go about his or her business without fearing for security. And since people generally centre their identity on their individuality rather than these partial solidarities, reason dictates that civil society and peace can result if the institutions of the state can guarantee equality under the law to individuals as rights-bearing creatures.

And so we return to Barbados' political evolution in the 30 years prior to independence – the backdrop of this book. Given the fact that restrictions on the franchise were financial and not racial, as Barbadians grew wealthier, the colony was able to follow a path of evolutionary reform. Even the 1937 riots did not force it down a revolutionary path. Eventually full adult suffrage and the open constitutional democratic system encouraged by Britain propelled the island past independence into its current status as one of the most developed of the developing countries.

But the question of what motivates people to form classes remains unanswered. Is it a refuge from the nudity of individualism in a world of selfish, dominion seeking humanity? Is it some other unknowable reason? Whatever the motivating impulse behind class consciousness, it is undeniable that in the Barbadian context, social distinctions derived from ownership of land and skin colour offered a readily available matrix into which the evident human instinct to pigeonhole individuals could be exercised. And in clear and simple terms, the island's entire political, economic and social system at the time of TT Lewis was oppressive to the vast majority of the population which either did not have access to land or which was the "wrong" colour. Or both.

In retrospect therefore the great achievement of the architects of Barbados' social revolution in the middle of this century was to recognize the lethal nature of race consciousness and class consciousness in the absence of state institutions to govern fairly and humanely. As architects, their efforts to build mechanisms to divert race- and class-based competition for resources through democratically governed organs of state power turned out to be a profound success.

NOTES

1. J.C. Tudor, "A.E.S. Lewis, an appreciation", in the *Daily Nation*, 31 July 1989. The phrase is borrowed from Thomas Gray's *Elegy Written in a Churchyard* : "Let not ambition mock their useful toil, / Their homely joys, and destiny obscure, / Nor grandeur hear with a disdainful smile, / The short and simple annals of the poor."
2. Aside from Lewis' birth certificate, additional evidence exists to tie his father to Drax Hall estate in that period. The Barbados Archives is in possession of the Drax Hall rent books. An entry for August 1903 shows that one Harry Lewis owed and paid $9.00 for 12 months' rent of land belonging to the plantation. Geoffrey Armstrong, owner of Hampton

plantation located not far from Drax Hall recalls hearing older relatives mention that Lewis' father worked as an overseer / bookkeeper at Drax Hall up to around 1910.

3. This fact poses risks for any numerical analysis of votes cast during the period of the property qualification. In one notorious case, four Skeete brothers – who owned Byde Mill and Bentley plantations which straddle the parishes of St George, St John, St Philip and Christ Church – were, on this basis, entitled to cast 32 votes among them.

4. The Voter Registration list contains 1,692 names for the year 1905. The numerical breakdown was as follows: St Michael (391), Bridgetown (347), St Philip (209), Christ Church (132), St George (115), St Peter (111), St Lucy (94), St Joseph (92), St James (60), St Andrew (52), St Thomas (50) and St John (39).

5. J.C. Tudor, "A.E.S. Lewis, an appreciation", in the *Daily Nation*, 31 July 1989.

6. The major absentee-owned estates at the time were: The Belle & the Mount (850 acres), Drax Hall (800 acres), Kendal (700 acres), Colleton (500 acres), Nicholas (400 acres), Cleland (400 acres), Pickerings (300 acres), Pool (300 acres) and Warrens (250 acres).

7. See appendix 3, parts 1–3.

8. See Bonham Richardson, *Panama Money in Barbados (1900–1920)*, University of Tennessee Press, Knoxville, 1985.

9. For a detailed account of some of the names of this elite see appendix 6.

10. By the middle of the nineteenth century, the worldwide expansion of the sugar industry had created major challenges to West Indian sugar supremacy. This prompted a need for industry rationalization which occurred through the process of estate amalgamation and incorporation on the premise that larger limited liability companies would be better able to withstand the pressures of the successive sugar crises which were then taking place. In the case of Barbados, the landed white planter families, were, for a variety of reasons, able to resist the pressure to changing the structure of their holdings until the last decade of the nineteenth century. However, from about the time of the sugar recession between 1890–1902, the process of corporatization was gathering pace. The island's merchants and businessmen had started to buy up estates and take a political interest in the colony's future by becoming assemblymen. In establishing Plantations Ltd in 1917 the planters were attempting to protect themselves from the growing monopolization of the import-export sector by the commercial houses. However, they were unable to sustain the effort. The merchants responded by setting up the Barbados Shipping and Trading (BS&T) Company in 1920. BS&T represented a holding operation where the "Big Six" commercial houses (see appendix 6) could continue to operate individually as family firms but with enhanced strength. This new agrocommercial elite also encroached on the old plantocratic families through marriage alliances and became Barbados' new ruling elite prior to the emergence of the pre- independence black leadership which followed the riots and the social revolution of 1937–66. For a full account of this process see Cecilia Karch, "From the plantocracy to BS&T: crisis and transformation of the Barbadian socioeconomy, 1865–1937", in Woodville Marshall (Ed), *Emancipation IV – A Series of Lectures to Commemorate the 150th Anniversary of Emancipation*, Canoe Press, Jamaica, 1993.

11. See appendix 6.

12. Most plantation overseers were white. The only other racial grouping whose members served as overseers were the coloureds or persons of mixed race. At this time, such persons would have accounted for about 5 percent of all overseers.
13. F.A. Hoyos, *The Quiet Revolutionary*, Macmillan Caribbean, London, 1984, 99.

CHAPTER TWO

The Formative Years

Lewis' formative years took place in the Barbados of the 1920s and 1930s. He was a young man with an active social profile. But his movements in the social scene give us few clues as to what formed his view of the way the world worked. Few young adults have clearly defined views on such matters.

As Lewis grows older, the ability of the interviewees to recall details about his characteristics improves correspondingly. His milieu is a colonial island society preoccupied with considerations of social status – derived largely, but not exclusively, from an individual's position along the colour spectrum. The "little ragamuffin" of the Kensington New Road years is starting to mature. He is joining social circles, sporting clubs and other groups that give him a profile among people whose names, while not belonging to the plantocracy or mercantile elite, were certainly not working class either.

As the picture of his formative years becomes clearer, the investigator finds more indicators of the

TT and I would often take a morning swim out from the Aquatic Club to the barge and back for exercise. I know that if TT had had too much to drink the night before he would recommend diving down ten feet and taking ten gulps of water to "purge the system" as he called it.
Donald Wiles (left) with TT Lewis in the early 1930s

development within Lewis of an attitude that later caused him to launch a challenge upon the island's prevailing social norms and customs. Lewis is drawn more and more to the company of people who questioned the way the colony was run. He starts moving in middle class "intellectual" societies of the sort that would eventually allow him to translate his iconoclastic views into political expression. Even so, before the end of the 1930s, the reformer with the social conscience is still visible only in outline.

LIFE OF THE PARTY

As would be reasonable to expect, few of the interviewees who knew Lewis as a young adult, sportsman and party goer paid much attention to his evolving political mind set. The portrait they paint of him is one of effervescence, wit and brashness. As the dawning of his political career approached, some recalled that he was a pleasant sort socially but possessed a tendency to go off on tirades about social justice.

TT Lewis (bottom left) with friends at the Bethel Hall (mid 1930s)

"TT was a very witty fellow. In fact, our group probably thought he was the funniest man in Barbados. It was only when he later entered politics that we discovered how serious he was." (Trevor Gale)

Those who knew him said that Lewis had a gift for making friends, for making puns and for reducing most topics to a joke of one sort or other.

... TT was a loveable character, with a highly developed sense of humour and a ready wit. He was, it is true, capable of biting sarcasm, as his opponents well knew and greatly feared, but his was a happy figure in any company, enlivening whatever group he happened to be among. (E.L. Cozier, in *Caribbean Newspaperman* [1])

You couldn't have a party unless you invited TT Lewis. He was a funny man. Let me give you an example: one day we went on a bus excursion to St Philip, and at that time, tradition held that when you got to Six Roads you were supposed to make a wish. When we reached the crossing,

TT got up and declared, "I wish somebody would be kind enough to pay my bus fare". (Kathleen Smitten)

Lewis is described as tallish, standing just under six feet. Although not a teetotaller he did not drink lavishly. Friends recall that until he got married he was a bit of a loner. While he was popular at parties and gatherings, Lewis appears not to have been involved in steady relationships with any of the women he knew. On the question of whether this was because he studiously avoided such liaisons, or because girls, fearing serious liaisons, avoided him, the jury is divided. Psychoanalysts could make much of the possible Oedipus complex that might have developed between Lewis and his mother and what may have caused this. Two sources confirmed independently that Lewis had had an intense love affair – long before meeting his eventual wife – with the wife of a sea captain and that when his mother discovered it, she was extremely disturbed by the news.

Theatre

By his early twenties, Lewis had long left the Kensington New Road area. He is reported to have lived briefly at a boarding house near St Patrick's Cathedral finally moving to a two-room rented flat in a house called "Clifton" on Bay Street. The dwelling is situated about 2 kilometres from the city centre and Lewis spent the remainder of his days in the Bay Street house as a tenant.

Here, he was just a few steps away from his old friend Frank Collymore who lived in Chelsea Road. In many respects, Collymore, a humanist and eventual Barbadian literary giant, would henceforth play the rather quixotic role of big brother, friend and intellectual companion throughout the rest of Lewis' life. Although it is difficult to point to the impact which his moderating advice may have had in any one specific instance, Collymore appears to have exerted a restraining influence on Lewis, providing cool reflective judgement on some of Lewis' more passionate ideas. Collymore's widow relates lengthy discussions between the two men on the issues of the day and on the content of upcoming Order Papers for the House of Assembly. Collymore also seems to have played the role of social facilitator

Frank Collymore (left) and Lewis at an east coast beach house in the early 1930s

for Lewis. It is reported that Collymore's house in Chelsea Road, which served as a thinking man's watering hole, is where Lewis first met the young Errol Barrow, eventual father of independent Barbados, as well as Guyanese Marxist and future prime minister, Cheddi Jagan. "Colly's [Collymore's] house was a *sanctum sanctorum* for almost everybody. The truth is that Colly found politics to be the most boring of activities. For TT, politics was everything. Therefore I could never really understand the basis of their great friendship." (Sir Alexander Hoyos)

Stage actor: Lewis (top hat) poses with players off the set of one of his several theatre performances in the 1930s

These were still the days of the horse and buggy, when the radio and the emerging cinema were the most prominent forms of mass entertainment. People interacted more during this period than they appear to have done following the advent of television, the video recorder and the technogame home. Far greater emphasis was placed upon generating entertainment for oneself and one's company. This included stage plays and the like. It is almost certain that Lewis was introduced to theatre by Collymore and, from the photographic evidence, he was actively involved in much of what went on stagewise in Barbados at the time. Photographs exist of Lewis as an amateur actor in several plays, none of which appear to have used West Indian scripts or featured island characters. A selection of stage parts found among Lewis' possessions confirms this. The Empire theatre had opened in 1922 in Bridgetown and it is said that Lewis performed in some of the short stage skits that usually preceded the screening of the feature film. Other plays would have been performed as complete pieces.

The social club that Lewis and his friends frequented at the time was the Aquatic Club which was becoming something of an institution for lower and middle income whites and coloureds of the period. Located adjacent to the more exclusive Barbados Yacht Club, it provided an opportunity for locals of more modest social background to congregate and entertain themselves. At the time, Frank Collymore used this venue to stage a number of skits and some plays in which Lewis featured both prominently and regularly as part of Collymore's drama group. They also performed plays at Combermere School, one of the island's prominent secondary boys schools, where Collymore was teaching at the time. What is particularly interesting about the photographs of those with whom Lewis performed is that they confirm the large presence of coloureds in Barbadian performing arts.

"TT [standing third from left] played polo at the Aquatic Club for a team called the Congers. Other teams at the time would have been the Flying Fish, the Snappers, the Sea Scouts and the Harbour Police." (Mike Foster)

The Aquatic Club also provided Lewis with other means of entertainment. He is described by those who knew him in the early years as keen at tennis, and a good swimmer – being both a player and referee of water polo.

THE PRE-WAR CRICKETING SCENE

Like most Barbadians, Lewis enthusiastically played cricket, the sport which is often compared to a national religion. Unlike most, he competed successfully in the island's First Division tournament as a fast bowler. However, his was no extraordinary talent. One surviving sporting vignette freezes Lewis in time, and captures in a metaphorical sense much of what was attractive about his style:

> ... Lewis ... was the last man to the wicket, and undeterred by the excitement which prevailed, he hit two consecutive balls over the boundary. These were shots of a brave man, and might well have been an index of his downfall, for, attempting another lusty drive he missed and skied the

ball. Parris was the bowler and on hastening to take the catch, he fell, and lying on his back, he took it. It was a phenomenal catch and such a dramatic dismissal was in keeping with the whole of the Pickwick second innings.[2]

In colonial times, Britain, as "Mother Country", routinely trumpeted the role of cricket as a builder of the bonds of empire. Its soldiers, teachers and administrators felt it their duty to use the game as a tool to impart and inculcate values such as discipline and gentlemanly conduct. Originally propagated by both expatriate Britons and British-educated sons of the local white plantocracy in the late nineteenth century, the expansion of the game beyond the confines of white plantocratic society had started, but had not yet gotten fully underway when Lewis first started playing in the 1920s.

At that time, the Barbados cricketing world consisted of very few clubs. And these tended to categorize themselves along very restrictive lines. Historian Keith Sandiford succinctly describes the situation then prevailing:

> The competition, in fact, was overly governed for a very long time by considerations of class and colour. Wanderers was the club for the wealthiest white families, Pickwick represented the clerical and commercial interests in the capital city, while Leeward and Windward were controlled by planter families from the rural parishes. The two leading secondary schools, Harrison College and Lodge, served as nurseries for all the other clubs . . . Spartan was founded in 1893 to meet the needs of middle class black and mulatto players. But Spartan itself was so exclusive that Empire had to be founded in 1914 to cater to the interests of lower middle class blacks with whom the Spartan players were reluctant to associate.[3]

First with Pickwick . . .

Lewis' face first graces the massive wall of photographs in Kensington Oval, home ground of both Pickwick and of the Barbados national team, as part of a picture of the Pickwick team which won the Challenge Cup in the 1924–25 season. Established in 1892, the Challenge Cup was the island's foremost cricketing tournament and it would have been a considerable sporting achievement for Lewis to be part of the winning team as he would then have been only 19 years old and is easily the youngest looking member of the team. In the constellation of existing cricket clubs, Pickwick was seen as one notch down from Wanderers, but was still an exclusivist club populated only by whites. In sociological terms, it is difficult to determine at what point Lewis may have started to ask questions about the nature of the class and colour structure within Barbadian cricket.

If you had any claims to social position and you were coloured, you played for Spartan. Empire was an offshoot of Spartan Club peopled by individuals who felt they would not be admitted there. If you were white and were a Pile, a Robinson, a Sealy or of similar social standing, you played for Wanderers. If you were not of the highest class (a Goddard, or a King for example) you played for Pickwick. (Sir Hugh Springer)

It is clear that in order to enter cricket at the highest level in Barbados, membership of one of the eight clubs was essential. Since Lewis was not of the social standing to gain membership in Wanderers, Leeward or Windward, and had never been to secondary school (ruling out Harrison College and Lodge), Pickwick, the club of "clerical and commercial interests", would probably have seemed to him, of all the white clubs, the most obvious choice. Added to this is the fact that Pickwick abuts the Fontabelle and Kensington New Road area. As a boy, Lewis would almost certainly have spent time watching cricket being played at Kensington Oval and would have developed an attachment to the club. Had Lewis joined either of the two existing non-white clubs, Spartan or Empire, such an action would have indicated an unusually early development within him of a social attitude deviating from the norm. If one assumes, on the other hand, that Lewis' attitude to society and concern for equality of access to the island's institutions developed later once he gained experience and a fuller exposure to Barbadian society, it is reasonable to conclude that being a young man interested in sporting success, he did not consider the matter of race very much at this stage. In any case, his journey with Pickwick was soon to come to an end.

Lewis (standing, second from left) as member of Pickwick Cricket Club in the 1924–25 season

TT was an up and down fast bowler – meaning that he bowled three good and three bad balls per over. As a result, he couldn't keep his place on the Pickwick first eleven. So, disenchanted with the club – probably more for cricketing reasons than for its white exclusivist policy – he went on to play for St Ann's and then YMPC [Young Men's Progressive Club]. (Tony Hinds)

Stanton Gittens, a former Barbadian fast bowler and wicketkeeper in the 1930s, is known to have described Lewis as someone who would "run up fast and bowl slow".

... then with St Ann's

For the duration of its decade and a half existence, after being founded in the mid 1920s, the St Ann's Cricket Club occupied the eastern end of the Garrison Savannah which was then and remains the island's only horse racing course. During the cricketing season, it borrowed part of the Turf Club building for use as a clubhouse. In terms of pedigree, it belongs to the second generation of established cricket clubs in Barbados. Even the term "established" is a bit of a misnomer since the club started out some time in 1924–25 and lasted for only a decade and a half before disbanding in 1941 as a result of financial constraints brought on by declining membership. According to one local cricketing authority, St Ann's "entered the second division and did so well that although it did not contain enough members to field a second team as the rules required, it was admitted to the first division in 1931."[4] Though St Ann's was a club comprised of white men, one former member who was interviewed added, "but it was a club for the ordinary white man not for the white managers and directors. That crowd went to Wanderers."

TT had apparently had an argument with some of the members of Pickwick Cricket Club and came to play for us at St Ann's. We were at the time extremely glad to have a fast bowler of some talent on the side. This was in the 1930s and TT then became a permanent feature of the St Ann's side. (Irwin Burke)

With St Ann's Cricket Club: Lewis (second from right in the back row) as part of the Second Eleven Cup Winners in 1931. (Third from right in the back row is Hammond Burke.)

Even after the passage of half a century, ageing members of the club were visibly resentful of the manner in which their club had to be shut down. They attributed it mainly to financial circumstances, saying that they had too few members and thus subscriptions, to cover expenses. The formation of the YMPC about one kilometre away, with fees lower than those of St Ann's, had the direct effect of siphoning off membership.

Although Lewis became a member of the YMPC, he never played cricket after he left St Ann's. It is likely that Lewis joined YMPC because some of the lectures and debates of the time, in which he was beginning to develop a particular interest, were being delivered at the YMPC. The available information shows that YMPC was a social club formed for the advancement of young men in the lower strata of white society, but paid for, ironically, by members of its upper class. Explanations for this curious development range from simple elite philanthropy to a perceived need to cultivate loyalty among lower income whites in the face of growing black clamour for civil and political rights.

This inevitably led some lower income whites to question the club's bona fides – a feeling that was sharpened during the years of the short-lived trade union of white and mulatto Bridgetown clerks which was formed in the mid 1940s (and is examined in chapter 6) to demand better working conditions for its members.

Though perhaps not central to the larger struggle then manifesting itself between the workers and the establishment – and thus largely ignored in historical literature – is the vigorous infighting within the lower stratum of white Barbados. It was most likely caused by the class pressures associated with the looming breakdown of plantocratic society. Many of these low income whites, some still alive, felt victimized by and immensely hostile to the white oligarchy. The resulting hostility they harboured but never openly displayed towards the white elite, was also directed at those of their own kind whom they considered to be stooges of that oligarchy.

Serving with the Barbados Volunteer Force

In July 1937, rioting occurred in Barbados. This event formed part of a series of working class protests which wracked the English-speaking Caribbean between the years 1935–38. The cause of the riots, as emerged in the testimony before subsequent hearings, was an explosive mixture of poverty and economic depression (then a worldwide phenomenon) combined with long years of imperial neglect and, in the case of many colonies, the restrictive political environment of development of Crown Colony (quasi direct) rule from London. Barbados was among the last of the British territories to explode.

Although it was the Royal Barbados Police Force which provided most of the firepower used to suppress the rioters (resulting in 14 deaths, 47 wounded and over 400 arrests), the Barbados Volunteer Force (BVF) was heavily involved in the efforts to quell the disturbances. It was called out, assembled and sent to man vulnerable locations within the island, as well as its own positions.

With the benefit of hindsight, what makes Lewis such a paradox is the fact that in his early years he was heavily involved in many aspects of Barbadian establishment society. Yet, he later emerged as a champion of those whom that same social structure was battering badly. Thus the apparent contradiction of his association with the BVF.

The BVF was a military unit formed in 1902 in anticipation of British military withdrawal from the island which occurred three years later.[5] During the Second World War, the BVF was absorbed into the Barbados Battalion of the South Caribbean Force, and after the war, was reconstituted as the Barbados Regiment in 1948.

Although it is known that Lewis was a BVF member, the paucity of available data on the force prevents us from knowing his exact dates of enrolment and discharge. As a consequence, it is not known whether he joined before the 1937

Scene from the 1937 riots: members of the Royal Barbados Police Force (upper left) make a baton charge up Broad Street, Bridgetown's main thoroughfare during the disturbances which claimed fourteen lives.

Company from the Barbados Volunteer Force in the 1940s dressed in mufti

riots, and if so, whether he was actively involved in the BVF's anti-riot operations. At the time of the 1937 riots Lewis would have been 31 years old, and just about to start taking politics seriously. His political views could not have failed to be influenced when these poverty-based riots swept through Barbados. If Lewis had chanced to pen his thoughts on this momentous occasion in Barbadian history, none of these writings survived. Any assessment of his views must therefore be speculative:

Author: Would it be incongruous for a man like Lewis, so much an advocate of working class rights, to have been a loyal member of the Barbados Volunteer Force – at a time like the riots of 1937?

Major Rudolph Daniel: If TT had been with the BVF at the time of a confused situation like the riots, he would have understood the causes of the grievances and probably sympathized but he was a man of honour and would have undertaken his duty. You know, the military trains you to be a cipher. One is trained to deceive, and to kill effectively and efficiently. All feeling is supposed to be drained out of you, allowing you to respond only to commands. After service they need to rehabilitate men. But this is never really done successfully.

At the time of the riots the BVF was structured along the following lines. There were two companies each comprising about 110 men and each commanded by a captain. These companies would themselves be broken into three platoons each commanded by a lieutenant. According to those familiar with the BVF at or just after this period, the racial composition among the privates and noncommissioned officers would have been 70 percent black and 30 percent white. For officers, the ratio would be the reverse.

The only reasonably reliable fix on Lewis' dates in the BVF comes from a colleague who served with him in the volunteers. He says when they were together in the BVF, Lewis would have been in his mid thirties. If true, this means that Lewis may have enrolled after the riots. This tallies with other, albeit fragmentary, evidence on the subject at the time.

Immediately after the riots, a new company was established. It was associated with the YMPC and most of the volunteers who joined were from the YMPC. The whole idea behind this expansion of the force was to get the citizen who was employed full time to spend time giving service to the community via the volunteer force. This was certainly the perspective of the merchants. As TT was a member of the YMPC it is likely that he would have joined around this time and may therefore not have been involved at the time of the riots. But I can't really say. (Major Rudolph Daniel)

The BVF was a voluntary set up. You had uniforms, and had to do four parades a year. The parades on the occasion of the Queen's (or the King's) birthday were the most spectacular. We also spent time in camp near Gun Hill. Then there were the usual marches and from time to time we would take the train to the beach by Belleplaine, St Andrew for shootouts using live .303 ammunition. A good few white boys were involved in the Volunteers. TT and I were in 'A' company which was considered the elite outfit. We communicated from Gun Hill to Queen's Park with flashing mirrors in daylight and with lights at night. TT was a private like me but we never went very far in it. (J.E.T. "Jonny" Bourne)

As Lewis' interest in social issues and politics grew it is unlikely that he devoted much time to his role as a volunteer member. Lewis never went far in the BVF; he would have ended his stint with them as either a private or perhaps a lance-corporal in charge of a section. Although it is not known when he was discharged, he is unlikely to have served with the BVF much beyond the year 1940.

SOCIAL CLUBS AND DEBATING SOCIETIES IN PRE-WAR BARBADOS

Following the end of his active involvement in cricket and the BVF, we see Lewis throwing himself into intellectual pursuits. Foremost amongst these was an extremely active participation in the literary and debating societies of the time. He appears also to have dabbled in theosophy and the Bahai movement – both religious approaches with links to India, emphasizing the spiritual unity of mankind under god. The degree of Lewis' immersion in what appears to be a quest for profound knowledge and answers to questions that were occurring to him at the time, probably reflects his own efforts to make up for years of lost schooling through intense reading and wide ranging discussions.

Little exists on the structure and subject matter dealt with by literary and debating societies in the Barbadian context, but it seems fair to assume that as for most such groups, their members would have met, read and discussed papers by the literary critics of the day. Literary societies had in fact thrived following the emancipation of slaves in 1838 and had served as an early source of quenching the thirst for knowledge and education which formal liberation had generated among members of the black and coloured population. This trend continued in Barbados up to and slightly beyond the period in which Lewis was active in such societies. The limited spread of education had created a Barbadian black and coloured intelligentsia which gained some access to travel and its mentally emancipating effect. Literary and debating societies were a logical parallel of this trend: they thrived with the spread of education among the small black and coloured middle class intelligentsia and may even have served as a substitute for those dissatisfied with their exclusion from the corridors of power.

Prominent clubs went by such traditional sounding names as the Riverside Club, the Forum Club, the Weymouth Club and the Young Men's Christian Association (YMCA). Contemporaries described these as essentially middle class institutions "where lawyers and reverends would come to meet the ordinary folk." Although Lewis mixed with all elements of society, contemporaries report that his black friends at this time were intellectuals. Lewis was at this stage just one step away from a close association with Hilton Vaughan's Liberal Association and a career in politics.

> **THE BARBADOS LITERARY AND DEBATING SOCIETY.**
> The Society will hold a meeting to-night at 8 o'clock at Bethel Hall. Subject of Debate will be "That in the opinion of this House the practice of Birth Control is to be continued." Speakers will be Mr. T. Branker seconded by Mr. F. Walcott who will propose the motion, and Mr. A. E. Lewis seconded by Mr. E. St.A. Fitzpatrick who will opose. The meeting will only be opened to members and their friends.

Newspaper notice in the late 1930s announcing a debate in which Lewis was taking part. The Bethel Hall was then quite popular as a forum for this sort of event.

I first got to know [Lewis] through the fact that we were both members of the Forum Club which met at Bethel Hall (later the Bethel Auditorium). This was the heyday of the social club – the only real form of local entertainment. The Forum Club had no well-defined purpose. It was a very sedate and grown-up affair. The racial composition was very mixed in terms of coloureds and blacks, but TT was the only white man there. The others were from several social strata. There were a number of solicitors . . . (Sir Hugh Springer)

Barbadian historian Sir Alexander Hoyos says that he first got to know Lewis in 1935 when both he and Grantley Adams were involved in a group known as the Barbados Literary and Debating Society. He claims that both he and Lewis were placed on a small committee to draw up the rules of the new society where Lewis is first reported to have displayed his widely known penchant for employing language that was not always chaste:

[Lewis] had a flair for detail that amounted almost to genius . . . he would question every sentence, every word, every comma and semi-colon. To make his point clear he would use language that was as noted for its vulgarity as its vitality. During one session, he kept illustrating his comments and criticisms with a widely used four-letter word until Grantley intervened with the remark that he had examined the rules most carefully and had found nothing suggestive of sexual intercourse. (F.A. Hoyos in *The Quiet Revolutionary* [6])

Lewis appears at this stage in his life to be a man who liked to be at the centre of events and very civic minded, but whose thinking had clearly not yet crystallized. We see a man torn by his legitimate desire for change, and yet one constrained by his colour in a racially polarized society to move primarily in white or coloured social circles.

Marge

One of the first casualties of Lewis' consuming passion for politics would be his marriage. Long hours of work and the abandonment of most aspects of domestic family life inevitably put a strain on the relationship causing several rows and breakups before the final separation occurred.

Marjorie ("Marge") Perryman came from the nearby island of Dominica. Her father, a white Barbadian had emigrated there, married a coloured Dominican and settled in the island to run a group of citrus plantations. In order to permit the completion of his daughters' secondary education, Perryman sent Marge and her twin sister, Constance, to board in a Barbadian friend's house while they attended their two final years at the island's top girls school, Queen's College. Although quite a bit older than Marge, Lewis was introduced through mutual friends and the two started seeing a lot of each other. Eventually they fell in love. Given that the twin sisters looked so much alike, the author could not resist asking the surviving twin, Constance, what she felt made Lewis go for Marge and not her. Came the modest reply: "Marge had the sort of qualities that would instantly attract any man in a room". Constance admitted that she was the quieter of the two. Several of the male interviewees reminisced wistfully about Marge's reputed good looks, especially her figure. One admitted to having had lustful thoughts about her.

Lewis with the Perryman twins, Constance (left) and Marge (mid 1930s)

TT was about 13 years older than Marge was, but they soon fell in love. She was effervescent and always so full of fun. She and TT got on well together despite their age difference. We then left to go back to our parents in Dominica. TT came down to Dominica, probably in November 1936 on one of his sales trips to sell thread, and asked my father for Marge's hand in marriage. Marge then returned to Barbados for the wedding. No one from Dominica was able to afford to come to the wedding as it was the time of the Great Depression. (Constance Younglao)

Because she was only 19 and therefore, according to the laws of the time, a minor, an official of the Catholic Church in Dominica had to give written permission for Marge to marry. Marge was also reported to have been the keener of the two to get married. The wedding took place in February 1937. Because Marge was a Roman Catholic, she and Lewis (who, though a baptized Anglican, was probably a religious agnostic) were married at St Patrick's Roman Catholic Church in Bridgetown. It was a small wedding: only a few people attended. It was also brief: "a ten-minute affair", recalled someone who was present. The reception was held at a suburban residence named "Artrament" in Flint Hall, home of the Gales (a well-to-do coloured Barbadian family with Dominican connections) where the Perryman twins had stayed while attending school. The surviving photograph of the reception was taken there. The honeymoon, to which guests apparently invited themselves briefly, took place at a beach house in Silver Sands on the island's then undeveloped south coast.

Constance Younglao, née Perryman (1992)

Within a year their first child, Sonya, was born in Barbados. Soon, thereafter, the strains set in.

Although reluctant to press for excessive detail owing to the fact that some of the persons involved were still alive, the author tried to piece together the details of this stormy relationship. There is a general consensus that the demands produced by Lewis' emergent political career are what caused the eventual split. Additional pressure would have resulted from the fact that by 1936 Lewis had worked his way up through the Central Agency to reach the position of travelling salesman[7] for the eastern Caribbean (Windward and Leeward Islands routes) and would have consequently spent a large portion of the year – probably about three months – away from Barbados selling threads and clothing materials. The comment below, offered by one of Lewis' contemporaries, is typical of those who proffered an opinion on the subject of Lewis' marital problems:

I always felt that TT separated from his wife because every night he would be having political meetings in his drawing room. His wife claimed she wasn't having a real married life since every night TT would be bringing home people to discuss politics. He was very much in the centre of the political arena and moved with the spirit of the times. He loved the action, but paid for it with his marriage and his job. (Christie Smith)

While his time-consuming political career may have been the underlying cause, the eventual marital breakup appears to have been caused by forces at work which were a great deal more complex. Contemporaries recall that Marge was given to flights of fancy and, possibly because of her good looks and inclination for frequent socializing, may have felt uncomfortable in the role of housewife and, possibly, young mother. Lewis' politics and long absences travelling abroad would certainly have caused much loneliness.

The demands placed upon Lewis' time during his first election contest in 1942 were stated as the cause of the first separation. In total, Marge would leave Lewis four times, always taking the children (a second daughter, Diana, was born in 1944), and always on the ostensible grounds of wishing to spend holiday time with Marge's parents in Dominica. During these rows, the couple would hardly speak to each other. A close friend of both reported that she was once used to convey to Lewis the news that Marge wished to return to Dominica. When Marge left Lewis in 1947, it would be the final separation.

Marrying Marge Perryman (1937)

In such a trying situation, infidelity inevitably crept in, with faults on both sides. Lewis, uncomfortable with long bouts of celibacy, is known to have sought affection elsewhere. Marge apparently did likewise, dealing with Lewis' long absences on business and his political campaigning by finding one partner to whom she became very attached. As a devout Roman Catholic, however, Marge never actively pursued divorce from Lewis and remarriage to the gentleman in question.

Survivor: Donald Wiles (right, in 1993) in exactly the same spot where he stood as Lewis' best man in 1937 (left). Marge is pictured on Lewis' left (with flowers).

Lewis would make an interesting case study for those interested in psychological history. His early family life is far from cosy. His father leaves home and eventually dies overseas. His mother struggles to bring up the family, but Lewis encounters difficulty in his relationship with her. Then there is the serious sibling rivalry with his brother Eyre. It is not unlikely that his attitudes to prevailing social mores were profoundly affected by these relationships. He has few, if any, steady girlfriends. He then gets married, but the relationship is combustible and eventually breaks down. As the relationship unravels, Lewis takes other partners.

In all this, Lewis appears as a man possessed of a powerful sexuality. Whether or not this is linked to the commonly observed tendency for politicians to have roaming sexual lives based upon notions of possession and a general power driven attitude to social relations, Lewis' needs propelled him to find affection where he could within the busy political schedule that was by then taking up most of his time. He was a member of the Hospital Board and is remembered affectionately by several of the nurses whose cause he is known to have championed at a professional level.[8] At least one of his liaisons appears to have been with a black woman. Although the author found no documented evidence of this, if Lewis had fathered a child by a black woman he would, in the eyes of local whites, have gone beyond the pale since, as a rule, sexual relations with persons of colour imposed tremendous strains on white Barbadian families. If true, this development would fit an emerging pattern of rebel social behaviour.

However, there can be no doubt that until the end of his life, Lewis felt a deep love for his wife. During the numerous separations he wrote consistently to her — every week, recalled most interviewees. Indeed, Lewis' thoughts at the time of his dismissal from the Central Agency in 1949 (the subject of chapters 7 and 8) come to us largely through the copious letters he sent to Marge detailing events as they unfolded. These letters are strangely unromantic and factual. But between the lines they convey a sense of profound affection and undeniable regret at the absence of his beloved daughters, the details about whose upbringing he avidly sought to be informed. The fact that Marge chose to keep so many of his letters attests also to the reciprocal affection she must have felt for him.

Lewis' letters to her were usually accompanied by money – whatever he could send, according to close friends. In this way he was able to provide for the support of his exiled family. Whenever he was unable to enclose a remittance he always explained why. Eventually a legal separation with Marge was arranged. Some time in the late 1940s, Marge and the daughters left Dominica to join her parents in St Lucia where her father had taken up a job with the Public Works Department in 1940. It was to Marge in St Lucia that the Barbados House of Assembly sent a letter of condolence on the death of Lewis in 1959. She was living in St Lucia when Lewis died there the day before the wedding of his first daughter whom he was preparing to give away. Marge would travel briefly to Barbados to attend Lewis' memorial service, but continued to reside in St Lucia until her parents died. In 1971 she moved back to Barbados where she herself died, two days before her 70th birthday.

Lewis and Marge with their first daughter, Sonya (1938)

NOTES

1. E.L. Cozier, *Caribbean Newspaperman: The Life and Times of Jimmy Cozier*, Coles Printery Co., Barbados, 1987, 54.
2. Extract from George C. Greaves, "At the cross roads – A survey of big cricket in the West Indies 1924–36" [undated pamphlet].
3. Keith Sandiford, "100 Years of organized cricket in Barbados, 1892–1992", in *100 Years of Organized Cricket in Barbados, 1892–1992*, Barbados Cricket Association, Bridgetown (1992), 5.
4. Charles Alleyne, "Later clubs", in *100 Years of Organized Cricket*, 39.
5. The local militia had started in 1640. It was to remain the only military force on the island until the late 1700s during which time it is noted for having engaged the naval forces of

Cromwell (under Ayescue) and of the Dutch (under de Reuyter). The British then set up in Barbados a headquarters and garrison for all their Caribbean forces shortly before the year 1800. The title "militia" was maintained until 1881 when it was renamed the Barbados Yeomanry Corps. It was then renamed the BVF in 1902 three years before the British pulled out their garrison from the island. During the 1914–18 war the BVF was mobilized and embodied to become a full-time unit of the British Army with some of its members fighting under the British West Indies Regiment. Following the war, it was demobilized. During the period of the 1937 riots, the BVF "went to the aid of the civil power", meaning that its men were put under the direction of the police force.

6. F.A. Hoyos, *The Quiet Revolutionary*, Macmillan Caribbean, London, 1984, 99.
7. A.E.S. Lewis, Memorandum to the Board of Enquiry, 2 February 1949.
8. According to one person who sounded suspiciously close to being an old flame: "TT would always attend the nurses' dances. All the nurses felt that a waltz with him was like . . . well, you would feel as if you were being wafted into heaven. It was like something sacred. Especially when you came to the last dance. TT was always admired as a 'dancer'. In those days, when a graduation dance was coming up, you would have to go to the head nurse to get an invitation. Whoever got in first would ask to invite TT. She would then more than likely say: 'Mr Lewis has already been invited.' So you would have to look for someone else . . . This would have been when I was in my early 30s, therefore in about 1943."

CHAPTER THREE

In the Freemasonic Brotherhood

Colly, you know what they have done? They've gone and made me a Master at Lodge and I've got to prepare a feast as part of the celebration. But, man, I don't know where I'm going to find the money . . . (TT Lewis to Frank Collymore in the 1940s as reported by the latter's wife)

One of the most intriguing aspects of TT Lewis' character is his connection with the world of Freemasonry. It is an affiliation he maintained, following his initiation some time in the 1930s, until he died, but which remains a mystery to those who see Lewis' radicalism at odds with the apparent pro-establishment inclination of Freemasonry.

The investigation into Lewis' involvement with Freemasonry centres on three questions. First, would Lewis' strong advocacy of the cause of many, especially blacks, have aroused anxiety in his lodge, which was, at that time an all-white group and whose membership came overwhelmingly from the planter class? Secondly, as a consequence of this apparent contradiction, did Lewis scale down his Freemasonic activities after he became active in politics in the early 1940s? Thirdly, did his Freemasonic connection help or hinder him during the intense battle waged by the island's merchant elite to dismiss him from his job in 1949?

THE FELLOWSHIP OF THE CRAFT

Much of the literature used to guide the novice Freemason towards the order's three great principles ("brotherly love, relief and truth") is no longer inaccessible to non-Freemasons.[1] Books and other published material (often produced by Freemasons themselves) have shed light on the inner workings of this secret society which relies heavily on the ancient methods of symbol and ritual to impart Freemasonic concepts.

Freemasons say that their order is neither a religion nor a substitute for a religion. Although it contains many religious concepts and principles, they claim it is not a religion as it has no doctrine of god, or man, of sin, grace or salvation – which are termed the primary concerns of every religion. It is certainly true that Freemasonry's concept of god is undefined in religious terms. Within the order, Freemasonry is described as "a system of morality, veiled in allegory and illustrated by symbols".[2] Before becoming a full-fledged Freemason, the candidate is expected to pass through initiation ceremonies which have existed for hundreds of years and through which every Freemason has passed. The elementary principles of Freemasonry are embedded in the three degrees[3] which all masons are expected to complete within a period of typically two years. The symbolism of the order is replete with references to architecture, geometry and, naturally, masonry. The emphasis is on building moral character and building relationships between oneself, one's fellow man and god that are akin to the legendary perfection symbolized by the temple of King Solomon of the Old Testament.

Members of the order claim that their brotherhood is a fellowship aimed at "making good men better". It is supposed to stimulate intellectual and moral improvement, friendship, morality and brotherly love. Freemasons are also expected to practise charity, but there is no fixed system dictating how much should be donated or how frequently. Each member is expected to judge what he can and should do to relieve distress. Whether this is done individually or collectively, Freemasonic gifts are always made without publicity even when these gifts are granted to persons outside the brotherhood or its members' families. While Freemasonry will admit members of all religions,[4] a prerequisite for all prospective members is that they believe in some form of deity. To demonstrate their commonality of perspective, Freemasons of the different religions refer to this deity as the "Great Architect of the Universe".

Although claims that the origins of Freemasonry go back thousands of years are not universally accepted, it is acknowledged that organizations of "operative" masons, or those who actually worked with stone, did exist in the Middle Ages. Their symbols and rites closely resemble those of modern "speculative" Freemasons. Speculative Freemasonry is the term used to describe men who do not themselves work in stone but who nonetheless preserve much of the form and spirit of the medieval guilds. Today, by this definition, almost all Freemasons are speculative.

Modern Freemasonry is thought to have formed initially among Scottish nobility about four centuries ago. While the order has adherents in all parts of the world, it is most popular in English-speaking countries and especially within the territories of the former British empire. The basic collective unit of Freemasonry is the lodge. In Barbados there are currently 11 lodges. Groups of lodges in a defined geographical area are generally controlled by a Grand Lodge. Each lodge is subject to the authority of the Grand Lodge of the country or region under which it holds its charter,[5] and the teachings of the order include obedience to the law of the land. For this reason, there is no international order of Freemasons: lodges in each country are independent of those in all other countries. While, in Barbados, Freemasonic lodges follow the constitutions of either the United Grand Lodge of England or the Grand Lodge of Scotland, neither of these Grand Lodges has any control over the internal proceedings of the Barbadian lodges.[6]

BASTION OF THE ESTABLISHED ORDER?

Freemasonry has encountered considerable opposition. Some of this has come from those who object to all secret societies, of which Freemasonry is undoubtedly one of the strongest. Within Freemasonry, custom is the supreme authority and Freemasons tend to carry out their activities in a deliberately cultivated atmosphere of ritual. Apart from mystifying and infuriating many of those who are excluded, secret societies, by the very clandestine nature of their activities, often prompt observers to draw an unfair comparison between secrecy and sinisterism. For this reason, members of the brotherhood often feel obliged to deny that theirs is a secret society, preferring to note, instead, that it is a society which has secrets. "Look, the only real secrets of Freemasonry are those things by which Freemasons are known to each other. All of our moral teachings are open. A Freemason is not a law breaker, but you are not allowed to discuss politics or religion in lodge." (Major Rudolph Daniel)

Nonetheless, the perception that Freemasonry's invisible hand has shaped and continues to shape most aspects of western history since the time of its original founding is still widely held. Given the apparent tendency of many Freemasons to deliberately fuel the consternation which their secret activities ignite among the imaginations of antagonists, it is unlikely that the debate will disappear. Even today, intense arguments will occasionally rage in the columns of Barbadian newspapers on the subject of Freemasonry. They usually take the form of shrill exchanges between those who laud Freemasonry's positive, charitable features and those who decry its secrecy and the alleged unhealthy influence it wields over society through its members who are typically well-placed figures in the community. And in an island whose citizens generally pride themselves as being God fearing, the debate will often descend upon the question of whether Freemasonry is compatible with Christianity.

Even if one discounts the claims of those who are convinced that the order has international conspiratorial aims, a cursory review of Freemasonry's local "who's who"[7] reveals a strong correlation between the order's highest members and society's establishment figures. In Barbados, top men in banking, commerce, agriculture, the civil service and the professions are well represented in the brotherhood. This, in turn, would seem to imply that it is through the maintenance of the established order that the Freemason is able to derive his influence in society. The picture that has emerged from interviews and research for this book is that the order would have had a similar pro-establishment leaning when Lewis was a Freemason between the 1930s and the late 1950s.

Freemasonry in Barbados

Freemasonry was introduced into Barbados in 1740.[8] Its oldest surviving lodge, Albion, constituted in 1790, is considered the sixth oldest in existence outside the United Kingdom. As the table following illustrates, of the total number of Freemasonic lodges in Barbados five follow the English constitution and six the Scottish.[9] When Lewis joined the brotherhood in the 1930s, there would have then been only six lodges in existence.

Despite its ambitious claim to be made up of men of high moral character, logic would suggest that Freemasonic lodges cannot be so distinct from the prevailing attitudes within society that they represent a code of conduct uninfluenced by changing social values. Lodges were, for instance, in operation in Barbados during the period of slavery. Interestingly, the justification for nonadmittance of slaves (or serfs and bondsmen in the United Kingdom) is not couched in terms of disqualification on the grounds of alleged moral or social inferiority, but in practical terms. It was claimed that the master, lord or lawful owner of the human property might call upon the man at any time (even out of lodge) thereby causing problems of attendance. Nevertheless, following emancipation, it took English Constitution lodges several years before membership requirements were changed from the stipulation that candidates be "free by birth" (thereby disqualifying members of society born as slaves) to "being a free man".

A review of the available Freemasonic literature charting the development of the order in Barbados suggests that the struggle of blacks and coloureds to make inroads into society's power structure also took place within lodge walls. The consequence of this successful struggle is that in the Barbados of the 1990s, all lodges now display a balance of the mixed racial composition of the island, although to varying degrees.

During the years when Lewis was a Freemason, however, this was not the case. There were quite definitely "black" lodges and "white" lodges. But Freemasonry was also seen to serve the purpose of strengthening social integration by permitting well-to-do coloureds and blacks to clandestinely mix and practise Freemasonry with their white brothers. In this way the order would cultivate the loyalty of these members, strengthen their ties to established social institutions and defuse possible resentment of white domination. Coloured or black members could, by being a Freemason, feel as if they belonged to the establishment.

FREEMASONIC LODGES IN BARBADOS		
	Lodge No.	Date of Foundation
UNITED GRAND LODGE OF ENGLAND		
Albion	#196	1790
Victoria	#2196	1887
St Michael's	#2253	1888
Union	#7751	1957
Amity	#9073	1983
GRAND LODGE OF SCOTLAND		
Scotia	#340	1884
Thistle	#1014	1906
St John	#1062	1909
St Andrew	#1062	1956
Unity	#1625	1966
Pelican	#1750	1983

It seems logical that despite the initial screening process, Freemasonic lodges, being composed of men from society, must form microcosms of the surrounding society replete with its distinctions of intellectual prowess, of rank, of class and of colour. The history of Freemasonry in Barbados confirms this. Barbadian Freemasonic lodges tend to faithfully reflect the profile of local society complete with all its delineations of race and class.

Until people dismantle the distinctions within society, you will continue to see these distinctions appearing in lodge. You wouldn't see this sort of stratification in Montserrat, for example, where there is only one Lodge. In Barbados we have eleven. Of these, Albion and St Michael, the older English lodges, remained white for some time. Occasionally these lodges would accept coloured people with a view to those coloured members eventually forming their own lodge. Victoria was an offshoot of Albion, as was Scotia. St John, also a Scottish Constitution lodge, was a lodge of poor whites and people who were regarded as not being well educated. (Major Rudolph Daniel)

It is into this 1930s world of Barbadian Freemasonry that Lewis makes his entrance. There is no evidence to indicate what prompted him to join the order. Interestingly, in the peculiar lexicon of Freemasonry, the term "Lewis" is used to describe the eldest son of a Freemason. Generally, fathers tend to encourage their sons to become Freemasons and the eldest son, or the "Lewis", is supposed to be eligible to join the order before reaching the age of 21, the attainment of which is a prerequisite for other prospective members. It is not known whether Lewis' father was a Freemason, but even if he had been, by the time Lewis joined in the 1930s, his father's earlier absence from the local scene and eventual death meant that he would have had no influence over Lewis' decision to join the brotherhood.

Since Lewis' life and work reflect a certain disregard for material enrichment, it would seem fair to assume that he did not seek to enter the order with a view to financial advantage. Given the fact that he later did much to dent the complacency of the established order in Barbados, it might also be inaccurate to credit Lewis with viewing Freemasonry as a way in which to enhance his status within the established community.

What does remain curious – aside from the fact that Lewis opted to join the Freemasons in the first place – is the question of why he should choose to join a lodge like Victoria, which at that time was not only an overwhelmingly white lodge, but was a lodge comprised mainly of sugar planters and their overseers.

Victoria Lodge

The irony of Victoria lodge, established in 1887, is that its founder, J. Jabez Warner, was a coloured man. He had sought admission to Albion lodge but had been "blackballed . . . only on account of his colour – and in the presence and hearing of three brethren who gave evidence, so stated his intention."[10] Within a few months of his rejection, Warner had formed his own lodge, named after the colony's monarch who celebrated her jubilee year in 1887, and started holding regular meetings in the Masonic Hall in Spry Street, Bridgetown. "In terms of its colour complexion, Victoria was originally a 'pass-for-white' or coloured lodge. If you look through the list of names of the original past masters in the Lodge in Belleville you will see the names of coloured men." (Major Rudolph Daniel)

Although the lodge was "founded to permit coloured brethren to become part of the Masonic fraternity",[11] white brethren also joined Victoria. During the years 1923–26, the lodge appears to have been embroiled in a turbulent period following the blackballing of a young coloured solicitor. Judging from the outcry at the blackballing, and reading the cold reaction of the then District Grand Master to what appeared to be a racist vote,[12] it is nonetheless possible to draw the conclusion that progressive ideas were alive within the Freemasonic community at the time. Nonetheless the overwhelming weight of the evidence points to the fact that:

> ... over a period of years Victoria had become known as the Planters' Lodge. Plantation managers, under managers and overseers had joined Victoria over the years and in turn had proposed fellow farmers for membership ... Pressures from its own members again mounted for the membership of Victoria to be 'more clearly representative of the community in which we live'. For many years no coloured member [*sic*] had been proposed for membership of Victoria.[13]

The lodge admitted the first black member for decades in 1987.

Lodges tend to consciously form within other lodges. Thistle, for example, was formed not for coloured men as such, but for a particular type of coloured man: the middle ranks of the civil service, the upper ranks of the health inspectorate and so on. Scotia was also a coloured man's lodge: but one formed for the established coloured man. It was the Spartan Club of Freemasonry; and Thistle was the Empire Club.[14] Now with relation to Victoria, since you already had an obvious resting place for coloured fellows, Victoria ceased to become a repository for them. This is why in TT's time it was almost all white. (Major Rudolph Daniel)

Major Rudolph Daniel (1992)

Access to Victoria lodge records proved difficult. So most of what follows comes from informed speculation as well as the available evidence. By the age of 31, Lewis had risen to become a Master Mason. We know this because he is described as being in the chair of Victoria in December 1936.[15] Barbadian Freemasons confirm that this would represent a rather remarkable achievement for someone so young. It would also imply that Lewis had been initiated when he was in his mid to late twenties.

Lewis' involvement in a lodge populated heavily with planters and overseers, and therefore likely to reflect pro-establishment values, might be seen in the same light as his participation in the all-white Pickwick and St Ann's cricket clubs and his having been a member of the BVF, probably just after the time of the riots.

The contrast between his activities in the Freemasonic brotherhood and his later espousal of views that would then have been deemed radical, also appears sharp. On the one hand, here is Lewis rising, presumably on the basis of dedicated work, to become the most senior officer within a lodge that celebrated its strong ties of loyalty to the sovereign. On the other hand we hear of a man loud in his aversion to racial discrimination and who is later allegedly asked to leave a military mess hall dinner for saying uncomplimentary things about the monarch.[16]

When directed to this contradiction, those Freemasons interviewed cautioned that the diversity of the order's membership means that it often contains people who possess a range of contending views on politics and religion. Under this interpretation, it would be possible for Lewis to be attracted more by Freemasonry's emphasis on fraternal good deeds and the requirement that its members be seen to possess integrity, than to be repelled by the likely political or social opinions of many lodge members. Lewis appears, for example, to have availed himself of the opportunity to use the network of Freemasonry and its fraternal associations with other lodges to foster contact with Freemasons from "black" lodges – or, generally, those which follow the Scottish Constitution. It is interesting to note that at some point in his Freemasonic career, Lewis became a member of Thistle Lodge.[17] "TT was so well loved in the black community that he was made a member of Lodge Thistle. This was a very important recognition of his status in the coloured and black community." (Major Rudolph Daniel)

Politics and the Brotherhood

Besides the mystery that shrouds the Freemasonic fraternity, the story of Lewis' involvement in Barbadian Freemasonry is doubly intriguing. First of all there is the apparent clash of his progressive ideas with those likely to have been held by his brethren.

As noted above, within the lodge, discussion of political or religious views is not tolerated. It is therefore assumed that a Freemason's political beliefs are not a concern of the lodge. But the innate conservative bias of Freemasonry is reflected in the fact that the Order is not inclined to accept a member whose political beliefs would lead him to subvert the peace and good order of society. One source of Freemasonic authority, called the "Antient Charges", describes a Freemason as "a peaceable subject to the Civil powers wherever he resides or works, and is never to be concerned in plots and conspiracies against the peace and welfare of the nation, nor to behave himself undutifully to inferior magistrates."[18] If therefore one accepts the view that Freemasonry is inherently pro-establishment owing to the fact that it draws its membership from the decision makers of society, then, the following question keeps recurring: would not Lewis' strong advocacy of the cause of the dispossessed, especially blacks, have aroused anxiety in Victoria Lodge, which was, after all, seen as a planters' lodge?

Sir James Tudor: I think they respected him so much that they would have given him latitude to make his various social commentaries. His integrity was certainly never questioned, nor was his logic. Probably he made them feel uncomfortable with his compassion and interest for the poor which may have shamed them.

Author: But would Lewis not have been considered a "traitor" by his white peers?

Sir James: Only in the sense that his intellect was wasted in fighting for the black people. They felt, no doubt, that he could have done better for the whole country – and, incidentally, for himself – if he had been with the governing elite.

This view was reinforced by a remark made by one other source and recorded on the condition that the person not be named: "TT spent far too much time in politics. And what did he get out of it? He lost all he had, his job, his marriage, and for what? For the benefit of the Negroid population..."

1933	B.A.T. WILLIAMS
1934	G.S.W. BAYLEY
1935	A.A. BELMAR
1936	A.E.S. LEWIS
1937	A.E MACKINNON
1938	F STC. OLTON
1939	H.D. GOODRIDGE
1940	J.E. BOURNE

Detail from the engraved Masters' Roll in Victoria Lodge, Belleville, St Michael showing Lewis "in the chair" in the year 1936.

The second question thrown up by the apparent contradiction of political views and associations made through the lodge is whether Lewis scaled down his masonic activities after he became active in politics in the early 1940s. It is impossible to get a sense of the pattern of his Freemasonic activities given the inaccessibility of documents or minutes from meetings where Lewis' involvement would have been noted. Judging, however, from the dates on those Freemasonic documents still in his possession when he died, the high point of his Freemasonic activities appeared to have been in the early to mid 1940s. Various documents associating him with both the Scotia and Albion Royal Arch Chapters as Mark Master Mason, are dated in the mid 1940s.[19] This would indicate that his Freemasonic involvement continued vigorously following his entry into politics.

The final question about Lewis' involvement with the Freemasons is whether his links to Freemasonry worked for or against him at the time of his dismissal

The facade of the building in Belleville which still houses Victoria Lodge (photographed in 1995)

from the Central Agency in 1949, an event which caused so much upheaval in his later life. This question, while intriguing, is one for which it is difficult to obtain answers grounded in anything other than informed speculation. Stephen Knight, in his work of investigative journalism on Freemasonry in modern society notes that perhaps the most "effective penalty [against a Freemason] doing anything displeasing to Masonry is to be shunned by the entire Brotherhood, a penalty adequate to bring a man to ruin . . ."[20] It would seem that this point carries special significance on the issue of Lewis' dismissal from the Central Agency, since it would be fair to assume that many members of the brotherhood would undoubtedly have belonged to the merchant elite which sought to engineer his dismissal. Some may have even been Victoria members. But in the interviews conducted for this book, none of the Freemasons or non-Freemasons raised the possibility of an anti-Lewis conspiracy organized by Freemasons against Lewis for his challenges to the existing social order. Nor, by the same token, was there ever mention of Lewis possibly availing himself of his Freemasonic connections in an attempt to rally support behind his cause and thereby thwart the forces clamouring for his dismissal. The answer to this question will therefore probably never be known with any degree of certainty.

Reminiscences

Lewis eventually rose to become Past Master in his lodge which is said to be the highest honour for a Freemason.[21] Given the difficulty of accessing the records of Victoria, glimpses of Lewis' Freemasonic activity emerge only from the interviews:

TT had a strong reputation for being strict in the accurate writing of the minutes. He was basically a decent chap. In the 1930s, all the Lodges met in the Masonic Hall on Spry Street. But it was during Lewis' active Freemasonic service that the Victoria Lodge was moved from Spry Street to Belleville. In fact, his was one of the five signatures required to authorize the relocation to the new site in Belleville.[22] (Aubrey Roberts)

In the Freemasonic Brotherhood

I was in the Chair of Victoria Lodge in 1940. I had risen through the ranks as secretary, and then junior and senior warden of the lodge before assuming the chair. TT had been in the chair long before then, and was quite an enthusiastic Mason when I was in the Chair. He regarded Masonry as a highly moral institution. (J.E.T. "Jonny" Bourne)

The masonic part of our connection was more subdued. TT and I were more familiar on political terms. But I do remember hearing that he was helpful to new Freemasons in helping them relate what they were being taught in the Order to the tasks and confrontations they faced in ordinary life. He made a practical connection between the Craft and life itself. (Sir James Tudor)

TT arranged to help with my schooling through his Masonic connections. He also helped me get my first job. (Ellice Collymore)

Although I didn't know him well, I always heard that TT Lewis had a reputation for being a rather irascible fellow. There is one celebrated instance where TT was acting secretary of a lodge meeting and was therefore obliged to take the minutes on behalf of the official secretary. When the official secretary resumed his duties the following week, the first point on the agenda was the adoption of the previous week's minutes and a discussion of the matters arising. Apparently everyone agreed that they were accurate – except TT. He described them as a 'shocking misrepresentation', I think they were the words used – of what had gone on the week before. He is therefore on record as the only man to have voted against his own minutes. (N.G.D. Atwell)

N.G.D. Atwell (1995)

Undoubtedly, [Lewis] did not care for wealth or social position, mingling freely and unreservedly with all classes and sections of the community. The operative word here is 'unreservedly', for, with TT, it was not a question of swallowing pride or overcoming prejudice. The plain truth is that he was genuinely without prejudice or false pride. He had neither envy toward the rich nor malice toward any man. He was a Freemason, and, I venture to say, lived up to the teachings of that brotherhood more than most. (E.L. Cozier writing in the *Barbados Advocate*, 2 March 1981)

Epilogue

Although possible, it is rare for Freemasons to resign from the brotherhood. In the period just before his death, he was reported to be rewriting either the rules or the constitution of his Lodge. As a mark of respect at his passing, his brother Freemasons from Victoria Lodge paid for the headstone which still adorns his grave in St Lucia.[23]

Given Lewis' inquisitive nature, his constant and very evident search for truths, it is possible to conclude that he entered the Freemasonic brotherhood at an impressionable age, and may well have liked the sense of camaraderie, purpose and moral insight it offered. Freemasonry also offered the opportunity to recognize the importance of devotion to country and it would have taught him the requirement for strict adherence to rules and customs – things in which Lewis seemed to take particular relish.

Rising from humble origins, it is easy to see why joining the Freemasons would have been for Lewis a powerful symbol of social acceptance in his early life. As his political views matured, turning a blind eye to the order's more conservative strain might well have been seen as a small price to pay. The fact that Lewis chose to live and die within the brotherhood meant that he did not consider these inconsistencies to be significant.

NOTES

1. Until recently women were not allowed to become members of the brotherhood.
2. Cited in a handbook for prospective applicants wishing to join the Freemasons: *The Applicant*, The Grand Lodge of Scotland, Geo. Stewart and Co. Ltd, Meadowbank Works, Edinburgh [undated], 3.
3. The three degrees of Craft Freemasonry are described as: (1) Entered Apprentice (2) Fellow Craft (3) Master Mason. Within Freemasonry, it is known that some chapters recognize 30 degrees in addition to the basic three, making a total of 33.
4. Despite a thoroughly Christian foundation, Freemasonry has had a particularly stormy relationship with the Roman Catholic Church, resulting in the fact that few members of the order come from that religion. The cause of this uncomfortable relationship appears to be the persecution which members of the original "operative" masons' craft guild suffered at the hands of the Roman Catholic Church. The original adoption of secret clandestine methods of mutual recognition (such as special words of recognition, handshake techniques and so on) among guild stonemasons, eager to protect their valued craft from interlopers in the late medieval period, is presumed to have clashed with the Roman Catholic Church's efforts to secure a monopoly of societal control.
5. In the case of Barbados, lodges operate under the Grand Lodge of the Eastern Caribbean which is based in Barbados but covers also the English-speaking islands stretching from Tortola in the north to Grenada in the south.
6. Grand Lodges do, however, have the power to revoke the charter of any lodge found to be conducting itself in a criminal or "immoral" manner.
7. See N.G.D. Atwell (Ed), *Yearbook of Freemasonry in Barbados and the Eastern Caribbean (Volume I)*, 1985, Coles Printery, Barbados and Editorial Committee of Research Lodge Amity, *Yearbook of Freemasonry in Barbados and the Eastern Caribbean (Volume II)*, 1987 (no other publication details).

8. The first lodge was founded in 1740 under the name of "St Michael's", but is not connected to the existing lodge which bears that name. Also founded in 1740, the Provincial Grand Lodge of Barbados claims to be the second oldest grand lodge under the jurisdiction of the United Grand Lodge of England outside the United Kingdom. (The oldest is located in Bengal, India.) In 1890, the Provincial Grand Lodge of Barbados was renamed the District Grand Lodge (the name it retains to this day) in line with the distinction then made by the colonial power which had adopted the practice of calling overseas provinces "districts" to distinguish them from English provinces. See *Yearbook of Freemasonry (Vol II)*, 48–54.

9. From this list of lodges, one is absent: the Prince Hall Lodge located in Graeme Hall in Christ Church. This lodge is not recognized by either the English or Scottish Constitution Lodges in Barbados for reasons which appear to be essentially legalistic. The origins of the Prince Hall Lodge are to be found in the United States from where, following that country's break with Britain in 1776, most other lodges repatriated their charters. Prince Hall Lodge did not do so, or at least did not do so within the required seven years and official ties were broken with them by the United Grand Lodge of England. This form of ostracism was followed in the territories adhering to the constitution of the United Grand Lodge of England. Interestingly, within the United States, the Prince Hall Lodge was formed by American blacks and Jews and was, by all accounts, formed in correct Freemasonic tradition. An eventual outmigration of Jewish masons ensued and it is now almost entirely a Lodge for black Freemasons.

10. P.M. Ross (Ed), *The Victoria Lodge: One Hundred Years of Masonic Work (1887–1987)*, 1987, Letchworth Press, Barbados, 6.

11. P.M. Ross (Ed), *The Victoria Lodge*, 14.

12. The District Grand Master, Professor J.P. D'Albuquerque is quoted as warning in 1924 that: "If one section of a Lodge now deprives another section of their [sic] fundamental rights, it commits an act of elemental as well as masonic injustice, and "Fraternity" would cease to have meaning. I therefore advise brethren to take counsel in order to remove the impression that the Lodge has abandoned the spirit of Freemasonry for its very antithesis, fratricidal strife." See P.M. Ross (Ed), *The Victoria Lodge*, 14.

13. P.M. Ross (Ed), *The Victoria Lodge*, 24.

14. See chapter 2, "The pre-war cricketing scene".

15. P.M. Ross (Ed), *The Victoria Lodge*, 16.

16. The following anecdote was retold to the author by Major Daniel: "Long after TT left the Barbados Volunteer Force, he was invited to the officers' mess as a guest at some celebration. After a couple of drinks, he made some remark about the Queen – not personal, but constitutional – probably something like 'Queen what? She has no influence in Barbados'. I was at the function at the time, but not in the room where the incident happened. Anyway some of the junior officers who had sworn loyalty to the Crown and its successors were so outraged by his comment that they manhandled TT down the steps and out of the compound." See chapter 2, "Serving with the Barbados Volunteer Force".

17. P.M. Ross (Ed), *The Victoria Lodge*, 22.

18. Quoted in *Yearbook of Freemasonry (Vol II)*, 64.

19. At that time these would have been two of only three Royal Arch Chapters in the eastern Caribbean: the other being Mount Lebanon based in St John's, Antigua.

20. Stephen Knight, *The Brotherhood – The Secret World of the Freemasons*, Grafton Books, London, 1985, 31.
21. This is, in fact, the highest position in Craft Freemasonry. However, the Ancient and Accepted Scottish Rite of the 33rd Degree carries on from the topmost rung of Craft Masonry. To be accepted into this Order (which is an entirely Christian order) the applicant must already be a Master Mason.
22. Victoria's transfer to the temple building on Pine Road in Belleville (built in the 1880s) occurred in May 1958.
23. In November 1960, Victoria Lodge agreed to place a headstone on the grave of "Worshipful Brother A.E.S. Lewis" in St Lucia. See P.M. Ross (Ed), *The Victoria Lodge*, 20.

CHAPTER FOUR

The Early Years in Politics

Anyone looking at Barbados' political structure following the 1937 riots would have found in place an apparatus that looked and operated essentially as it had for the previous 300 years.[1] Earlier efforts to break the mould of Barbadian politics through mass meetings and consciousness raising, which for instance had characterized the work of Charles Duncan O'Neal's Democratic League (formed in 1924) had changed little. It was the riots of 1937 that shocked the established order out of its stupor. The testimony of the post riot Deane Commission laid embarrassingly bare the causes and extent of the troubles that had given rise to the unrest. What appeared to loom ahead were the twin paths of revolution or reform.

Perhaps the single most impressive accomplishment of Barbados' political leadership during the following quarter century was the ability and foresight it demonstrated in moving the political system out of its ancient trappings. The new Barbados would eventually be characterized by independence, stable two-party politics, an established system of trade unionism, and, most crucially, a state based on the precepts of constitutional government which, by imposing genuine limitations on the actions of the power holders, guaranteed the political rights of the ordinary citizen. This achievement was realized gradually with those who stood to lose out under the new arrangements always considering themselves to be under siege but never under threat of extinction.

Looking back at Barbados in this particular period, one gets the sense of a white oligarchy reluctantly coming to terms with the view that its political ascendancy was no longer sustainable. One sees its members fighting a rearguard action to protect long-held privileges. One sees them reluctantly submitting to black mass-based demands for greater civil and political rights. But one never sees them capable of breaking the siege and recovering lost ground. Because the basis of the franchise qualification was economic, not racial, attempts to reform and eventually abolish it did not have anywhere near the level of ideological rancour that similar efforts did elsewhere. If one compares, for example, the Barbados of this period with the South Africa that was in 1948 codifying its politically exclusivist and racially grounded apartheid system, one sees, apart from the other considerable differences between the two countries, that the two dominant racial groupings in Barbados are prepared for better or worse to seek compromise – to allow demands for significant changes to be accommodated in a peaceful way. As a result, Barbadian whites are able to see a future for themselves in the island, while blacks are able to obtain long coveted political goals.

The path chosen would thus be reform. Adopted with enthusiasm and gritty determination by one side, and with dogged reluctance by the other. But it would be reform. And once the process got underway, the scale of change was remarkable. It showed how much could have been accomplished earlier had there been sufficient will to effect it. The smoothness of the transition can probably be traced to three interrelated factors. First, there was the pace of the transition – deliberate and gradual – allowing the elites to come to terms with it. Secondly, the quality of the leadership offered by men like Grantley Adams and Errol Barrow and the catalytic role played by insightful governors such as Sir Grattan Bushe. Thirdly, the general political culture based on the Westminster model which at the time did not exhibit an overly adversarial nature.

Despite the laudable efforts of the Congress Party towards the beginning and the Democratic Labour Party at the end of the period 1937–66, the main movers for reform, at the centre of it all, were the Barbados Labour Party and its "Siamese twin" the Barbados Workers' Union. Their particular partnership would last from 1941–54. Political analyst Patrick Emmanuel writes convincingly that:

> . . . the early BLP–BWU cooperative worked for socioeconomic endowments for the working people with first small, later larger success. Demand followed demand for changes in law and custom in such specifics as enforceable wage agreements, workmen's compensation, holidays with pay, factory supervision, shorter shop opening hours, higher pensions; free and compulsory education, free books, free school meals; promotion of peasant agriculture; slum clearance and housing development; state ownership of public utilities, oil and natural resources. By 1966, this agenda had been substantially addressed through the exertions of the two major parties and the prevailing workers union. The rest has been Any Other Business . . . [2]

The Early Years in Politics

Lewis Joins Hilton Vaughan's Liberal Association

For someone seeking entry into the politics of the late 1930s in Barbados, there were few organized groups under which one could run. Charles Duncan O'Neal's Democratic League had by then become defunct. The Barbados Labour Party, though formed in 1938 (and almost immediately renamed the Barbados Progressive League – or BPL), would not enter candidates until the 1940 election. The enduring era of political parties, brought on by the organizational demands of the mass-based political movements which were a consequence of the disturbances, had not yet arrived.

Milling around at the starting gates during this period of Barbadian political awakening, and attempting to garner a following for its centrist programme, was the Barbados Liberal Association. "Here was a group of people, both black and white – and certainly not a large group – who were beginning to examine in a nonpartisan way, how Barbados could be improved. It was anti-planter and anti-Broad Street but was not revolutionary. It sought a middle way." (Sir James Tudor)

In his autobiography *The Quiet Revolutionary*, Sir Alexander Hoyos recalls that both he and Lewis joined the Liberal Association when it was formed some time in the late 1930s. Although the Association was not founded by H.A. Vaughan, the latter became the first, and possibly only, president during its short lifetime. Vaughan, described by Hoyos as imperturbable and unobtrusive, was elected to the House as an independent in the 1936 election and twice thereafter successfully defended his seat.

Although short lived, the Liberal Association would provide Lewis with his initial exposure to an organized political grouping. Hoyos claims that the Liberal Association was a political party which

H.A. Vaughan (1930s)

implies that it had a constitution, a programme and a set of procedures governing the election of officers. Curiously, Vaughan never campaigned as a member of the Liberal Association, but only as an Independent. Hoyos says both Lewis and himself were looking, in the Liberal Association, for a middle way between the politics of the left and the right, and through this, for a solution to Barbados' existing social problems.³ Lewis canvassed for Vaughan in at least one election, helping him to secure his seat in the House as a representative of the City of Bridgetown. This exposure no doubt provided Lewis with a wealth of knowledge which he would later apply in the successful 1942 campaign to clinch his first seat in the House – as senior representative for the City of Bridgetown.

In the absence of other written or oral records on Lewis' activities at the time, Hoyos' reflections become the only available source to try to trace the development of Lewis' thinking on the burning issues of the day, foremost among which stood the quest for social justice. Hoyos hints at Lewis' growing reluctance to accept anything other than forthright measures to resolve the colony's social problems, though he does not exactly specify what Lewis' views were. He states that Lewis moved into politics as an independent "when he could not persuade [the Liberal Association's] members to adopt more thoroughgoing Liberal, if not Radical, measures."⁴ Lewis never contested an election alongside Vaughan however. In 1940, at the age of 35, he may have considered himself too young to run, although his appetite for politics had doubtless been stimulated. As for the Liberal Association, referred to disparagingly by BPL leader Grantley Adams as a "Mexican Army" – all generals and no soldiers – it died a natural death in 1940 after Vaughan, victorious in retaining his seat, nonetheless left politics to take on a judicial appointment. Thereafter, Lewis moved on.

Flirting with the Elector's Association

... [Lewis] had joined the [Elector's Association], but his crashing indiscretions disturbed the members who regarded him not as an asset but as a grave *menace*.⁵

There is little other than passing reference in most of the literature on pre-independence Barbadian political history to the conservative grouping known as the Barbados Elector's Association (BEA). The BEA was formed in 1941, interestingly, the same year that the Barbados Workers Union was registered.⁶ Its members contested elections for several years starting with the election of 1942, and, well into the year 1954, references were still being made to it in the local press. The name of the group then disappears. Conservative interests are championed thereafter by a party which carried the oxymoronic title "Progressive Conservative Party" (PCP). This party contested the 1956 elections. Its name would again change in 1958 to "Barbados National Party" (BNP). Essentially, all three bodies represented the island's conservative interests.

At the time, the BEA did not however organize itself as a political party.[7] Its members were still described as "independents" in the House.[8] The group viewed itself as an association primarily formed to give financial aid to those of its members seeking election. To the extent that can be gathered from the speeches of those members, the BEA appealed to traditional values and were little influenced by grassroots attitudes and opinions.

BEA campaign advertisement from the 1940s aimed at white voters – who then constituted a majority of the electorate – and depicting a scene designed to reassure them. Prior to 1950, the franchise was restricted to owners of property or persons earning a certain level of income per year.

However, unlike the BPL, whose perceived menace the BEA was formed to counteract, the BEA appears to have possessed no clear cut set of policies, and no two members stood on the same platform.

With hindsight, the onrush of labour's political power in the 1940s makes all of the BEA's peculiar organizational arrangements seem strangely irrelevant. Excluding one abnormal electoral success in 1948, the BEA and its successors were doomed, by the twin forces of franchise reform and demographic pressure, to receive an ever decreasing percentage of the electoral vote.

In terms of platform substance, those associated with the BEA gave the appearance of being very much persons reacting to events. Seen in this light, the BEA could be considered a mechanism designed to give conservatively-minded members of parliament, and similar members of the wider society itself, an opportunity to protect their interests at a time when organized parties were becoming the vessels of future political power.

It was the move to greater adult suffrage that caused the Elector's Association to be formed. They were a conservative party. Their name evolved from the Elector's Association to the Progressive Conservative Party and then into something else – I think it was called the Barbados National Party. I never agreed with them attaching "Progressive" to the title. The name should have been kept as the Conservative Party. (Herbert Dowding)

The reasons why Lewis joined the BEA are unclear. Hoyos himself gives no explanation. And in terms of the general trend of Lewis' ever leftward political migration, this affiliation appears quite anomalous. It is possible that Lewis was at this stage dabbling around with various ideas and political groupings. Based on the reflections of E.L. Cozier, outlined below, aspiring members may have initially been naïvely unconvinced of the essential conservative nature of the BEA. But this misperception did not last long. Importantly, Lewis would have been in need of financial support for his electoral endeavours, and, as noted, the BEA was aimed primarily at providing such support. Cozier infers that Lewis realized that the price for such support would undoubtedly have been the advocacy of views which, while not part of any official BEA ideology, reflected a strongly status quo sentiment: views which Lewis did not share.

E.L. "Jimmy" Cozier in the 1940s (left) and the 1980s (above)

At the same time, the BEA seems to have viewed its newly arrived nonconformist member rather warily. Cozier relates how, during the BEA general meeting immediately prior to the January 1942 elections, it became clear that the party was not interested in proposing Lewis as one of its two candidates to contest the seat for the City of Bridgetown even though Lewis was a BEA member and was known to be planning to come forward on his own. Moreover, one of the two candidates they were proposing for that constituency was *not* a BEA member at all. Cozier says he succeeded in persuading the BEA's Executive Committee to withdraw the nonmember's name " . . . and the suggestion was made that if Mr Lewis would accept, his name [would] be substituted. TT thanked the members, but said that . . . as an official BEA candidate . . . his chances would suffer!"⁹

Cozier goes on to reveal his own doubts about the quality of democracy which appeared to be on offer within the BEA when writing about its draft constitution:

When I joined the BEA, I had high hopes for a political reformation, but I must admit to some disappointment . . . [The draft constitution itself] was an amazing production, and, in my opinion, then and still, an affront to democracy. Membership was divided into four classifications, based upon ability to pay. Thus plantation owners paid according to acreage of estates, so much per ten acres: big business according to directorships held or some other measure of financial importance; professionals and other well off middle class members, if memory serves, $20 a year; and we, the lowly *hoi polloi*, were to be charged a modest five shillings per annum. All this would have been well and good, even highly laudable, but for one little snag: in return for their generosity in funding the Association, Classes A, B and C enjoyed an outrageous advantage on the Council, the ruling body, whereas Class D barely had a toehold. The Draft Rules stipulated . . . that Class A should have the right to eight seats thereon; Class B, six; Class C, four; and we, underlings, two. This would never do. I . . . am happy to say that [a colleague] and TT managed to have sanity prevail. The seats were apportioned 4–4–4–4; which still made for conservative control under the practical political circumstances of the day, but prevented us from being completely swamped."[10]

Against this backdrop, Lewis decided to campaign as an Independent. Cozier volunteered to be his political agent.

Occasionally during the interviews the observation was made that regardless of the underlying trend in Barbadian politics where an increasingly enfranchised citizenry clamoured for leadership which would both represent a complete break with the past and represent their interests fairly, there was still room for a conservative party to counterbalance this trend.

In my view, the period 1946–51 was probably one of the most important in this country's political life. During this period, things could have gone several ways. For example, if members of the Electors Association like E.K. Walcott, who was the kingpin in the period 1946–47, and E.D. Mottley had modified their dictatorial methods and pushed conservatism more sensibly then the BEA could have been more easily recognized as a natural alternate party to the Labour Party. The Elector's Association would therefore have been

Herbert Dowding in 1946 (left) and in 1995 (above)

able to have more of a say in politics from the beginning of the period after [universal adult] suffrage. Instead, what we ended up with was two labour parties. (Herbert Dowding)

That there is a clear conservative vein running through Barbadian society and its politics is often recognized. This said, it is nonetheless far from certain that such a vein could have been tapped by a party which, without at least a reformist agenda, did not represent a break with the past but only a continuation of it.

What men like Walcott and Mottley were worried about was the challenge to the status quo. The elite gave no credit to the intelligence of the average working man. They didn't realize that even a properly constituted trade union movement would provide the solution to many of the then problems. And what has happened since then? We've now got the adult franchise and has any of the doom they predicted occurred? (John Wickham)

In the context of the 1940s and 1950s, the BEA and its successor parties were seen as an attempt to rally the forces of conservatism in a country, most of whose citizens wanted progressive change. This caricature proved impossible for the BEA to shake off, and, as full adult suffrage loomed, the fate of the party and of its successors was sealed.

The 1942 Election: Getting into the House

I was the one who nominated TT . . . As a ratepayer, I was entitled to nominate someone. It wasn't yet full adult suffrage. I was paying a certain amount in taxes per month and I was also paying occupancy tax as a young businessman – a shopkeeper. This gave me the qualification. So I made a speech on behalf of TT. At that time I was quite proud to have been in a position to be able to nominate someone for the Assembly. (Owen T. Allder)

It was a plucky thing to seek political honours as an Independent. TT was determined that the electors should accept him for what he was and what he stood for. He refused to conduct a campaign which sought to buy votes by distributing rum and corned beef. His representative was EL (Jimmy) Cozier, who worked heroically on election day to transport many people to the polling stations in his American Baby Austin, reputed to be the smallest car on the island at the time." (F.A. Hoyos in *The Quiet Revolutionary*[11])

In his autobiography, Cozier relates how in 1942 he became political agent for Lewis' first contest for the House of Assembly. The details of Lewis' first encounter with the people's will are recounted by Cozier in the following manner:

The counting of the votes gave a clear picture of the voting. The boxes were filled, and were opened and upturned for the slips to spill out onto the table, so that early votes were counted first. For the most part the early voters would be the senior businessmen; our . . . boys and their friends would be [voting] either during their lunch hours or after work. We'd done quite a job of getting the young people on the voter's list, and they all turned up plumps. At the beginning of the count, all we could hear was "Pierce, Tudor" [names of the BEA candidates]. As political agent, I was sitting quite close to the Sheriff, keeping my own score. I don't mind admitting that I was getting a little anxious until the plumps (solid votes for one candidate only) started to come in for TT. Then we heard "Lewis," "Lewis," "Lewis, Pierce," "Lewis," and I began to breathe more easily. It was a decisive victory. Lewis, 399; Pierce, 360; Tudor, 200; Johnson, 29; Allamby, 20; Yard, 16. The last three were nuisance candidates meant to upset TT's chances . . . In the event we won the election, TT becoming senior member for Bridgetown, much to the too evident chagrin of the BEA." [12]

The result appears to have been generally received with astonishment. According to the *Barbados Advocate*: ". . . In the City a new and little known candidate in the person of Mr Lewis topped the polls, wresting the senior position from Mr Pierce who, it was thought, would have outdistanced his nearest rival by many votes."[13]

The convening of the House following the election on 26 January would start what would be the longest session in the history of the local Assembly to that date. Ending in November 1944, the sitting would last almost three years. The extra year was added, in part, to assist with the registration of newly enfranchised voters following the lowering of the income qualification, and the enfranchisement of women, in 1943.

The characteristic thirst for democracy in countries which do not possess it in full measure was apparent in Barbados at this time. The lowering of the franchise to include persons annually earning $96 (down from $240)[14] had the immediate and dramatic result of increasing interest in public affairs among the general population.

In early 1942 the world was at war and it would take another year before the tide turned decisively in favour of the Allied forces. In the colony of Barbados it was a period of "war conditions" with the Imperial Emergency Powers Act of 1939 in force. The day after the election, the seeming irrelevance

> ### PLUMPS
>
> The election process in Barbados prior to that country's political awakening in the 1940s was essentially a sedate and ritualized affair. Sir Keith Hunte describes the type of ceremony that had gone on for hundreds of years as follows:
>
> "There were relatively few contested elections at the constituency level. Mass meetings were rare. Shortly before nomination day each year, candidates established and/or renewed contact with their constituencies, visiting influential constituents; paid canvassers did much of the necessary leg-work and solicited votes on behalf of their candidate. On nomination day, in the Vestry Room candidates were formally nominated and seconded for the twelve double-member constituencies across the island and the opportunity was taken to give account of stewardship, make promises, field questions from electors attending; and then a vote of thanks to the Sheriff would be moved and seconded, and he would be congratulated on the smooth handling of the ceremony. Since quite often not more than two nominations would be received per constituency, the results of several of the twelve constituencies would be declared at that time. On polling day, electors would return to the Vestry Room to cast their ballots in cases where three or more candidates had been nominated. Each constituent had two votes. He was free to vote for two candidates, or to exercise one vote only and 'plump' for his favourite candidate. The latter move gave the preferred candidate a decided advantage."
>
> Extract from Keith Hunte, "The struggle for political democracy: Charles Duncan O'Neal and the Democratic League", in *Emancipation III: Aspects of the Post-Slavery Experience in Barbados*, Barbados, 1988, pp. 23-24.

of that event was manifested by the puny article devoted to the subject on the front page of the *Barbados Advocate*, then the island's only daily newspaper. Quite characteristically, that particular edition devoted the bulk of its front page, and certainly the lead stories, to matters relating to the war effort.

And yet the local political scene had perceptively entered a period of transformation. The early pre-war consequences of the 1937 riots – the establishment of the Barbados Progressive League in 1938 and the passing of the Trade Union Act in 1939 – had been quickly followed by the entry into the House of Assembly of the first group of five progressives in 1940 organized as a disciplined political party, and, in 1941, the formation of the Barbados Workers' Union.

Lewis' arrival in 1942 coincided almost perfectly with this evolution. For here, in the form of the man from the poor end of Kensington New Road was the first bona fide employee ever to grace the floor of the House. Henceforth, the House could not claim that its membership was exclusively drawn from the plantocracy, or the Bridgetown professionals and businessmen or the self-employed. Merely by entering the House with this sort of background, Lewis had created a first of sorts. However, his status as an employee brought with it no discernible advantages other than a politically appealing sense of earthiness. Indeed, his total financial dependence on a single salary paid by a large Bridgetown firm closely linked to "Broad Street",[15] rendered his position extremely vulnerable. Given the calamity that was later to befall him, his tenaciously independent and outspoken attitude appears astounding – even naïve. In this light, Lewis' nomination speech in 1942 (excerpted from the *Barbados Advocate* in reported speech which was then the customary style) is ominous: "It had been said that it was presumption on the part of an employee to come forward and offer his services to the electors . . . It had been said that he was sure

---

VIEWS ON TT LEWIS AS AN INDEPENDENT

TT's forte was that he was a great critic. He loved to criticize almost anything. He didn't suffer fools gladly and saw through a lot of the nonsense spouted at the time. He was inclined, however, to go overboard in some of his criticisms. He was best when he was an independent member of parliament. This is when he was able to show his true worth to Barbados. (Trevor Gale)

TT was a no-nonsense type of fellow. He was not a party satellite. He would not vote "aye" and then go and grumble about it in his mind. Instead, he would vote "no". (Tony Hinds)

As an independent in the House of Assembly, TT was fearless in the course he elected to follow. He opposed what he thought was wrong and supported what he considered right. He proceeded on his way without fear or favour. (FA Hoyos, *The Quiet Revolutionary*, p. 100)

to be victimized for having done so. Well, he was very pleased to tell them that he had no evidence of that so far . . ."[16]

THE CITY CONSTITUENCY

At the time when TT Lewis entered the political fray, the constituency in which he chose to run contained the best and the worst of Barbados. Though it was only the third largest constituency in terms of population after St Michael and Christ Church, it nonetheless represented the throbbing heart of the island – serving as the commercial and communications centre, as well as the seat of its political authority.

Bridgetown linked Barbados with the world. Ships riding at anchor in Carlisle Bay would offload their foodstuffs, firewood, coal, building wood and manufactured items onto sturdy mini barges manned by black "lightermen" who ferried the merchandise by oar to the Careenage and would later row back out to the moored ships with the precious sugar exports which then formed Barbados' lifeblood. Roads, the railway line and the 40-minute schooner service to Speightstown all fanned out from Bridgetown. At the popular Savannah Club, the local white elite would indulge in its social antics. Broad Street and Roebuck Street would bustle with commercial activity and the governor's residence, the legislative chambers and the parliament buildings would serve as the focus of political activity.

But there was another side to Bridgetown. At the lower end of the social spectrum lay the plight of the urban poor rubbing shoulders in the Bridgetown slum tenantries of Pine Estate, Bay Estate, Carrington Village, Phillips Tenantry, Emmerton, Lakes Folly and Chapman Lane. The squalor and disease which prevailed in these areas was captured vividly in the report of the Moyne Commission that was set up to investigate the causes of the working class riots in the colony in 1937.

The final report described housing conditions in the following terms:

In many homes overcrowding exists – large families of two or three small families living in the same house. This condition although present in the country areas, is more serious in the City. Here, small houses are often subdivided into small cubicles, partitioned off, merely by curtains and rented out to men and women. The living conditions in these 'lodging houses' are very bad and the sanitary arrangements very primitive.[17]

Slum tenement in 1940s Bridgetown

On public nutrition:

The nutrition of the labourer is definitely inadequate, especially is it lacking in the so-called protective foods. The manual worker is accustomed to a bulky carbohydrate diet and at his present salary it is impossible to supply a satisfactory diet which at the same time includes a sufficiency of the protective foods.[18]

On public health:

The endemic prevalence of typhoid fever [is particularly acute] in the parish of St Michael (in which Bridgetown is situated) where from 50–66 percent of the total cases occur in a population estimated at 30–35 percent of the total.[19]

Just five years after the commission reported, Lewis fought and won the election in this constituency as senior representative of the City of Bridgetown under the two-member constituency system.

Having spent so much time in the Kensington New Road area as a youngster, Lewis would have built up a number of friendships and alliances. This might have convinced him that he stood a reasonable chance of election to the City seat. Many of those interviewed proffered similar explanations for Lewis' string of successes in this highly contested constituency.

Cecil Hutchinson (1992)

TT always used to address his political gatherings with arms outstretched saying: 'Nothing in my hands I bring, simply to the cross I cling.' In essence he was saying that all he had to give them was himself and that they couldn't expect him to dole out any money or corned beef. So they had to take him for what he was. (Cecil Hutchinson)

It is interesting to note that long before the election of H.A. Vaughan in 1936, the City of Bridgetown had been represented in the House of Assembly by one of Barbados' most distinguished sons, the coloured Samuel Jackman Prescod, widely regarded as the father of franchise reform in the island.

TT was a very likeable person. He had to be, if not, he would never have gotten a seat at that time in the City where there was a lot of poverty. TT came from humble beginnings and would have suffered the same as blacks. He circulated with coloured people and was forced to spend a lot of his time among us. One of TT's great advantages was his ability to build up a relationship with those he met. I daresay that he appeared to be more popular with the blacks than the whites and this is reinforced by the fact that he could obtain the votes of people in Cats Castle, Chapman Lane and the New Orleans area. (Owen T. Allder)

Owen T. Allder in the 1940s (left) and in 1992 (above)

Upon entering the House, Lewis immediately became embroiled in the debate over the weighty issue of franchise reform, a topic that clearly delineated the representatives of the old order and the progressives. Lewis' involvement in the fight for social and economic justice in Barbados, aside from contributing significantly to the general increase in political consciousness at the grassroots and the improvement in working conditions for poor Barbadians – black and white – also yielded two clearly identifiable legislative triumphs. The first was the battle for the abolition of the Occupancy Tax. The second was the struggle to achieve access for all Barbadians to free secondary education. Lewis would push this latter measure loud and hard over the next decade and a half. It would never be passed under his name, nor even in his lifetime. But when it was passed those who enacted it claimed that the law had Lewis' fingerprints all over it. This fact has been forgotten or omitted by many who have written on the subject in the media over the past few years.

FRANCHISE REFORM IN 1943

The question of the franchise and its reform is central to the evolution of Barbadian democracy. Prior to the arrival of universal adult suffrage, franchise reform was seen as *the* primary vehicle for the advancement of working class rights.

The question of lowering the franchise had not been dealt with decisively since 1884, following the Confederation Riots when an act was passed lowering the qualifications for voters, but not the qualification for candidates vying for places in the House of Assembly.[20] Even after the violence and confusion of the 1937 riots, it took a considerable effort to push the legislature towards full political rights for the entire population of the colony. The gradual and constitutional encroachment on the white power base through legislative reforms would be finally embodied in the two successful reforms of the franchise in 1943 and 1950.

In the entire hundred years prior to the 1943 franchise reform, the number of electors, when taken as a percentage of the island's total population, had hardly changed at all. Samuel Jackman Prescod had reported that there were 1,100 electors in 1841 (of which, he noted, approximately 200 were non-white).[21] In the year 1905, the official register of electors shows that the number of citizens registered to vote had risen to only 1,692: less than one percent of the entire population.

By 1918 all men in Britain, the 'mother country', were entitled to vote. By 1928, universal adult suffrage had been attained in that country. But by 1942, Barbados' features as a representative democracy were visible only in outline.

The 1940s produced a number of political firsts. Even before Lewis gained a seat in the House and became the first elected employee, J.T.C. Ramsay (pictured above) won a seat as the first tradesman. Ramsay, a carpenter, caused an uproar when he entered the House for the first time in 1940 dressed in overalls as a mark of working class origins.

Almost inevitably, one of Lewis' first contributions to the debates of the House of Assembly is recorded in connection with the extension of the franchise – a matter under discussion in 1942 at the very first meeting of the reconvened House following the election. It was Grantley Adams who two years earlier, in 1940, had returned the question of franchise reform to political centre stage. Having gained a foothold in the Assembly – the electoral breakthrough of his Barbados Progressive League ushered five labour candidates into the planter and merchant dominated chamber – Adams would attempt to enlarge the electoral base, from which his party and the working class interests which it represented, stood certain to benefit.[22] The measure which Adams introduced called for the provision of full adult franchise as well as the abolition of the property qualification for membership of the House. The measure was predictably rejected by the House. And although Adams reintroduced his franchise reform bill in the 1942 session as a private members' bill, the Government countered with a bill of its own, tabled to amend the 1901 Representation of the People Act. It was this latter

The Early Years in Politics

measure that would eventually be passed in 1943, reducing the annual income qualification from $240 to $96 and enfranchising women.

Lewis was not a member of the BPL, but he instinctively supported a bill that clearly, if insufficiently, advanced the idea of universal adult suffrage in which he believed. In addition, he argued, it would have another positive effect on political life. According to him, it would:

... hasten the day of real party politics in this island, and it will expedite legislation. I have been told that it is very necessary for members of this House to make speeches on every occasion that a Bill or Resolution comes up, if not, they are charged by their constituents as being neglectful. If we hasten the day of party politics, we may cut that out and get down to the very serious business in an expeditious manner.[23]

Clearly, if a member felt it necessary to ramble on, as a matter of course, on every legislative measure that came up before the House, proceedings would take rather longer than if organized political parties could nominate spokespersons on certain subjects who would argue the issue in a less time consuming fashion. Lewis' point was echoed two years later in the pages of the *Barbados Advocate*:

If political parties do nothing further than decide to depute certain members to speak on certain issues, instead of each member

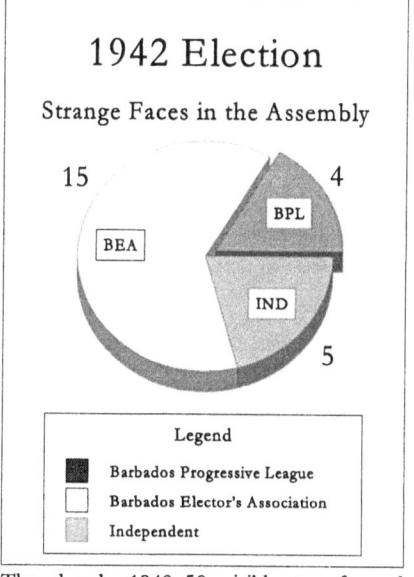

The decade 1940–50 visibly transformed Barbadian politics. The 1940 elections had witnessed the first ever election of black politicians in an organized party with a progressivist outlook. The election of 1942 and subsequent ones would serve to reinforce this trend, reaching its culmination in the elections following the attainment of universal adult suffrage in 1950.

assuming the role of gramophone record, [party politics] will be to the benefit of the Island. By this manner of conducting debates, the time occupied over the measures on the Order Paper could be considerably reduced.[24]

Here are some of Lewis' first recorded words in the House, spoken on the subject of franchise reform:

I thought that at least some young member of this House should make his contribution to this debate, and I thought that mine will be of some assistance to this House ... A Bill of this nature places honourable members in the position of judging the intelligence and political ability of their fellow creatures. That is a grave responsibility, but I am going to accept mine, and I am going to discharge my duty according to the dictates of my conscience. I feel that the only thing I can do is to give my assent to a Bill that embodies universal suffrage. I feel that that is what we owe the community. If there are any members of this community that are unable to read and write, or unable to earn an income qualification, this House is in a large measure responsible for it. This House of Assembly is older than any member of the community, and if previous members of this House had accepted their responsibilities no member of this community would be thought to be outside the qualifications of a voter for a representative Chamber . . . I beg to support this Bill, and I hope that it will in reality extend the franchise. (Cheers.)[25]

Lewis also addressed himself to the widespread concern among progressives about one possible retrograde consequence of the female franchise. An act allowing women the vote, but retaining a property qualification, would thereby only enfranchise women of the upper class who could be expected to vote conservatively. In tackling this delicate issue, Lewis expressed the hope that women falling into this category would: "feel it is their duty to see that it is universal adult suffrage they are fighting for, and not to penalize the less fortunate among their sex."[26]

Essentially, the question of the franchise qualification was seen in starkly contrasting terms by the conservatives and the progressives. The latter quite openly viewed any measure placing property restrictions on candidates' eligibility to contest elections as a rearguard action by entrenched elite interests. And such a rearguard action was in fact mounted by the conservatives. Prior to the passage of the bill, they tabled an amendment to the effect that while the franchise itself would be lowered, the income qualification for members of the House should not only be raised, but that the law should be changed on the matter of proof of eligibility to sit in the House. A heated exchange ensued. What follows are selected quotes from that debate. They reflect the sullen mood prevailing in the House in June 1943 over the issue:

. . . what is creating a certain amount of ill feeling in this country – and I am going to be frank now – is that certain sections of the community [i.e. black candidates] who have hitherto come forward and offered themselves as candidates for election to this House have been challenged at the elections and asked to swear to their qualification while nothing is ever asked of other sections. This has created a bitter feeling." (E.S. Robinson) [27]

I have heard it suggested both inside this House . . . and outside it, that the tone and dignity of this House is tending to be lowered. I do not believe it . . . It was only fear engendered by the sudden influx of strange [i.e. black] faces in 1940. (Hugh Springer)[28]

I am moved to condemn the amendment more particularly because it would seem to me to be an amendment based on fear – fear that if you lower the qualification for a voter and do not retain the qualification for a member you are still likely to have in this Chamber someone whom you would not like to see in it . . . I counsel honourable members that if they signally fail to extend the honour and responsibility of membership of this House to other than those persons possessing the qualifications which have been existing for the past 300 years, and merely concentrate upon offering further restrictions because they are afraid that by giving the voter his right he is likely to bring in someone to displace them, it would be a disservice and a dishonour to themselves. (A.E.S. Lewis)[29]

Do we feel that at a time when the Colonial Office is broadening the franchise in every West Indian Colony we will be permitted to assume a reactionary spirit in Barbados? Are we so stupid as to think that the Imperial Legislature is really so afraid of us, or so anxious not to crush our corns, that they would not provide some means whereby the reactionaries of this island should not be able to persist in retarding the forces of progress? Can any one have any doubt whatever that, if we persist in this sort of thing, as soon as the war is over, we will have an Imperial Statute giving universal suffrage to the whole of the West Indies, completely wiping out every qualification for membership of the Assembly, and making it impossible for them to have retrogression to the unhappy days when a few persons in financial position were able to maintain the status quo? . . . Those who feel as I do have always been impotent in this Assembly. We could do nothing by way of argument. When questions with regard to the franchise come before them, honourable members sit and vote silently against any progress, feeling absolutely sure in their minds that their financial position is so secure, and the class which goes with it is so great, that in spite of what may be said, in spite of the opposition of a few of us in this House, they have a majority which they expect to have for years to come. (Grantley Adams)[30]

> ## A VIEW FROM THE OTHER SIDE OF THE HOUSE
>
> In the House of Assembly in those days there was not so much an idea of party lines or toeing the party line. And TT was without question the best example of this. He was someone who, when he had something to say, would say it – regardless of party loyalties. As a result, he found himself as somewhat of a loner. I never really felt that TT was a party man. In fact, he moved through many parties. Nevertheless, you can get the idea that I very much admired TT and would have liked to see him come over to our party. I personally disagree with the concept of the political party and I think that we'd be better off with individuals representing a constituency without party affiliation. Politics should be about serving the community. I believe that the two-year term, when it was in existence, was an extremely good system of governance. Within two years you should certainly be able to tell if the person you have elected can serve the constituency well enough to return him again. I really think TT was more knowledgeable than many senior party people about the business of running the country because, owing to his training in business and bookkeeping, he had a good sense of balance sheets. (Herbert Dowding)

These remonstrations were not sufficient to prevent the amendment. But Adams' contribution to that debate gives a strong flavour of the extent to which persons whom he termed "reactionaries" were prepared to go in order to limit the reforms, conjuring up, at the same time, the old image of the recalcitrant planter dominated assembly challenging the imperial parliament in the manner it had done over the Confederation issue three generations earlier.

An interesting, even ironic footnote to the entire franchise debate as it related to Lewis himself is the fact that Lewis' enemies would later seek to use the income qualification as a weapon to deny him eligibility to sit in the House once he had been fired from his job. Though he did not know it at the time, the instinctive thoroughgoing contempt which he, and others, demonstrated towards the retention of any type of income qualification for electors or representatives was to prove well founded.

Views on Censorship

Lewis cut his political teeth during the war years when the colony was beset by wartime restrictions of various kinds. One highly restricted commodity was information. Based on the "careless talk costs lives" admonitions being broadcast throughout the British Empire, the colony of Barbados and its citizens placed certain restrictions upon themselves, among which was the censorship of public material deemed crucial to the security of the empire.

In this context, the vexed questions of censorship, its scope and its relationship to matters of security were all debated in the House between July and September 1942. At issue was whether the powers of censorship were being abused by the Chief Censor for ideological and political aims. The protagonists were Lewis and the Chief Censor, George Birt Evelyn, a conservative and senior representative for Christ Church. Eventually Grantley Adams would enter the fray on Lewis' side.

Clearly risking the stigma of unpatriotism, especially at a time when censorship rules governing Britain were themselves also highly restrictive, and when it was by no means clear which way the war would turn, Lewis chose to challenge the government's censorship measures. The specific issue was the banning of the pro-Labour Trinidadian *Vanguard* newspaper from the colony of Barbados by the Chief Censor. Lewis spoke as follows:

> . . . It has been told to me that it would appear to be humanly impossible for someone who is interested in sugar factories and plantations not to take his duties seriously in the condemning of the circulation of the information which was contained in the particular newspaper. [Moreover], dissatisfaction has arisen because of the fact that the Chief Censor of Barbados is a man widely and variously mixed up in the political and economic life of this colony . . . It is his connection to the economic and political life of this colony rather than his unfitness which make it impossible for him not to be charged with partiality in dealing with some of the information which must come before him in the normal course of his duties.[31]

Despite having the audacity to raise the matter, Lewis' presentation on the subject was halting, and, no doubt due to his apprentice status in the chamber, tended towards equivocation. Lewis' line of attack was that while the Chief Censor himself was above reproach, his business and professional ties to the establishment prevented him from taking a disinterested stance on what was or was not fit to be published. Lewis' challenge was furthered by Adams in an altogether more robust fashion:

> I emphatically disapprove of the present censorship practice. I disapprove of any banning of a publication because you are of a particular party and certain publications happen to be published by persons who differ from you in politics. To my mind, the war has reached a stage when the publications which should be banned are publications like those issued by the Primrose League.[32] Anything which aims at perpetuating the Old Order is, to my mind, the only danger to the Empire... What is the object of censorship? To ensure that no military information... should be made public... and thereby enable the enemy to destroy life and property in any part of the British Empire... Censorship has been put into the hands of people with extraordinary conservative views... And I am going to ask the Chief Censor a direct question. Has there been any non-Labour publication which has been prohibited into this colony? I am perfectly sure he is going to answer "No". If he prohibits periodicals or books or other reading matter with a Leftist tendency, he is doing just the thing that we, in common with other parts of the British Empire, believe to be one of those evils that the Allied Nations are fighting against.[33]

ATTITUDE TOWARDS THE SECOND WORLD WAR

In the absence of clear written evidence on the matter, Lewis' views on the war are difficult to determine clearly. Differing impressions on how Lewis stood on such a momentous issue were given by those interviewed for this book.

What is known is that despite having served in the BVF during the 1930s, Lewis did not volunteer for service in the Barbados Battalion of the South Caribbean Force, which was constituted in 1942 in response to the war and which was to play a support role in the campaign against Hitler's forces in Italy before being decommissioned after the war.

Lewis' nomination speech of 1942 referred to the ongoing war, but quickly linked the struggle against Nazi Germany with the need to secure freedom from fear at home in Barbados. The following excerpt from that speech is taken from the *Barbados Advocate* newspaper, again in reported speech.

> He [Lewis] had seen two wars and he had been able to take a keener interest in the one that was going on. The employees of Bridgetown – to a great extent the clerks of Bridgetown – were offering themselves to die for their country, they were going to keep the lanes open for those

at home in this island to be able to carry on their commerce and he did not see why the electors should not feel proud to have one of them occupying a seat in the Legislature. (Cheers.) [Barbadian clerks] were going to carry out what [British Prime Minister] Mr Churchill had promised them, a freedom from fear – and if they could go and die for freedom from fear then it was necessary that they should eradicate fear in Barbados. (Cheers.)[34]

Likewise, his contribution to the debate on the message of support for the Red Army, cited below, suggests also that like most Barbadians, he was moved to see the war as a struggle for freedom against tyranny. If this is so, then one questions why Lewis, as a young man with militia experience, did not choose to volunteer to serve with the South Caribbean Force. Judging by his later health problems, it is possible that he proved not to be fighting fit. Yet, the real reason is likely to have been financial.

The BVF was mobilized three days before the British declaration of war on Germany in September 1939. The governor then ordered the BVF into the barracks and from this moment on for the duration of the war its expenses were paid by the Government of Barbados. The BVF was not required to serve outside Barbados. But when the Barbados Battalion of the South Caribbean Force was constituted in 1942, the latter became a full unit of the British Army under the

Some of the Barbadians who volunteered to fight with the Royal Air Force during the Second World War. Note the young Errol Barrow (later prime minister of Barbados) in the back row on the extreme right of the photograph.

control of the War Office in London. Several members of the BVF went over and joined.

To become a member of the Barbados Battalion, the volunteer had to sign a document entitled "Imperial Service Contract" which exposed him to the possibility of serving anywhere in the world as a British soldier. After 1942, the BVF was "stood down" and those members who did not elect to go into the Barbados Battalion of the South Caribbean Force were encouraged to join the local Home Guard.

Those of the interviewees who served with the Barbados Battalion recall that volunteers generally came across from the BVF at their existing rank. Thus, if you were a private in the BVF but had risen to a senior position in the local business community you would still go across to the Barbados Battalion as a private and get a private's pay. On the other hand, if you stayed in the BVF (or the Home Guard after 1942), your employer generally paid your salary when you were called away from work on exercises.

The British constituted the BVF into the Barbados Battalion, South Caribbean Force and staffed it with British officers and sergeant-majors. Some of the officers of the BVF went in. At that time the South Caribbean Force had become a full-time force, sleeping in barracks and so on. BVF members tended to transfer across at the same rank. So I would suspect that if TT was in effect managing an agency, it would have been financially difficult for him to go in as an enlisted man, which was probably his rank in the BVF. It was not necessarily a lack of patriotism. Most of those chaps who did go in the South Caribbean Forces were getting pay much higher than they could get by working as a carpenter or a joiner. Unless he went in as a commissioned officer, as I did, it would have made no sense. (Sir Fredrick Smith)

In any case, Lewis had just become an elected member of the House in 1942 and would probably have thought he was serving the cause of eliminating injustice by locking horns in Barbados with the group he most identified as the historical opponent of the poor.

Lewis, like most of the ranks of the progressive representatives in the House, was stirred by the role of the Soviet Union in the war. Without question, the single most important force in turning the tide of war against the force of Naziism was the Soviet Union's Red Army. Approximately three out of every four German soldiers who died would do so on the Eastern Front. The Red Army's decisive stand at Stalingrad in the winter of 1942–43 and what this feat symbolized, implanted in many onlookers grateful and affirmative feelings towards the Soviet Union and its people. Lewis shared those views and would probably have also wanted to be considered among the ranks of a generation that looked favourably upon the Soviet Union as the world's best hope against Hitler's Germany, Mussolini's Italy and Franco's Spain.

What must doubtless have added to the enthusiasm of the progressives in the assembly for the Red Army was the fact that the Soviet Union, despite having entered into a short-lived strategic alliance with Nazi Germany from 1939–41, was still widely perceived as holding on offer a social system alternative to bourgeois capitalist society. Hugh Springer, then a sitting member of the Barbados Progressive League, no doubt reflected the views of the progressives when he stated:

> I am not a Russian nor a Communist, but I am a patriot in the best sense of that much abused word. I want to see the best for the people of whom I form a part, and in these days of turmoil – I am speaking not only of the war – of upset and disequilibrium of our economic and moral life, when we are looking in all directions for a plan and a system which will bring order out of chaos, I have always felt that any system which makes a bold and brave attempt to organize our disorder is worthy of the closest study and the most sympathetic consideration, and that the only solution for our difficulties will be found along the lines of bold experimentation where they seem hopeful of success. It is for that reason that I look towards Russia with mixed feelings. We are being told . . . that the Russian system is sheer tyranny under which the masses of the people are being ground for the benefit of the few; that it could not stand the slightest shock from outside because of the hollowness of its structure . . . The heroic resistance of the Russian Army and people is proof positive that although there may have been defects, and may still be, in the embryonic Russian system and government, whatever faults, however crass, the Party in power might have committed, in the name of the Government of the people, there is sufficient guidance in it to claim the unstinted loyalty of the masses of the Russian people whose resistance has been such that nowhere in the world has it ever been on such a scale . . . My sincerest hope is that . . . we may at this time be prepared to look with unclouded and unfrightened eyes at Soviet Russia, draw from it whatever lessons it has to teach us and decide on them on their own merits. (Cheers).[35]

The question of paying tribute to the Red Army, which had just accepted the surrender of the last Germans at Stalingrad in February 1943 and was now starting to turn the tide against Hitler's forces, was raised in the House. Predictably, whereas the progressive members of the chamber were unequivocal and even euphoric in their support for the Red Army, conservative members were reluctant. This prompted Lewis to remark bitterly:

> I, therefore, have much pleasure in the passing of [the resolution congratulating the Red Army's victory, which is] nothing more than a compliment to ourselves and an expression of our gratitude to a noble Ally. (Cheers). In doing honour to that Ally, I feel that we are doing honour to ourselves, and it is with deep regret that I look around this horseshoe table and see so many seats vacant. Vacant seats are an eloquent testimony to man's inhumanity to man. The moment that we do not feel there is an impending danger, we are prone to be ungrateful. It is with deep regret, I repeat, that an Address of this sort is passed in other than a full House [as it is] nothing

more than a vote of thanks to those who are aiding us in what we firmly believe to be a good cause.[36]

Additional and possibly contradictory light is shed on Lewis' attitude to the war through his contribution, in 1946, to the debate on what sort of occasion would befit the celebration of the first anniversary of Victory Day, to be held in Barbados on 8 June 1946. Flying in the face of the general consensus even among progressive members that the celebrations should be held despite the food shortages that were then affecting the island, Lewis challenged:

> I would like to know what we are celebrating. Is it victory over right, victory to get justice, or is it merely the cessation of hostilities so that we can start an economic war? Is it that the War Criminals of one nation will be able to try those of another nation? . . . I regard this celebration as nonsense . . . I am not desirous that the people of this colony should have any interest in war . . . It has been suggested that there should be Thanksgiving Services for peace that has come to the world, but I would like to say that there is no such thing as peace in this world today . . .[37]

His remarks were brought to an abrupt end through a polite admonishment by Adams: "I congratulate the honourable senior member for the City on his speech, but I would like to say that in 1937 Mr George Lansbury[38] made an excellent speech on the same lines. That speech, however, did not prevent a War."[39]

Given the scale of the devastation brought about by the Second World War in which an estimated fifty million perished, the very identifiable source of the aggression, and the fact that the war had been won by those championing open, as opposed to totalitarian, forms of government, Lewis' remarks would have been deeply shocking to probably all members of the House. They would certainly have been considered disrespectful by those Barbadians who had lost kinsmen in the Allied forces. Nonetheless, his strength of feeling displays a deep pacifism and his words probably drew heavily upon the then much publicized United Nations War Crimes Commission, established in 1943, which had introduced the new category of "crimes against humanity".

On the war, then, Lewis appears to be a man torn by the conflicting impulses of patriotism to his native Barbados (then part of an empire at war), and a pacifist inclination bolstered by a sense that the real enemy was not an antidemocratic idea waging war on the Allies on distant continents, but a very visible enemy fighting to preserve an antidemocratic political structure within the confines of the island itself.

The Constitutional Radical

From the vantage point of the end of the century, it is possible to identify the great intellectual contest of twentieth century politics as the struggle between forms of totalitarian[40] rule on the one hand and those of constitutional democratic governance on the other. In this battle, Lewis comes down squarely on the side of the latter.

Lewis never put his thoughts on political theory down in writing. It is therefore difficult to reliably ascertain which political thinkers he chose to draw inspiration from, and, more importantly, what portions of their thinking he found appealing. It is known for example, that Lewis never tired of quoting Bertrand Russell's *History of Western Philosophy* and admired (reportedly to the point of reverence) the ideas of the Irish Fabian socialist George Bernard Shaw. Shaw's famously withering critiques of the British establishment stood side-by-side with his fawning misperception of Soviet society during the 1930s – a period of widespread man-made famine and of Stalin's terrifying purges of the intellectuals and the army. The breadth of Shavian writing on politics, referred to by contemporaries as literary terrorism, would have offered a vast cornucopia for the intellectually hungry Lewis. It is not clear whether Lewis understood how far some of Shaw's extreme and intolerant views were straying from leftist orthodoxy: Shaw sided, for instance, with Mussolini against Ethiopia and he advocated the overthrow of the US constitution. So the best one can settle on is that Shaw's irreverent portrayals of capitalist society in the 1930s and 1940s, being in line with the radical chic of the times, would have strongly appealed to Lewis' nonconformist instincts.

In the interviews, a number of other names were mentioned as having had an influence on the development of Lewis' political thinking. Since nothing which Lewis may have written or said, drawing on these thinkers has survived, their names, like that of Shaw, can serve only as general reference points for a pattern of political thought.

As he left school so early, TT must have spent a lot of time educating himself. Unfortunately, he read a lot of communist literature and was a great admirer of Leon Trotsky. TT used to quote Laski a lot. TT was a great fan of George Bernard Shaw, whom he was not alone in describing as the best brain of the twentieth century. However, I believe that even though TT used to consider himself a socialist, he was a true democrat without really knowing it. (Trevor Gale)

Leon Trotsky, Russian revolutionary and exiled opponent of Stalinist dictatorship, may have held special intellectual appeal for Lewis on account of his authorship of the theory of "combined and uneven development". This held that

The Early Years in Politics

it was possible to envisage a direct transition from feudalism to socialism, skipping or bypassing the interim capitalist stage required by orthodox Marxist theory. Thus the impetus for anticapitalist revolution could come, not from the proletariat within capitalist societies themselves, but from revolt in underdeveloped countries sustained through the linked doctrine of "permanent revolution".[41] Trotsky was speaking of Russia, but Lewis may have considered the point applicable to other territories under colonial control, like Barbados in the depression years.

Harold Laski, influential British political theorist and precocious leader of the British Labour Party in 1945–46, is of particular interest as a supposed intellectual parent of Lewis. As a socialist, Laski faithfully denounced the capitalist system, argued that the ownership of property ought to be related to duty and held that the right to work and decent wages were the obligations of a compassionate society to provide. But in a manner similar to Lewis' own position, Laski's writings reveal an ultimate inability to reconcile his socialist leanings (which intensified as he recoiled from Hitlerian fascism) with his strong individualism and liberalism.

Of considerable influence nearer to home was the superb pioneering journalistic work of Clennel Wickham, with whom Lewis corresponded. Wickham's lucid and penetrating prose had in the 1920s exposed, among other things, the social failings of the Barbadian plantation economy. By the time Lewis had gotten to know Wickham, the latter's radical writings had essentially been tamed through their author's loss of a libel case which separated him from the *Herald* newspaper and effectively exiled him in neighbouring Grenada.

Clennel Wickham shaped a lot of TT's political thought, and he had a high regard for the man. Once, I visited TT at Colly's [Frank Collymore's] house and TT produced a magazine called *Outlook* from which he proceeded to read an article by Clennel Wickham. TT had nothing but praise for the man. TT said he had all the copies of the magazine. Wickham, editor of the radical *Herald* in the late 1920s, developed a reputation for being one of the foremost critics of the plantocracy.[42] (Trevor Gale)

Trevor Gale in the 1940s (left) and in 1992 (above)

So little direct evidence exists on which to pin Lewis as a categorizable political entity that to try to do so risks oversimplification. However, a broad brush portrait seems possible. Writing in 1981 – almost a decade before the Cold War would come to an end – E.L. "Jimmy" Cozier, columnist and lifelong friend of Lewis, reported that the latter "considered himself to be a Socialist, and in those far-off days before the exposure of Communist opportunism and intransigence, would not have been offended at being termed Communist."[43]

Yet, the essential tenet of communism is that all property should be held in common and that ownership should be confined to the means of consumption, while the means of production and exchange should be owned communally. This view is nowhere to be found among what one can identify as the armoury of Lewis' ideas. As regards the label "socialism", if one leaves aside its more restrictive Marxist definition as a transitional stage between capitalism and full communism, it is possible to find a definition of socialism that fits the political perspective of the Barbadian progressives among whom Lewis counted himself.

Unlike the conservatives who viewed the political system in Barbados as a means to preserve the traditional order of things, the progressives saw the state and its machinery as a tool that could be fashioned to redress social imbalances and perceived injustice. Key planks in their socialist platform were the advancement of welfare entitlements (like workmen's compensation and holidays-with-pay), redistributive justice (land reform, better wages, progressive taxation) and the elimination of hereditary privilege (as then manifested in the restricted franchise). Private property would be permissible, but its excessive accumulation in the hands of a few could not be allowed since those who possessed inordinate amounts of wealth would thus be in a position to threaten the balanced interests of society as a whole. Hence the reasoning behind the progressives' idea of nationalization.[44]

Like most of those who inhabited the world of pre-independence Barbados, Lewis was never recorded as having ventured into deep debate on the subject of how he categorized himself politically. Concepts such as class struggle, would have no doubt been as familiar to Lewis as they were to other progressives, but one never sees in the House debates references to phrases like "proletarian internationalism", "vanguard party", "dictatorship of the proletariat", "dialectical materialism" and other bits of jargon used by Marxist-Leninists. And while the sights of Lewis and his other progressive colleagues were clearly fixed upon oligarchs and upon poverty and injustice, their approach was reform not revolution. Social amelioration would have to take place in a constitutional, not an unlawful, manner. Throughout his career in politics Lewis stood faithful to the concept of constitutional rule.

I don't know if it is right to call him a socialist. He never repudiated private property. His approach was one of trying to get to the root of political and social issues. He would always want to know why social institutions were the way they were. He was not a revolutionary. He was a constitutional radical. (Sir James Tudor)

Because Lewis worked within the framework of the constitution he was not vulnerable to the disappointment typical of failed revolutionary hopes. The labour movement in Barbados was never used as the vehicle for a revolutionary overthrow of the capitalist plantation economy. It served, instead, as an agent of progressive change from within. The evolution of liberal democratic constitutional government in Barbados in the post-1937 period consistently confounded those who overestimated the level of ideological radicalism in the workers' movement. The fundamental success of the era's progressive leadership – sometimes scorned as British educated and "petty bourgeois" – was that it managed to combine a solid programme of social (and socialist) reform with a commitment to parliamentary democracy. This separates Barbados from many other former colonies. It undoubtedly places the Barbados progressive movement firmly within a characteristic "western" socialist mould and laid the basis for the considerable social improvements for subsequent generations.

In the early stage of Lewis' political career, however, the label "socialist" seems amiss. He clearly exhibits an abhorrence of social injustice of any kind but the essentially socialist mindset that characterized many of his speeches and actions would come a little later.

As would have been the case with many Barbadian political luminaries of the time, the ideas which Lewis may have held on the sweep of great issues from the first half of the twentieth century – wars, feminism, totalitarianism, national liberation movements – having never been written down, were subsequently lost. Nonetheless, the main issue which preoccupied reformist minds in Barbados – the struggle to improve the conditions of the working class in the colony – fills the pages of the official records of the House of Assembly and bears rugged testimony to this great battleground of the island's social democratic inheritance.

NOTES

1. See appendix 3 (parts 1–3) for graphical representations of the evolution of Barbados' governance structures to 1960.
2. Patrick Emmanuel, "Shifts in the political balance of power: trade unions and political parties" in *Emancipation III: Aspects of the Post-Slavery Experience of Barbados,* Barbados, 1988, 107.
3. F.A. Hoyos, *The Quiet Revolutionary*, Macmillan Caribbean, London, 1984, 99.
4. F.A. Hoyos, *The Quiet Revolutionary*, 100.
5. F.A. Hoyos, *The Quiet Revolutionary*, 100.
6. E.L. Cozier, *Caribbean Newspaperman – an Autobiography: The Life and Times of Jimmy Cozier*, Literary Features (Caribbean) Ltd, Barbados, 1985, 55. See also P. Emmanuel, "Shifts in the political balance of power: trade unions and political parties" in *Emancipation III*, 95.
7. Curiously, there seems to have been an unwritten taboo about attaching the word "party" to the names of political organizations in Barbados prior to the mid 1940s, even though organized political parties had existed in Britain for decades. Indeed, the concept of a political party appears itself to have been only timidly embraced in Barbados. Local conservatives labelled their grouping an Elector's Association in 1941 before changing the name to the Progressive Conservative Party for the 1956 election, and the Barbados Labour Party effectively started its work in 1938 under a banner titled the Barbados Progressive League. As mentioned earlier, seekers of a "middle road" banded together under the Barbados Liberal Association banner. Finally, Charles Duncan O'Neal's reformist political activism had involved him in what was called the Democratic League in 1924.
8. This fact causes considerable difficulty for anyone attempting to trace party allegiance to the BEA for it mixes those who were true independents (like Lewis, Crawford and Brancker in the 1942 election) with conservatives linked to the BEA. In an attempt to arrive at reasonably clear distinctions on the matter, this book describes those associated with the BEA as BEA candidates and not Independents.
9. E.L. Cozier, *Caribbean Newspaperman*, 57.
10. F.A. Hoyos, *The Quiet Revolutionary*, 100.
11. F.A. Hoyos, *The Quiet Revolutionary*, 100.
12. E.L. Cozier, *Caribbean Newspaperman*, 57.
13. *Barbados Advocate*, 27 January 1942, 6.
14. See chapter 1 for details on electoral entitlement.
15. The commercial and shopping centre of Bridgetown. The term is used as a euphemism for the island's commercial interests.
16. *Barbados Advocate*, 20 January 1942.
17. See *West Indies Royal Commission: Proceedings of the Investigation in Barbados*, (Reproduced from the *Barbados Advocate*), Advocate Publishing Company, Bridgetown, 1939, 176.
18. See *West Indies Royal Commission: Proceedings of the Investigation in Barbados*, 176.
19. See *West Indies Royal Commission: Proceedings of the Investigation in Barbados*, 170.
20. Anthony Phillips notes that "attempts were made in 1930 and 1931 to lower the franchise, but the measure was rejected by the Legislative Council. Only those who had 'a stake in the

country' would be allowed to vote. A similar attempt to extend opportunities for political participation failed in 1936." See A. Phillips, "The Parliament of Barbados, 1639–1989" in *The Journal of the Barbados Museum and Historical Society*, No. 4, 1990, 436–37.

21. Quoted in Warren Alleyne, "Black Barbadian landowners", *Sunday Sun*, Bridgetown, 11 October 1992.

22. Little detailed analysis exists on Barbadian electoral results in the early years of party politics in Barbados (1940–51). A review of the scanty published information reveals considerable variations in the election results reported in these publications. For instance, one reference in the literature suggests that in the 1942 election, all non-BPL members of the House were "conservative" (see Emmanuel, 95). While it is difficult to be definitive about how many of the non-BPL House members belonged to the Elector's Association (since none of the BEA records, such as they were, appear to have survived), it is well known that politicians such as Wynter Crawford, J.E.T. Brancker and TT Lewis were all non-BPL members, but would hardly qualify as "conservative".

23. *Hansard*, 24 February 1942, 58.

24. *Barbados Advocate*, 29 November 1944, 4.

25. *Hansard*, 24 February 1942, 58–59.

26. *Hansard*, 24 February 1942, 59.

27. *Hansard*, 22 June 1943, 1042.

28. *Hansard*, 22 June 1943, 1043.

29. *Hansard*, 22 June 1943, 1043.

30. *Hansard*, 22 June 1943, 1042–43.

31. *Hansard*, 8 September 1942, 506–507.

32. A British based conservative league originally set up in the previous century by Prime Minister Disraeli to flatter Queen Victoria.

33. *Hansard*, 8 September 1942, 507.

34. *Barbados Advocate*, 20 January 1942.

35. *Hansard*, 23 February 1943, 792.

36. *Hansard*, 23 February 1943, 792.

37. *Hansard*, 14 May 1946, 1005.

38. George Lansbury was a leading British socialist and Labour MP in the period 1922–40 (party leader 1932–35). It is claimed that Lansbury was an individualist who championed causes which won him few votes (support for women's suffrage; opposition to the First World War from the outset). He was also a pacifist. The incident to which Adams refers occurred in April 1937. Although loathing Nazi dictatorship, Lansbury visited Hitler in a vain attempt to improve Anglo-German understanding.

39. *Hansard*, 14 May 1946, 1005.

40. Defined as a system in which the political rulers control every aspect of public and private life in a society where there is a totalist ideology enforced by a single party and its fully-developed implements of monopolistic control including mass communications and a secret police. See Karl Popper, *The Open Society and its Enemies*, Routledge & Keegan, New York,

1945 (1966); Leonard Schapiro, *Totalitarianism*, Pall Mall Press, London, 1972 and Hannah Arendt, *The Origins of Totalitarianism*, New York, 1958.

41. See M. Lowy, *The Politics of Combined and Uneven Development*, New Left Books, London, 1981 and Ernst Mandel, *Revolutionary Marxism Today*, New Left Books, London, 1979.

42. *Outlook* was the journal produced by Clennell Wickham (1895–1938) after the earlier forced closure of his *Herald* in 1930.

43. E.L. Cozier, "The man "TT" Lewis", *Barbados Advocate*, 2 March 1981.

44. Interestingly, Adams had proposed to the Moyne Commission in 1939 that the sugar industry in Barbados be nationalized, and that the plantation system (if at all maintained) should have individual estates with lots cut up into five and ten acres apiece. See F.A. Hoyos, *The Rise of West Indian Democracy: The Life and Times of Sir Grantley Adams*, Advocate Printing Co., Barbados, 1963, 85.

CHAPTER FIVE

With the Congress Party (1944–1948)

WYNTER CRAWFORD AND THE CONGRESS PARTY

What is fascinating about Lewis' political career is not only that it spanned the generation which witnessed the most profound transformation of the Barbadian social and political order, but that for much of that period, Lewis himself was in the thick of the fray. The fact that he, as a white man, chose to stand for the Congress Party which was then seen to be even to the left of the Barbados Labour Party (or Barbados Progressive League, as it was still called up until 1946), bears testimony to his keenness to champion the tenets of socialism. "Before long, [Lewis] joined the Congress Party because it seemed to him to be the most left-wing organization of the day. Lewis, however, had no intention to abandon his sturdy individualism. In spite of party affiliation, he remained a full-blooded and warm-hearted Independent in politics."[1]

The West Indian National Congress Party was formed in 1944 from disaffected members of the BPL. The party would contest elections in 1944, 1946, 1948 and 1951. And although there is no date on which the party is known to have been formally disbanded, the records show that it took no part in the 1956 elections, by which time its erstwhile leader, Wynter Crawford, had joined the Democratic Labour Party, itself formed a year earlier from among individuals who had broken away from the BLP.

In the one interview he granted to the author, Crawford, who had been a founder member of the BPL in 1938, seemed to have felt betrayed by Lewis.

Indeed, his single most vivid memory of Lewis as a Congress member was of Lewis getting up in the House at is first sitting following the 1946 election and opposing a motion brought forward by another Congress member. Lewis was not Crawford's main worry at the time, however. Nor, would it seem, was the main named enemy of the time – the white oligarchy which, since 1941, had sought electoral protection under the banner of the conservative Barbados Electoral Association.

Wynter Crawford in the 1930s (left) and in the 1980s (above)

Following the neck-and-neck 1944 electoral successes of both Crawford and his former political leader Grantley Adams, the two men were rapidly becoming bitter enemies. It is possible that each had come to the conclusion that with the white political establishment now on the verge of retreat, with the full franchise seemingly inevitable and with the power of demographics on their side, their fight was nothing less than a battle for the future political leadership of the colony.

But with the advantage of hindsight, the intense contest between the leaders of the two labour parties seems absurd, taking place as it does during an epoch that would otherwise have seemed to call for consensus and consolidation within the ranks of the progressive movement. Thus, the perplexing feature of the political landscape in 1944–48 when Congress held a favoured political position is that the two chief representatives of the labour movement were prepared to permit squabbling to a degree that would split the labour vote, thereby allowing conservative interests to maintain a position of strength in the House.

It is even possible to argue that the introduction of the Bushe political reforms in 1946 designed to advance the aim of accountable and responsible government in Barbados, by dangling the inducement of executive power in front of Adams and Crawford, had the paradoxical and negative effect of inadvertently fuelling this intense rivalry between the two men, and thereby harming the progressive cause.

The immediate effect was to delay political development towards full adult suffrage, self-government and ultimately independence. It has been argued, for example, that internal wrangling over power-in-prospect also slowed the progress of Barbados towards full internal self-government and independence, when compared to the other prominent British West Indian colonies.² However, to lay the blame for this deviation from common purpose at Crawford's feet is to ignore the fact that Adams' forceful personality also later sparked off two other politically significant divisions within the labour movement – first with Frank Walcott, General Secretary of the Barbados Workers' Union and then with Errol Barrow, who eventually became the prime minister of independent Barbados under a breakaway party. Both men would leave Adams' BLP well before the 1956 election, as would TT Lewis, on account of his own altercation with Adams.

An interesting perspective on this division is that though it may have slowed constitutional advance, the split within the ranks of the labour movement was healthy from the point of view of checks and balances on political power. According to this argument, the split would have headed off any tendency towards creeping dictatorship by the Adams forces.

Little is known about why Lewis joined Congress. For a man of decidedly progressive views the option existed to join either the BPL or Congress. Central planks of the BPL's programme were adult suffrage, self-government and West Indian federation, land reform involving a breakup of the plantation system, state ownership of factories and minimum wages set by law.³ A report following one of the first meetings of the Congress Party stated that the core of party policy was to "fight for the improvement of the working classes".⁴ Any conclusion as to why he joined one and not the other must remain speculative. Lewis may have felt comfortable with what was then the reputed greater degree of intellectual depth found on the Congress Party's platform. Electorally, they were doing just as well as the BPL. Ideologically, they were committed to the same views he held. "Crawford's Party would have been the more radical of the two labour parties at that time. It may not have had the power base of the agricultural and waterfront workers, but it did have a little more of an intellectual understanding of the issues than the BLP [*sic*] had." (Sir James Tudor)

THE 1944 ELECTION

The 1944 election took place on 27 November. Politically, November was an unusual month to hold an election in Barbados. The reason for its postponement from the traditional first quarter of the year was to allow the electoral machinery to work in registering the newly enfranchised voters. While only 6,050 persons were registered to vote in 1938, the reduced franchise meant that as many as 15,400 could cast their ballots in 1944. The seemingly practical and innocuous proposal to extend the life of the assembly appeared to Lewis to be wrong; and he opposed it in a characteristically rules-based, almost puritanical style:

> I cannot go along with those who would, by their acts, make themselves members of this House for another five months, six months, nor any period at all. I should never feel this House a representative Chamber under conditions of that sort... I feel sure that [my constituents] would not agree with me if I, having been elected here for two years, should take it upon myself, during that period to make it more than two years and to rob them of the opportunity of saying whether or not they approve of what I have done.[5]

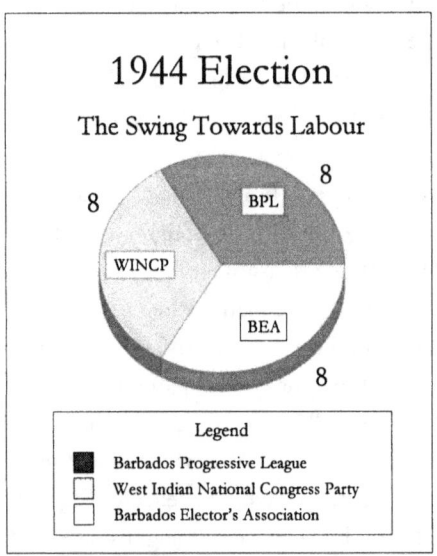

As a result of increased political consciousness, and the larger electorate following the franchise reforms of 1943, the colony elects a substantial number of labour representatives. In a system without full responsible government at this time, the participation of labour members in the Executive Committee – the island's principal instrument of policy – is limited to the BPL's leader, Grantley Adams.

The proposal to prolong the life of the Assembly was nonetheless carried through.

It was Owen Allder who again nominated Lewis for the 1944 ballot. Allder had nominated Lewis almost three years previously and said he was doing so again because Lewis had shown his true colours in giving his unstinting support to every progressive measure brought before the House.[6] Backing such as this from Allder, a black small businessman of modest origins in the rural parish of St John, would have been of immense political benefit to Lewis fighting in the depressed environs of the City of Bridgetown. In the event, Lewis repeated his electoral triumph of 1942 by securing 515 votes (with 171 plumpers) to Pierce's 465 (81 plumpers).

From the standpoint of the political analyst, the campaign for the 1944 election broke new ground. Hitherto unfamiliar issues were raised. Would Barbados be large enough and mature enough to accommodate the politics brandished by organized political parties which were crowding out the more independent brand of political representation? The *Barbados Advocate*, though loud in its support for the extension of the franchise as a long overdue measure, nonetheless had second thoughts about the new voting regime. Interestingly, it was worried about the possibility that newly enfranchised workers might be "cajoled or coaxed into voting this particular way or the next".[7]

The diminished income qualification for electors meant that the stranglehold of the wealthy and propertied class on the Barbadian political system was considerably slackened. All newspapers were reporting increased interest in politics and political participation by people from every walk of life. The electoral consequences were dramatic; the swing towards labour decisive. For the first time in its history there was a predominance of labour representatives in the House: sixteen in all, equally divided between the BPL and the Congress Party with Lewis in its ranks.

Congress surprised all pundits by scoring eight wins despite putting up only nine candidates. Although characterized by differing degrees of organizational coherence and internal discipline, the three forces which contested the 1944 election served notice that party politics had arrived in the colony. Indeed, it was argued that one reason for the declining fortunes of the BEA was that it had not constituted itself as a political party:

The failure of the Elector's Association can be traced to the fact that it is primarily an Association to give financial aid to certain members of the Association who may be seeking election. It is not a political party . . . A political party with a definite policy, although the members, when elected to the Assembly, may deviate from this policy, will always have an advantage over an association which is simply an organization where the electorate can meet and air their views."[8]

Opinion on whether party politics was good or bad for the colony continued to be divided. Some worried about the " . . . threat to . . . individuality in the creation of small parties by power-lust politicians . . ."[9] But a progressive editorial of the *Barbados Advocate* optimistically opined that a sharp division in the House between conservatives and progressives would "prove to be the life-giving force which the Legislature of the Island sadly needs if it is to awaken from its three hundred year sleep".[10] Because of the importance of the arrival of party politics in Barbados, the significance of the 1944 election in this regard, and the effect of all this on the political prospects for labour, it is worth quoting extensively from a local press account written by celebrated *Barbados Advocate* reporter of the time Joe Broome:

If we really subscribe to the need for reform, then we will be really progressive. And there are very few who would publicly deny the need for improvement. There is still a small but ineffective minority who would deny the crying need not merely for change, but for improvement. This is where the new house, with its strong mandate from the people, can do much to assist in improving the conditions of our people. And it is not a difficult programme either. The British government, aware of the necessity for this change, has done much to facilitate it. The programme of the government and the desires of the people are, for all purposes identical, therefore the representatives of the people should not find it difficult to satisfy their supporters. This does not mean that there must be any blind following of any government programme. It must be subjected to the same critical analysis as any measure introduced from private sources. The new House, with its predominance of labour representatives will, however, have a much greater responsibility than has been thrown on others in the past. It is the first time that there has been a predominance of labour in the House of Assembly and it is for them to prove that they are worthy of and fully alive to the responsibility which they now shoulder.[11]

The evident success of the two disparate wings of the labour movement in Barbados during the 1944 election, brought forth a rush of hope for the future. Here is Joe Broome again, reflecting on the extent of the changes that had been brought about within only a generation:

The founding of the now defunct Democratic League by Dr Charles Duncan O'Neal in 1924 coincided with the institution of a system of free elementary education. A peculiar combination has had its effect in the General Elections of 1944. During these twenty years, there has been a series of changes unperceptible at the beginning but marking, none the less, definite stages in political and economic evolution. I have heard them described, according to the speaker, as retrograde steps and alternately as movements of real democratic progress . . . Twenty years ago when Dr O'Neal started preaching the need for political education and economic relief he was characterized as an obstructionist by some of the very people who have since benefitted from his agitation . . . The predictions of a precipitate flight to ruin have been proved all wrong.[12]

Early Champion of Free Secondary Education[13]

I always credit TT as the man who gave Barbados free secondary education – even though this was brought about later on. He was always bringing in resolutions about this in the House. The legislation we have was definitely the brainchild of TT Lewis. As was the legislation to remove the Occupancy Tax. The most striking thing about him? His fairness, honesty and his love of the underdog. (G. Vernon Marshall)

Education has played a generally liberating role in Barbadian history. Originally, formal schooling was the prerogative of the planter class which – for the members of this class who could afford it – sent its progeny off to be educated in fee paying schools in England. In the pre-emancipation era, the planter-dominated elite was generally hostile to the idea of providing education for slaves fearing the disruptive consequences of notions of upward social mobility on those they owned. Private schools for the children of poor whites were started through bequests during the course of the eighteenth century. The nineteenth century witnessed somewhat increased educational opportunities for poor blacks, with a leading role played by the Anglican Church and Bishop Coleridge. It is not surprising therefore that the basis of the curriculum was religious education, typically rote learning and the regurgitation of passages from the Bible.

Following slave emancipation in 1834, the number of schools increased and the British government started to provide support (through its Negro Education Grant) for the education of the children of the newly emancipated citizens. The Barbados Legislature made its first grant towards the education of its citizens in 1846. Those knowledgeable about the development of education in Barbados generally claim that the education commission appointed in 1875 and presided over by Bishop Mitchinson gave the first effective and coherent direction to educational policy in Barbados. The commission's report, which laid the foundations for the Education Act of 1878, was a watershed, not least because between the lines of its several clear-sighted recommendations, it illustrates how education for all citizens would be a desirable social good.

The liberating role of education in Barbados society derives not so much from the intellectual freedom it bestowed on those fortunate enough to get access to it, but from the options it offered to those yearning for an alternative to direct involvement in the plantation economy. For reasons already explained in chapter 1, the Barbadian plantation economy experienced little upheaval following slave emancipation. One of these reasons was the scarcity of arable land available to the ex-slaves to purchase or rent under a tenant farmer system. This compelled the majority to remain economically wedded to the plantations. With education, however, other options became possible – principally via the professions. Thus there was great demand for it. Interestingly, the push for state-sponsored education was coming from many sources. One scholar even argues that cheap child labour was forcing many men out of work and that this proved an impetus to search for solutions to mop up surplus juvenile labour.[14] One such solution would have been organized education.

The legislation which followed the Mitchinson report established an Education Board and committed the government to provide primary school (elementary) education and some secondary education to Barbadians. The Board was given legal authority to incur expenditure on education and it had the authority to set the various curricula. Between this date and the introduction of ministerial government in 1954 (which placed responsibility on a member of government for the education portfolio), there existed a dual management system whereby the state took on responsibility for certain schools while the running of others was left either to the church or to the semi-autonomous governing bodies in the case of the older and more established schools. Both the Marriott-Mayhew (1932) and the Moyne (1938) commissions pointed to weaknesses in the system of schooling then prevailing in the colony.

It is not difficult to discern the important parallel development of political and educational enfranchisement in twentieth century Barbados. As a general trend, the extension of the franchise went hand-in-hand with the election of representatives with a broader social mandate. This gradually led to greater agitation in parliament for the extension of education to all the citizens of the colony as both a right and a key to future development. But the process was by no means uniform and focused. As a reflection of the limited parameters within which possibilities for meaningful social development was seen at the time, the *Ten Year Development Plan for Barbados: 1946–1956*, written when a majority of the Members of Colonial Parliament (MCPs) were labour representatives, had this to say about the prospects for overall social improvement:

> ... we are compelled, therefore, to look for assistance to the Comptroller for Development and Welfare and the Secretary of State [both located in London], at the same time making it as clear as we can that there is little real hope in Barbados of raising the standards of health, education and social welfare and general well being, in the sense envisaged in the Secretary of State's circular despatch of November 12, 1945, unless and until colonial cane sugar production is placed on a more satisfactory basis.[15]

Hardly a declaration fired by revolutionary, or even reformist, zeal.

Here is the educational picture Lewis and his contemporaries were looking at, as described in a recent study:

> By 1933 the path through the Barbadian educational system led from the elementary (or primary) system which was available to most Barbadians between the ages of 5 and 14. However, appreciable material deprivation within the lower class and other deficiencies in the culture that constitute social barriers to educability such as poor parental motivation, aspiration and indifference, kept some children out of school ... [T]he number of children in the age group 5–14 in 1945 was 34,281 with 29,695 enrolled in elementary schools ... [Barbados still featured] a non-compulsory system of schooling ... In 1933–34, the path from elementary to secondary education in Barbados narrowed significantly. Fee requirements, the onerous costs of uniforms and textbooks and the forces of prejudice and snobbery kept an appreciable percentage of the school age population from enjoying the benefits of a secondary education.[16]

In 1934 the number of children enrolled in primary schools who proceeded to the secondary level of education was 4.7 per cent. Ten years later, the figure had risen to only 7.5 per cent.[17]

To be sure, TT Lewis was not alone among those seeking to make education free at the secondary level. However, parliamentary records of the time and the testimony of those who remember mark him out as one of the most vociferous and dogged parliamentarians in his pursuit of this goal.

Many contemporaries interviewed ascribed the fathering of free secondary education to Lewis even though it eventually came about a generation later, after his death. In 1943, when he was still an Independent member, Lewis had made his first contribution to the great debate over free and compulsory secondary education. Here are Lewis' words on the subject as recorded in the House at the time:

> I think that we should say that we must have compulsory education and not say that we cannot afford it. We ought not to have people growing up in this community without a modicum of education; that is disgraceful and we should go all out to provide everybody with some form of education . . . I am saying that we must do our best to find the means by which the schools can be built and let the people see that we are not content with taking our responsibility in this matter so lightly that they can be allowed to go without some form of education . . . I think that we, in this country, have been too willing and too contented in the past merely to say that we have balanced our budget and I think that we have been able to do so by shirking our responsibility.[18]

In a *Barbados Advocate* report on Lewis' nomination speech for the 1944 election, Lewis makes the case for progress in this respect.

> Then there were some things that were left undone by the House of Assembly. As regards compulsory education, they knew that an Address was passed to the Governor in the matter. He [Lewis] felt that compulsory education was necessary and in his opinion, it should be enforced before an attempt to try out the scheme of age grouping in the schools was made. *Then there should be free education in all the schools – elementary as well as secondary* – and if the Government worked with the Workmen's Compensation Insurance themselves, they would find the money to do a great many of these things that were to be done.[19]

Again, in 1946, Lewis compares the educational system then existing in Barbados with that existing in Britain:

> I have spoken with someone who lived in England and he tells me that you can get free secondary education in England (Cheers) so that even if you have to pay a little more in Income Tax and you have to pay a tax for occupying a house, you do not have to pay a great deal in school fees as is the case in Barbados. Some people seem to think that secondary education here is very cheap; I do not believe that.[20]

In March 1947, Lewis makes a powerful (one MCP present at the time said "reckless") pitch along the same lines – this time for free secondary education. On this particular occasion, Lewis was responding to a Bill proposed by Ernest Deighton Mottley, the senior member for the City to amend the Education Act (1890) to enable the St Michael Parish Vestry to increase the number of Exhibitions granted. At the time, the main avenue for working class children to gain access to secondary education was by means of scholarships awarded by no less than twelve awarding bodies.²¹

He would be a brave man in this House to oppose a Bill of this nature, but I would just like to warn the House that they are merely creating an occasion for parochial patronage. *The proper thing for this House to do is to give free secondary education to the peoples of this colony who are in a position to have it.* I do not think that it should be put into the hands of the Education Board, the Vestry or anybody else to walk around and dispense this form of charity as parochial patronage to the children of parishioners who are in straitened circumstances. This is absolutely wrong. I cannot get this House to see that a mere £15,000 or £20,000 a year will provide secondary education absolutely free, and people will not have to beg for scholarships for their children. That is the most degrading form of charity that I know of . . . I say that it is time that secondary education should be given free. By doing that, you will put everybody in the same position. One person can pay for his child, another cannot pay, and when the War comes down both children have certificates, and both of them go to die for the country! I say that it is a degrading form of charity to make a child beg for its education while its father goes and votes for a Vestryman. I raise my voice in the hope that free secondary education will be given to those children in the community who can use it. In this year 1947 a House of Assembly like this should insist that the Government introduce a bill to make provision for free secondary education and get it passed.²²

The point which Lewis was trying to make was that tinkering with the scholarship system was a waste of time. The entire system needed a profound overhauling so that scholarships would no longer be needed at all. A cynical political observer would no doubt also conclude that Lewis would have been concerned over the possibility that his principal rival for the City seat, E.D. Mottley, could through the proposed legislation, enhance his political popularity through use of funds from the Vestry.

Ernest Deighton Mottley and the Vestry System

The parish vestry system had been instituted immediately following the administrative division of Barbados into parishes in the 1630s. The idea of local government in Barbados was presumably rooted in the fact that road communications between the rural parishes and the capital, Bridgetown, even in an island so small, were impractical for many of the day-to-day aspects of running the island's affairs. The vestry system lasted until 1969. Its influential position in society derived from the fact that it was empowered to levy local rates raised by an acreage tax on land ownership, an occupancy tax on houses and a trade tax. An additional, and eventually highly controversial source of revenue, was the rental of designated church pews to wealthy families. The money obtained from all these sources went towards the maintenance of the parish church and the

With the Congress Party (1944–48)

LEWIS VS. MOTTLEY: STUDIES IN CONTRAST?

Lewis would run against Ernest Deighton Mottley in four successive elections starting in 1946. Little is known of their views of each other. Their relationship appeared to be one where each of the two rivals understood the politics of the other, did not particularly approve of those views, but equally and importantly agreed to coexist on that particular political constituency called the City.

TT was no doubt ranked among the three most popular men of the time. In my estimation these were: Ernest Deighton Mottley, Grantley Adams and TT himself. (Christie Smith)

... Another thing that made me enchanted with TT as a personality was that I could not understand how a white man could represent a working class constituency like the City and stand his ground against a man like Ernest Deighton Mottley who had a completely different ideological outlook. These two men were studies in contrast but were also excellent foils of each other. Mottley's approach was that of the pork barrel. He controlled the vestry and used it to dispense largesse. TT's approach would be to patiently teach self-respect. He never made it his aim to give away handouts to the voters – because he himself didn't have very much of anything. You see, if a poor woman were to walk up to Mottley and say "Could you help me, I have nothing to feed my children . . .", Mottley's approach would more than likely have been to ask her to come down to the Board of Guardians weekly meeting where the Poor Law Church Warden and two guardians sat to hear cases of distress and give immediate relief. These took place on Wednesdays, I think. Mottley would be sitting there with the guardians on each side of him and would listen to people and determine on the basis of what they said whether they could find a few dollars to give them. I think TT, and others, felt that this whole arrangement was rather feudal. TT on the other hand would probably have told this lady that he would look out for someone who, perhaps, wanted a maid. His design would have been to raise her dignity and self-respect in the absence of largesse. And yet, as I said, they complemented each other extremely well. Those were the days of the two-member constituency. It was as if the City constituency had a split personality – there is really no better way to describe it. One half, the TT half, was radical. The other half was imbued with a sense of patrimonialism. Mottley satisfied people's immediate wants, but TT gave them a sense of themselves. The curious thing was that they campaigned against each other without ever seeming to need to get involved in muckraking. Mottley probably thought that TT's approach was good for the future and TT that Mottley's was good for the moment. (Sir James Tudor)

A.E.S. ("TT")Lewis (1946)

E.D. Mottley (1940s)

payment of church officials. It was also channelled into the upkeep of roads, sanitation, almshouses, as well as the education of the poor – through the awarding of Vestry Scholarships, for example.

Owing to the large taxation base available in the city of Bridgetown, the Vestryman of this constituency had access to considerable sums of money. The temptation to use these funds for the purpose of political gain was correspondingly high. This fact, combined with a tremendous oratorical appeal, served as the power base of Ernest Deighton Mottley. First elected to serve the Vestry in 1942, Mottley would faithfully follow his white predecessors in ensuring that the funds amassed within the confines of his vestry were used for no other purpose than to support those who "belonged" to that particular vestry.

At the level of national politics, Mottley, a real estate agent by profession, entered the fray as a canvasser for the conservative Elector's Association in the early 1940s. But his unrivalled strength lay at the Vestry level. Following his first election to the local Vestry, Mottley topped the polls in every subsequent local government contest until the Vestry system was abolished. During the years of his great contests with Lewis, Mottley's power lay in his ability to dispense patronage – through poor relief and food distribution. Consequently, he could count on the loyalty of the poor.

After Lewis faded from the political scene, Mottley – two years his junior – went from strength to strength. His personality was such that he impressively took over effective leadership of the conservative party and changed its name from "Barbados Elector's Association" to "Progressive Conservative Party" in an attempt to show that the grouping was no longer a white-dominated body out of tune with the times. He became affectionately known as "the City Father" and was a power in the City in the late 1950s and early 1960s. The abolition of the archaic Vestry system pulled away Mottley's power base from underneath him. Though he eventually became the first Mayor of the short-lived local Municipality of Bridgetown, in his final years in politics Mottley was, like Lewis, a shadow of his former self. He died two years after resigning from the House in 1971.

THE 1946 ELECTION

In 1946, the Second World War was over. Barbados' political machinery, with its excessively adversarial relations between government (comprised of the British governor and those who advised him through the Executive Committee) and Assembly continued to be unwieldy and unresponsive to the needs of party politics and greater demands for responsible government. The existing constitutional arrangements exhibited a certain awkwardness, amply reflected in the fact that although, following the 1944 elections, the BPL and Congress each accounted for eight seats in the House, there was no automatic mechanism in place to ensure that either party had a voice in the Executive Committee. (It was purely a result of the governor's decision at the time that Adams, for example, had been appointed to the Executive Committee in 1942.) This, as a consequence, made the government (or executive) unrepresentative and it was deemed preferable to establish an automatic mechanism to remove this handicap which regularly resulted in the deadlock of parliamentary business owing to lack of legislative support for government initiatives.

Immediately prior to the 1946 election, the outgoing governor of the island, Sir Grattan Bushe, introduced a unique experiment into the island's governing machinery. The so-called Bushe Experiment strengthened the link between the legislature and the executive. It increased the power of the legislature to propose measures through fuller representation in the government (the Executive Committee) and thereby minimized the risk of the government not having corresponding support for its legislative measures in the House of Assembly. This streamlining had the effect of bringing the elected members of the House of Assembly to bear more of the burden of government. Government would thus become "responsible government". In this way the Bushe experiment laid the groundwork for the later arrival of full ministerial, and eventually, cabinet government.

At its core, the Bushe Experiment set in place a semi-ministerial system through which the governor would send for the person best able to command a majority in the House of Assembly and ask him to pick and submit names of House members he wished to have sit with him on the Executive Committee. Under the new system, the direction of House members' accountability would be reversed. The 1881 reforms which had originally set up the Executive Committee had established that once appointed to serve on the

Sir Grattan Bushe, Governor of Barbados (1941–46) after whom the famous Bushe (pronounced "bush") Experiment is named. Bushe emerges from this period as a man who was able to read the future and interpose himself between the rising black leaders and elite whites who were looking for "responsible" blacks to whom to hand over power.

Executive Committee, House members were accountable to the governor who had appointed them. Under the new rules, the leader of the largest party in the House (or the person best able to command a majority), would, based on an electoral mandate be charged with selecting a handful of other members to sit on the executive. Ideally, he would choose these persons from among his own party. This group of men, each charged with the affairs of particular government departments in the executive and in the House, would then be accountable not to the governor, but their own leader and party colleagues in the House and ultimately to the electorate. Thus according to Bushe:

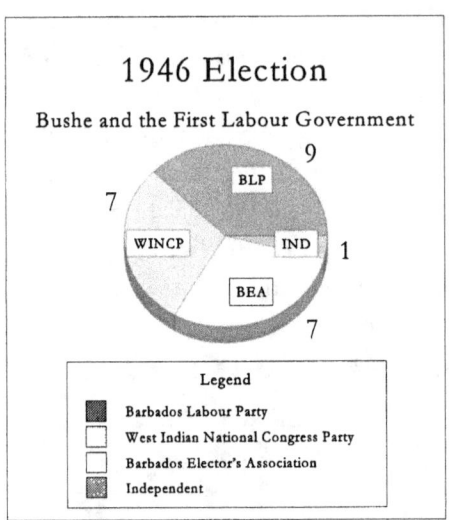

Following the Bushe reforms and with the prospect of the island's first labour leader ("premier"), the degree of political fever was the highest it had ever been in the colony. Barbadian voters return the two labour parties contesting the election with roughly the same number of representatives as two years earlier. Governor Bushe's Experiment in semi-ministerial government provides an opportunity for these parties to fashion a government in 1946, but leadership rivalries paralyse it one year later.

> The Executive Committee will then in practice cease to be merely a collection of individuals nominated by the Governor for the purpose of advising him, and will become an effective organ of Government accepting collective responsibility for policy, though the Governor must under the constitution as at present existing retain ultimate responsibility . . . At present the House can reject Government measures, refuse supply, and confound Government policy in the calm assurance that Government will carry on notwithstanding. That is what I call irresponsibility. The duty and responsibility of Parliament is to support, if not one Government, then another, or to face a dissolution with all its consequences . . . The Executive Committee . . . must be prepared to resign if they lose the confidence of the House.[23]

Unfortunately, the first session administered under this arrangement did not work well. Owing to the fact that no party emerged from the 1946 election with a clear majority, a coalition was required between the two uneasy rivals: Adams and Crawford. The result was an unhealthy spate of bickering and time wasting. Paralysis set in towards the end of 1947. However, once a clear majority winner emerged from the 1948 and 1951 elections, legislative matters moved along smoothly under the Bushe system.

With the Congress Party (1944–48)

Assisting in the 1946 election count: Lewis stands behind the sheriff (sitting). To Lewis' left are Charlie Thomas a supporter from the Barbados Clerks' Union and politicians T.O. Bryan and E.D. Mottley.

The 1946 elections took place on 18 November. Their result could easily be described as having delivered the party system with full force into Barbados. In the years immediately prior to 1946, three recognized political factions had risen to compete for the voters' ballots now that everyone seemed to have woken up to the important role which organized political parties would play in Barbados' future political landscape. These elections also ushered in the first Labour government – albeit coalition government – in the history of Barbados. Newspaper headlines screamed "Election Fever" and claimed that there had never been so great a degree of interest in political issues in the colony. They talked about the keen enthusiasm of the hitherto politically excluded.

The ferocity of the two-horse race between the BLP and Congress increased as it became clear that the parties were again running neck-and-neck. Talk before election day centred on questions like: Would any party emerge with a clear majority? Would the Progressive League or the Congress form the first Labour Government in Barbados? Would Adams or Crawford be the colony's first "Prime Minister"? Although Adams is the name most people remember from this era, the Adams vs. Crawford race could, in 1946, easily have gone either way. Crawford was just as popular as Adams at this time and he was gaining in popularity. Crawford had the middle class as well as labour behind him. But political observers recall him squandering his opportunity in 1946.

Barbados Labour Party supporters in the 1946 election.

Three weeks before the election, he went off to a conference in one of the French islands, instead of staying and canvassing – an action that appears to have made no strategic sense. In his absence, Adams made great political capital and in the end he narrowly ousted Crawford.

Of the over 1,700 eligible voters for the City constituency, over three-quarters would turn up to vote. When the dust had settled, Lewis kept his seat but lost his position as Senior Member for the City to Ernest Deighton Mottley, the black real estate agent and vestryman who was to become a considerable force in local politics over the next generation. Mottley obtained 674 votes to Lewis' 553, almost exactly the same number the latter had received in 1944.[24]

According to the new rules, Adams was sent for by the governor and asked to name his selection of representatives from the House to sit on the Executive Committee. These were, from the BLP, Hugh Springer and himself; from Congress (with whom he was obliged, by dint of not having achieved an overall majority, to share a coalition government) Wynter Crawford and H.D. Blackman. Hoyos, writing on the composition of the 1946 "cabinet" under his pseudonym "Bystander", mused that Lewis and not Blackman would have deserved a seat with Crawford as the representative of Congress in the Executive Committee, had he not been "prevented by the nature of his occupation [a travelling salesman], from accepting office".[25]

Grantley Adams (1940s)

With the Congress Party (1944–48)

Lewis with jubilant supporters on lower Broad Street following the announcement of the 1946 election results.

ATTACKING THE "PERNICIOUS" OCCUPANCY TAX

The tax was pernicious because it required you to pay a tax for simply living in a house – it was purely a naked attempt to raise money. (John Wickham)

TT's part in the removal from the statute books of the Occupancy Tax is the equal to what the Reverend Francis Godson did for the introduction of the Old Age Pension scheme into Barbados. TT was a great fan of Reverend Godson because Godson was a white man with a social conscience . . . (Sir Alexander Hoyos)

Although Lewis is well remembered for a principled stand on workers' rights which cost him his job, and as the man who did more than anyone at the time to further the idea of free secondary education, when the question: "What do you consider Lewis' most important legislative achievement?" was put to interviewees, a large number of responses centred upon the abolition of the Occupancy Tax – a statute which was seen to be particularly oppressive to those who did not own property, and who as a consequence were forced to rent. The Bridgetown clerks, largely low income whites and coloureds were, as a group, especially hard hit by this form of taxation. Its removal is certainly one of the reasons why many low income whites of the time saw Lewis as a hero.

As the law stood at the time, all persons occupying houses – whether chattel or real estate – with an annual rental value of $48 or more were obliged to pay a tax called the Occupancy Tax. So stated the Vestries Act of 1911. Consistently, following his entry into politics and until the successful passage of his bill to contravene the act in 1949, Lewis hammered away at what he saw as the essential iniquity of the existing taxation regime for rented property. He did so in terms that sought to emphasize that the system in operation was one which placed an even greater disadvantage on the backs of those who were not fortunate enough (himself no doubt included) to own property in Barbados.

The essence of Lewis' objection to the Occupancy Tax system was twofold. First, it formed part of a system of double taxation. It amounted to approximately one month's rent and was imposed on top of the traditional ownership tax. The latter would already have been paid by the owner but recouped by him or her from the occupier through the monthly rent. The Occupancy Tax had to be paid by the occupier to the Vestry once a year and typically represented an entire month's rent. Secondly, and worse still, it was a regressive form of taxation. It was levied on persons who did not possess property, and who were thus obliged to live as tenants. These were the people least able to bear such a financial burden. In essence, Lewis considered it a property tax charged against persons who did not possess the means to own that property.

The tax was variously labelled iniquitous and pernicious by contemporaries. It is even possible that Barbados was the only British colony where such a tax existed on the statute books. And although the bill to remove it was passed only in late 1949, most of the legislative steering work was done by Lewis in the three preceding years. The effort to abolish this tax appears to have been a primary driving force in Lewis' early political career. It seems to have been one of the main accomplishments he set out to achieve upon entering politics and, as a subject, features prominently among those things he targeted continuously throughout his legislative career.

In February 1946, Lewis brought the matter before the House in a Bill under his own name. In doing so, he was directly challenging the powerful interests of the vestry. And in an island where there was still a great cleavage between those who owned property and those who did not, the Occupancy Tax issue rapidly became a *cause célèbre* pitting Lewis against the propertied class. It was for Lewis a matter of protecting the interests of the poor against a system that was levying an unjust burden on them.

Though the casual observer of this period in Barbadian history might regard the effort to remove the Occupancy Tax as no more than a curiosity, it was in fact a process that defined both the nature of the economic order and the character of a man who stubbornly refused to let the matter drop until it was settled to the benefit of the disadvantaged.

What made the matter all the more controversial was the fact that the Vestry which stood to lose most from the abolition of the tax – St Michael, accounting for 80 percent of rented accommodation – was represented by Lewis' chief political rival for the City seat, E.D. Mottley. In St Michael, the collection of the Occupancy Tax would have amounted to a very appreciable sum of money. On the question of abolishing the Occupancy Tax, House records show Mottley equivocating until 1949 when alternative revenue to replace the loss of this important source of Vestry income had been identified. In that year, Mottley conceded:

> ... I think we have to agree that this tax creates a hardship on persons who are compelled to rent houses, but we also realize that unless we had some definite recommendation to offset that system of taxation ... we would not have taken it upon ourselves to advise the abolition of this Tax.[26]

No doubt Mottley was seized by the realization that it would be financial folly to support the abolition of the tax. Yet it was something for which a majority of voters were clamouring.

What follows are the principal arguments used by Lewis in the House of Assembly to carry across his point. They are not chronological, but have been arranged by the author to provide a common thread:

> The reason why this Tax has not been removed before is that the Voters' Lists for the Vestries was made up chiefly of house owners and [they] ... get somebody else to pay their taxes and put people in the Vestry to see that that system is perpetuated ...[27]

> ... the vast majority of occupiers are people who have no hope of owning a house and they should know that their monthly rental includes all the taxes and the Vestries should realize that it is wrong to collect virtually a property tax from a non-property owner (Cheers).[28]

> The last point is this: if all these evils that we hear about are going to befall owners of rented houses if the occupiers do not pay taxes, the owners have a simple remedy. If they find it easier and cheaper to rent than to own let them get rid of the headaches which they think the renters do not have by putting a notice in one of the newspapers like this: 'I have come to the conclusion that it is much easier and cheaper and very comfortable to my mind if I rent a house, and therefore I am willing to give mine away ...' If they want to change over from owners to non-owners and occupiers, they can do it in the very easy way that I have indicated, but if the occupier wants to change his status to that of an owner, it is a very difficult task indeed. In this community, many people have been known to die in the effort; many people have been known to set out on an adventure which should give them the opportunity to become owners of houses and portions of land which they would eventually leave for their children, and in the end they have lost all the deposits and payments they have made and they end up by owning nothing at all.[29]

In supporting the bill, Congress colleague Edwy Talma said the following:

> There is only one point which has beaten everybody and it is this: if you happen to live nowhere you are deemed a rogue and vagabond, and because you happen to live in a house which brings a rental of $60 [a year] or thereabouts, because you try to keep your head up and try to be as decent as possible, as decent as your means allow, because you try to avoid being deemed a rogue and vagabond, you are called upon to pay this Tax . . . I think that if there is only one measure that the Legislature [should have] passed and to which we can point, it should be this one.[30]

One thing TT should be credited for is his prominent role in seeing that the Occupancy Tax was abolished. This tax didn't seem very fair as it was a tax that had to be paid on top of all your other taxes. It was due from those who rented property. If you rented a house, or a room, then you paid occupancy tax. (J.E.T. "Jonny" Bourne)

Lewis stated that the matter was of such importance to the Clerks Union members that it was put to them. He said that they met and voted by a majority that the Occupancy Tax should be abolished.[31]

In those days the vestries were important and responsible for maintaining things like the St Michael's Alms House. One of the taxes they imposed was a thing called the Occupancy Tax. This was considered to be an "iniquitous" tax – that was the word used at the time. It was especially harsh on the clerks in Bridgetown who felt that because of the tax they were paying the equivalent of 13 months' rent a year. You see, there were only a handful of clerks who owned the properties they lived in, most of the others rented houses near to town in Chapman Street and so on, so they could be near their work. The tax amounted to about $5 and always fell due in December. Now, for a fellow getting only $20 a month, you could see the problem, it was a case of hand-to-mouth. Anyway, the Clerks Union had a meeting – big crowd – to discuss the matter and decided that the tax should be removed. It was decided that Mr Lewis should go to discuss the matter with Mr E.D. Mottley at the vestry. Mr Lewis argued the case and Mr Mottley proved very sympathetic. The tax was removed shortly afterwards. (Christie Smith)

Lewis Leaves the Congress Party

The coalition government created through the Bushe experiment – comprising two BLP and two Congress members sitting awkwardly together – was doomed to a short life. By October 1947, halfway through the two-year parliamentary term, it had run its course. What little harmony had existed following the creation of the colony's first labour government in 1946 had by this time evaporated to the point where Crawford no longer participated in meetings of the Executive Committee. As reported by Hoyos, himself no sympathizer of Crawford, the latter's objections to the way the Executive Committee was constituted centred on the fact that Adams had been invited to form the government. As such, it was Adams who had been given the power to select members of the House for appointment to the Executive Committee. This applied even to the choice of representatives from Crawford's own Congress Party. Crawford was angered that he had not been sufficiently consulted on the choice, claiming that had he been consulted, J.E.T. Brancker and not H.D. Blackman would have been chosen.[32]

In October 1947, Lewis, along with two Congress colleagues crossed the floor and joined Adams.[33] Possibly, Lewis sensed that the future lay with the BLP. All three were probably approached by Adams who then needed only three seats to add to his existing nine to achieve a majority in the House. With this he could form a government without Crawford. The migration of the three Congress members gave Adams enough parliamentary support to form a BLP government on its own. According to the new Bushe arrangement, Adams was now entitled to select representatives for the Executive Committee from among his own party. Interestingly, the two other Congress members who crossed along with Lewis, Blackman and Talma, joined (or in the case of Blackman, rejoined) the Executive Committee. This was presumably the reward for their new-found loyalty. On Lewis' role in the switch Hoyos writes: "along with Hugh Blackman and C.E. (later Sir Edwy) Talma, [Lewis] resigned from the Congress Party and joined Adams' political organization. It is characteristic of TT that he made this decision without any promise of office or any hope of reward."[34]

As to the reasons why Lewis left, none of the interviewees appear to have known for certain, but a couple of suggestions were proffered. "TT left Congress because he felt that our support came from the countryside whereas he was fighting the City seat and would need the backing of Adams and his union – especially the waterfront workers who were the backbone of the union." (Wynter Crawford).

Oddly, this explanation takes no account of the fact that Lewis had managed to attract a considerable number of nonagricultural workers in three previous elections.

There may have been a disenchantment with Mr Crawford. I don't know. But since TT's convictions lay with the working class majority he would have probably seen greater opportunity for promoting their interests through working with Adams' more mass-based political organization. He contested the 1948 election with Adams. (Sir James Tudor)

Lewis may have become disillusioned with the effect the paralysed government was having on the passage of progressive legislative measures. But even after the political logjam was broken with the formation of a new BLP government following the three defections, that delicate position was again threatened by the confusion surrounding what was then dubbed the "twelfth seat" issue. This mini-crisis developed following the resignation of Hugh Springer on 7 October 1947 to take up a job in academia. When the BLP failed to retain the seat thus vacated, there were rumours that the Congress Party and the BEA (effectively the radicals and the establishment) had tactically joined forces to keep the BLP from winning this seat. Grantley Adams made a fiery speech saying that the Congress Party had linked up with the devil in an unholy alliance to take Barbados back into the middle ages. According to Hoyos, Lewis appears to have come to the same conclusion:

> [Lewis] had been bitterly disappointed by the result of the 1947 by-election when the BLP failed to retain the seat vacated by Hugh Springer. He was convinced that the Conservative and Congress parties had formed an unholy alliance to prevent the Labour Government from obtaining a working majority in the House. I remember the startling and almost violent courage with which he condemned the coalition of the Right and the Left on that occasion. He felt so strongly on the matter that he insisted I publish [Hoyos was leader writer at the *Barbados Advocate* at the time] the speech made by Adams after the result of the by-election was announced. He went to a great deal of trouble to get the full text of that speech and I readily accepted both his advice and his assistance.[35]

In the event, it appears that Adams was able, in the remaining months of the 1948 session, to keep a government together, despite his party again being in a minority position. In the elections which took place at the end of 1948, the BLP won a full twelve seats at the polls. This gave it the right to form a government on its own. Lewis was with him among the winners.

NOTES

1. F.A. Hoyos, *The Quiet Revolutionary*, Macmillan Caribbean, London, 1983, 100.
2. See F.A. Hoyos, *Barbados: A History from Amerindians to Independence*, Macmillan, London, 1978, 225, and Patrick Emmanuel, "Shifts in the balance of political power: unions and parties" in *Emancipation III: Aspects of the Post-Slavery Experience in Barbados*, Bridgetown, 1988, 102.
3. Patrick Emmanuel, "Shifts in the balance of power", 99.
4. *Barbados Annual Review*, 1944–45, 54.
5. *Hansard*, 31 August 1943, 1150.
6. *Barbados Advocate*, 21 December 1944, 7.
7. *Barbados Advocate*, 22 November 1944, 6.
8. *Barbados Advocate*, 29 November 1944, 4.
9. *Barbados Advocate*, 3 November 1944, 4.
10. *Barbados Advocate*, 29 November 1944.

11. *Barbados Advocate*, 29 November 1944.
12. *Barbados Advocate*, 2 December 1944, 6.
13. This subject is dealt with in greater detail in chapter 10 under the section entitled "Laying the groundwork for free secondary education".
14. Earle Newton, "Education policy and human resources development in Barbados – a case study", unpublished study prepared for UNESCO/UWI Workshop on Methodologies used in Educational Policy Analysis as related to Human Resources, Planning and Management in the Caribbean, 1991, Bridgetown, 4.
15. Quoted in Sir Keith Hunte, "Twenty-five years of education in an independent Barbados: a critical review and the future agenda", unpublished Memorial Lecture in Honour of Rudolph Greenidge, 1991, Barbados, 2.
16. Ralph Jemmott and Dan Carter, "Barbadian educational developments (1933–1993): an interpretive analysis", unpublished, 1994, 4.
17. Jemmott and Carter, 5.
18. *Hansard*, 17 August 1943, 1137.
19. *Barbados Advocate*, 22 November 1944, 5.
20. *Hansard*, 19 February 1946, 809.
21. According to Jemmott and Carter (p.5), "These included the 'Foundation' Scholarship awarded by the Governing Bodies of the Schools and Scholarships awarded by the Education Board and the Eleven Vestries. In addition, there were a few private bequests like the Armstrong Scholarships to Harrison College established in 1927.
22. *Hansard*, 4 March 1947, 209.
23. Quoted in Lionel C. Hutchinson, *Behind the Mace: An Introduction to the Barbados House of Assembly*, Bridgetown, 1951, 36.
24. *Barbados Advocate*, 20 November 1944, 4.
25. *Barbados Advocate*, 27 November 1946, 4.
26. *Hansard*, 8 November 1949, 875.
27. *Hansard*, 19 February 1946, 810.
28. *Hansard*, 19 February 1946, 811.
29. *Hansard*, 19 February 1946, 810.
30. *Hansard*, 19 February 1946, 811.
31. *Hansard*, 21 May 1946, 1028.
32. F.A. Hoyos, *Barbados: A History*, 221.
33. R.L. Cheltenham, "Constitutional and political development in Barbados (1946–66)", PhD dissertation, University of Manchester, 1970, 47.
34. F.A. Hoyos, *The Quiet Revolutionary*, 101.
35. F.A. Hoyos, *The Quiet Revolutionary*, 101.

CHAPTER SIX

The Clerks' Union

There was a lot of fear in those days. TT was a giant of a man for fighting the cause of the clerks. (Hammond Burke)

Very few citizens born into post independence Barbados have heard of an organization called the Barbados Clerks' Union (BCU). Like the Barbados Workers' Union (BWU) which predates it by four years, the BCU was established to defend its members against the employment conditions prevalent at the time. Because the Bridgetown clerks tended mainly to be drawn from the lower income white and coloured segments of the population, the BCU's ranks were filled with such people.

The fact that to this day Lewis remains a hero for many former BCU members who are still alive, challenges the notion that he was interested only in improving the lot of the working class black man. Lewis' own origins, social background and evolving view of the way the world worked made it inevitable that he should number the clerks among those he saw as being victimized in colonial Barbados, and his involvement in the BCU demonstrates the importance he attached to workers of all colours organizing themselves into a union to fight for better conditions.

The cause of the Bridgetown clerks was among the first he championed in the field of politics, and this is traceable to some of Lewis' earliest pronouncements. Here, for example, is an extract from his 1944 election nomination speech, as reported in the pages of the *Barbados Advocate* at the time.

The Clerks' Union

The first executive of the Barbados Clerks' Union photographed in 1945. Pictured in the back row are two interviewees: Christie Smith (third from left) and Laurence Small (second from right).

As regards the clerks in Bridgetown, he understood that a great number of them were dissatisfied about the salaries which they were receiving; they had asked for bread and had been given stones. He would like to point out to these clerks that until they came together and formed themselves into an association they would never get adequate salaries and proper remuneration for their services."[1]

The BCU was founded one year later in 1945. Two years prior to this date, trade union legislation had been liberalized somewhat and the formation of the BCU was clearly a result of this. The organization was headquartered in what is now the YMCA building just off Pinfold Street in the city. At its peak, it probably numbered about 500 members.[2] According to its constitution, one of its aims was "to obtain and maintain just and proper rates of wages, hours of work and other conditions of labour, and generally to protect the interests of members."[3]

Some of these "conditions of labour" under which the clerks then worked are described in this recollection of the time by Hoyos:

I knew of the discontent that was due to the low standard of wages which were paid in many occupations. I knew of the clerks in Broad Street – many of them poor whites – who received salaries of $4 to $5 per month and in a few cases $10 to $12 per month. If they were ill, they went without pay; and if they were given any holidays – at most two weeks a year – they received no salary at all.[4]

Irwin Burke (1992)

A former clerk explained the vulnerability of their position in the following terms: "The clerks in those days were treated the same as the porters. You had no right of appeal. People were lining up to take your job so you were not expected to set your sights too high." (Irwin Burke)

The nostalgic reverence with which many lower income whites of the time viewed Lewis is captured in this observation by Cozier looking back on the period: "[Lewis'] greatest achievement was to bring and keep together the clerks of Bridgetown, and helping them to wring better conditions out of their still Victorian employers."[5] Although it is known that Lewis was involved in the establishment of the union, he did not actually become President until 1948, succeeding Vincent St John and Charlie Thomas in that order.

Vincent St John (left) and Charlie Thomas, the first and second presidents of Barbados Clerks' Union (respectively).

But the overall story of the BCU is far from happy. In the emerging struggle for political control of the colony and for economic enfranchisement within it, the lower income whites in the 1930s and 1940s suffered, as a group, from a paralysing "in-betweenity". Although the broad aims it intended to secure for its membership – improved service conditions for clerks and office workers – were sufficiently laudable, the BCU was always dogged by a heavy dose of ambiguity. From its very formation, the BCU was reportedly riven with suspicion and factionalism. Night time meetings were convened in the grounds of the BCU's Pinfold Street headquarters, but members feared speaking out. The feeling was that if they vented views on perceived victimization, their words would be faithfully ferried back by fifth columnists or "snipers" to senior management in Bridgetown the next day.

Here was a bunch of very uneasy, suspicious men, formed to increase the wage levels they were getting, but prone to endless discord and infighting, basically because no one trusted anyone else in the group. These clerks, many of whom were coloured, felt that if they trusted the senior white clerks they would be sold down the river. On the other hand, if they remained undecided, they would not reap any benefits from their association. Most would be worried about speaking

The Clerks' Union

out because they feared the presence of snipers in their midst. If it got back to their employers, they might have lost that promotion or be overlooked for something else. I believe that the employers were, actually, inspiring some senior clerks present at those meetings to create havoc. (Sir Alexander Hoyos)

This story was repeated in the interviews. Suspicion everywhere. Difficulty in convincing members that the union made sense. Every meeting breaking up in disorder. In the interviews, the frustration and anger of individuals involved in this seemingly futile exercise still burned strongly. It was known at the time that many who joined the clerks' union insisted that they not be identified as members. Some did not want to pay through a payroll where their names would be noted. Instead, they paid their dues to the union in cash after payday.

The BCU's essential conservatism, a characteristic of labour aristocracies worldwide, is best reflected in its timid response to the firing of its president, TT Lewis, in 1949. Aside from the fact that Christie Smith, then BCU Secretary, attended an initial hearing on behalf of Lewis, the union took no action. Its members themselves proved unwilling to come out and visibly support their president in the massive demonstrations organized by the BLP and BWU to reinstate him.

Sir Frank Walcott, former General Secretary of the BWU gave the author his views on the BCU's central dilemma as follows:

Frank Walcott in the 1940s (left) and Sir Frank Walcott in 1993 (above)

Author: How would you characterize the central problem besetting the BCU?

Sir Frank: The problem with the Clerks' Union was that it was not independent enough and was certainly not strong in character. Their leaders were not leaders. Their organization did not build up the characteristics of the individual. The clerks were men who worked on Broad Street on a "Yes, Sir" basis.

Author: What was meant by the term 'snipers'?

Sir Frank: Basically, these were union members who would run back to their boss the next day and reveal what was said the previous evening at the Clerks' Union meeting. It stopped people from speaking their minds. For example, someone who would be in line for a position as a senior clerk would jeopardize his future by making critical comments about big business. The laws of dismissal at the time were very easy. You didn't have to serve a lot of notice on employees. The rest of us saw the clerks as being a privileged lot.

Bridgetown Business in the 1930s: A Clerk's Perspective

Hammond Burke (1992)

Hammond Burke died while the author was carrying out the interviews for this book. The final interview with him occurred in 1992. Burke, then 78, was living with his wife and several members of the Burke family in the area of Upper Bay Street popularly known as "Burke's Beach", located opposite the flat Lewis had rented in the 1940s and 1950s. Burke said he got to know Lewis when they were both clerks in Bridgetown in the 1930s. At the time, Burke worked for a lumber and hardware firm by the name of C.S. Pitcher which, after a couple of corporate mutations, became the company known today as Manning, Wilkinson & Challenor.

Over drinks, Burke was preparing a little anecdote about events which took place the day after the Clerk's Union was formed. Cautioned by his wife that he should not be too forthcoming he responded: "Nuh'body can't tell me to shut up now – I too old." He continued: "In those days, stores opened at 7 am. Bannister, the man who was the store boss at C.S. Pitcher, walked in, turned to Greenidge, a supervisor, and says, 'I've heard that that man Lewis has gone and formed a union with the Clerks!' I don't say anything. I keep my head down. [He asks someone next to me.] 'Have you joined, Greenidge? Are you a member?' Came the reply: 'No sir, I would never join that lot.' Bannister is now behind me. 'Ahm, what about you, Burke? Have you joined that union?' I swivel on my chair: 'Yes, I was one of the first to join. I am a founder member. I am number eight on the membership list.' Bannister is now climbing down. 'Well, I suppose the union is an alright thing.' I don't say anything more. I continue on with my work.

"You see, the problem with the 'big boys' was that they not only wanted to control you, they also wanted to think for you. You had no right to be thinking for yourself. They formed this thing called the Elector's Association. I remember one election . . . I can't remember which one it was . . . Anyway, these people would pass lower class whites in the street and wouldn't give them the time of day – man, they would walk right past you in broad daylight and wouldn't say 'buff'. But they knew who you were on election day . . . I had just got a raise which took me over the \$20 a month needed to vote. It was about two o'clock on election day when the phone rang. It was one of the directors:

'Ahm, [pause] Burke, have you been out to vote yet?'

'No, sir, not yet. We're very busy down here.'

'You don't mind about that. Get someone to replace you and take a couple hours off and go vote . . . of course, you know who to vote for, don't you?' – meaning people like [conservative] Harold Austin and so on.

'Yes, sir.'

"When I got to the polling station, there was Harold Austin sitting in a chair at the top of the stairs just as you go in. Cork hat and smoking too. He nods his head and I nod mine. In those days you could vote for two people, but my vote was not for Austin, it was for people like TT Lewis."

Hammond Burke outside the Central Agency, then in Hincks Street (1942).

The Clerks' Union

Author: So they were a distinctive upper strata of the working class – a sort of 'labour aristocracy'?

Sir Frank: I suppose you could say that. But their jobs could have been taken away in a flash. And that is the price TT paid because his job was taken away from him. TT had a difficult struggle because Barbados was then not a true democracy, it was a little oligarchy. Because TT was seen as having pull with the black crowd the oligarchy felt that they had to let him have it.

Author: Would the black workers have been less 'victimizable' than white clerks at the time of the Lewis demonstration?

Sir Frank: Yes. The black longshoremen and porters were different. They had no stake to lose other than their jobs, and their jobs could have been taken away with impunity anyway. In those days, nobody had to write to anybody about a firing. You just fired the man. Just so. So demonstrative behaviour in support of TT could only have come from the man at the bottom who had nothing to lose.

Similar views are expressed by others:

Scared, man. They were scared. The black man would have felt he had nothing to lose. They, on the other hand, would have felt "if I behave myself, I will get promoted . . . whereas if I join the wrong group I will miss out . . ." (Sir Alexander Hoyos)

Author: Is it fair to argue that whites and coloureds in the Clerks' Union could not march on TT's behalf in 1949 on the grounds that they would certainly have lost their jobs if they had done so?

Ronnie Hughes: Yes, clerks who marched would have lost their jobs the next day.

Author: Would not the blacks who marched also have lost their jobs?

Hughes: No.

Author: Why not?

Hughes: First, for the most part, they would have been lightermen, longshoremen, and general labourers. It is unlikely that they would have been recognized by the members of the elite who would have done the firing. Secondly, they would have been protected by the BWU which, through the TT Lewis march, was demonstrating its power amongst the rank and file in the land. Third, a clerk working at Cave Shepherd, for example, would not have gotten the support of the BWU.

Author: Wasn't Lewis from that group?

Hughes: Yes, but he was a recognized member of the BLP and was widely seen to have been dismissed for his political connections. Adams had a personal interest in the outcome of this march. On the contrary, even though TT was a founder member of the Clerks' Union, that organization was riven with factions.

The view of the time seems to be as follows: black workers provided merely a pool of labour; and anyway, views unsympathetic of the ruling class were to be expected of them; the lower income whites and coloureds, on the other hand, were a smaller more targetable group – action by any one of them would have singled that person out. This is what makes Lewis' action such a profound statement. Alone among whites, his courage lay in a willingness to stand up and be counted against the powerful forces of the merchant elite.

Christie Smith, BCU Secretary, in the 1940s (left) and in the late 1980s (above)

Through his involvement with the Bridgetown clerks, Lewis emerges as a man driven by the same motives of self interest common to everyone: job security and a decent standard of living. But there was something in what he did that distinguished him from most of his colleagues in the Bridgetown clerks. More than simply trying to survive within this climate of fear, Lewis was motivated to fight and eradicate the situation which his own kind, the lower income whites, faced every day in a work environment controlled by the Bridgetown merchants. His weapons were language and leadership. He had called for freedom from fear in one of his first platform speeches in 1942.[6] His evolving socialist outlook and assessment of the local situation would have convinced him that the discrimination then assailing the island was a product of that society's class bias, and not its race bias.

The climate of fear which Lewis denounced was characterized by a code of conduct where everything was thought and nothing was said. Through inertia, individuals facing injustice became victims of their own silence. Victims would not protest unless they were under immediate threat. And sometimes not even then. It was in response to this type of dilemma that the first labour movements and trade unions were formed in Barbados and elsewhere. Yet this dilemma wracked the BCU even after formation.

Judged in these terms, the ineffectiveness of the BCU becomes obvious and its actual achievements become difficult to point to. While no doubt the BCU lobbied its conservative employers for improved working conditions, it never engaged in any strike action or peaceful picketing. Nor is it known ever to have threatened to do so. The only traceable legacy that the author was able to link to the BCU was the initial securing of a holiday from work (the first Monday in October) which has been part of the Barbadian calendar ever since. One is therefore left with the conclusion that the reason why so little is heard today about the BCU is because it achieved practically nothing.

CLOSURE

In the end, realizing its basic impotence to effect serious change, or even to seriously protest blatant victimization, the BCU died a natural death. The view, expressed by some interviewees, that the BCU merged with the BWU appears to be false since neither of the unions' constitutions were amended to effect such a merger. What probably happened is that BCU members keen to maintain a union link would have moved over to the BWU which was then enjoying considerable success as a labour organization.

Lewis had no doubt already written off the clerks as a meaningful agent for social change in Barbados. He could not have failed to recognize that it was the working class – "organized labour" – which had backed him up in his march. He must surely have conceded that this was where the future strength of the democratic movement's struggle against the white oligarchy lay. The final failure of the Clerks' Union and its essential ambiguity were captured by Lewis in a letter to his wife in 1949 written shortly after his dismissal. It refers, in a disillusioned manner, to the token support which he received even though he was then their president:

> Last night we had a meeting of the Clerks' Union and they admitted they could not do anything to help me more than offer me their sympathy for which I thanked them. In the end, they decided that the present position of the Clerks' Union was farcical and so they decided to go and join the Clerks' section of the Barbados Workers' Union.[7] In this they will be linked up with all types of workers in the Island and in this way they will get their strength. I am to make the arrangements for the transfer of allegiance. (A.E.S. Lewis, Letters, 13 January 1949)

Though numbered, the days of the Clerks' Union did not end officially in 1949. It is known that Lewis was re-elected president on 31 March 1949 at their annual general meeting.[8] There is reference to yet another annual general meeting taking place on 28 March 1951. This time, however, Lewis was not among the officials elected or even mentioned. After this, all contemporary written reference to the Clerks' Union ceases.

RACE OR CLASS?

In all fairness, the characteristic of a paralysing in-betweenity cannot be ascribed only to lower income whites and coloureds. When offered an opportunity to use the vote to elect progressive members to the House, newly enfranchised Barbadian property owners and wage earners of all colours often felt constrained to exercise this right because of bread-and-butter considerations. Even though voting was done by secret ballot, one writer states that such newly enfranchised citizens felt a sense of economic insecurity as they sought to gain access to jobs, loans and mortgages.[9] As a result they considered themselves extremely vulnerable to pressures exerted by the ruling class. According to this analysis, class and not race is the overriding factor.

And yet – leaving aside the fact that modern genetics questions whether one can speak of separate races in a scientifically acceptable sense – considerations of race are an integral part of the Barbadian psyche. They are, indeed, a persistent causal factor in West Indian history. The sense of entitlement that skin colour has traditionally given white Barbadians would have led even the poorest of whites in Lewis' day to see equally poor blacks as the "others" with whom they would have deemed they had little in common.[10] It is presumably this reason which explains why the clerks saw it necessary to form a union of their own separate from the BWU in the first place.

Its inability to choose sides in the ongoing struggle for better working conditions meant that the BCU would last fewer than ten years. It was eclipsed by the black

> ## A Digression: The White Community Then and Now
>
> Considering the observations of those among the white Barbadian community interviewed for this book, and examining white Barbadian society of the 1990s, one is left with the conclusion that half a century ago the white Bajan community, though far more in control of Barbadian affairs than it is today, was at the same time considerably more stratified. Sternly applied social hierarchies mattered and were much in evidence then. There are a number of possible reasons to account for the relative disappearance of stratification within the white community today. Only one, however, is particularly relevant. White society is now really so small (currently 4 per cent of total population down from 10 per cent at the turn of the century) that it is difficult to maintain rigid stratification. There is consequently a greater sense of minority status. The white community now seems to regard itself as being sidelined by black politics. This has prompted a correspondingly higher level of cohesion among members of the white group – linking both the lower income and high-white groups with a considerably enlarged white middle class community.
>
> Anecdotal evidence captures the mood of this change. Although the Royal Barbados Yacht Club is still seen as a bastion of the white establishment it has, over the past generation, undergone a radical change in the structure of its white membership. Two interviewees offered the following comments on the institution:
>
> Half of the people who you now see as members of the Yacht Club would not have been admitted by the high white community not even twenty years ago. In those days, it was class – not colour. (Irwin Burke)
>
> There are white people that are Yacht Club members today who, forty years ago, could have only gotten in to deliver a message. (Ronnie Hughes)

trade union which had emerged following the labour disturbances of the late 1930s and which would become both a class and a political movement. When socialism and its trade union consciousness were making headway throughout the Caribbean, the pervasive and powerful white Barbadian belief in social hierarchy based on skin colour made whites resist joining the tide.

Ronnie Hughes in the 1940s (left) and in 1993 (above)

The actions of lower income whites stubbornly serve to confound classical Marxist prediction that the emergence of class consciousness among the proletariat comes inevitably as a result of struggle with the ruling class. According to Marxist theory, the capitalist forces of production in Barbados should in principle have generated class struggle between the white planter bourgeoisie and the combined group of working class blacks and whites. A society polarized along these class lines would inevitably suffer what is called a "crisis of capitalism" and would collapse under the ensuing revolution. The fact that lower income whites generally tended to keep their heads down when the struggle for workers' rights was taking place in Barbados offers evidence to contradict this line of thought.

Even though Marx did not write extensively on colonial societies, his intellectual successors have traditionally encountered problems with the concept of race as a determinant of political action. The simple reason for this is that race suggests a form of social bonding distinct from those arising from considerations of class. And it is the latter which form the basis of Marxist theorizing about society.

Weighing the relative importance of class and race as factors that motivate political behaviour is an inherently difficult task, especially in those situations where – as in Barbados – class structure does not correspond tightly to the racial breakdown of society. Nonetheless, a Marxist analysis of post slavery Barbadian society would hold that lower income whites – because they do not fully belong to either the exploiting or the exploited classes – would tend to group together simply on account of their having been subjected to similar types of exploitation. Not because they perceive a mutual racial affinity. Moreover, there has been a general tendency for Marxists to dismiss political action demonstrably deriving from race or ethnicity as a transient form of 'false consciousness' which will disappear with time. But this argument is inadequate. For, as in the case of Barbados, the evidence inconveniently suggests the existence of a pattern in such behaviour rather than a series of aberrations. The example of paralysing inbetweenity referred to above is probably best explained by way of considerations of loss or gain to one or other racial grouping.

The evidence thus appears to show that race and class are both very much factors at work in the political mind of the nation, and that they are linked – but that neither is driven by the other in an exclusive or deterministic way.

The great weakness of the BCU as an agent for change in Barbados was its essential ambivalence and wavering in the winds that were then sweeping across the island. Because they shared a numerical minority status along with their racial 'betters', lower income whites genuinely feared being swamped by a growing tide of black discontent. They felt it was in their interest to preserve the status quo and this led them to find areas of accommodation with these racial 'betters' even when acts of discrimination and injustice were perpetrated against them. Little connection appears to have been made between securing justice for themselves and securing a broader justice for black citizens. This is why it is ironic that, with hindsight, some of the most visible beneficiaries of the 1937 riots were the lower income whites. These individuals, principally plantation overseers and Bridgetown clerks privately supported labour; and when the dust had settled, they inadvertently gained better access to a middle class that had by then started to grow and become visible in Barbados.

NOTES

1. *Barbados Advocate*, 22 November 1944, 5.
2. The figure comes from Francis Mark, *The History of the Barbados Workers' Union*, Advocate Commercial Printing, Bridgetown, undated [but probably 1966], 75.
3. *Rules of the Barbados Clerks' Union*, undated, 1.
4. F.A. Hoyos, *The Quiet Revolutionary*, Macmillan Caribbean, London, 1984, 51.
5. E.L. Cozier, *Caribbean Newspaperman: The Life and Times of Jimmy Cozier*, Coles Printery Ltd, Barbados, 1985, 54.
6. See chapter 4, "Attitude towards the Second World War".
7. It is unknown how many of those clerks who joined the BWU, if any, would have been white.
8. *Barbados Annual Review*, 1948–49, 81.
9. K. Hunte, "The struggle for political democracy: Charles Duncan O'Neal and the Democratic League" in *Emancipation III: Aspects of the Post-Slavery Experience in Barbados*, Barbados, 1988, 27.

10. In an insightful series on the poor whites of Barbados, local historical researcher Edward Stoute cites the reflections of two visitors to Barbados in 1838 on the status of the very poorest whites in society at that time – the so-called "Redlegs" referred to earlier in chapter 1. Their attitude, claimed to be determined by considerations of race above all else, is relevant to the point under discussion. Although the relevant text depicts Barbadian society one century earlier, it is worth quoting in its entirety:

"We passed numbers of men and women going towards town with loads of various kinds of provisions on their heads. Some were black, and others were white – of the same class whose huts had just been shown us amid the hills and ravines of Scotland [the Scotland District]. We observed that the latter were barefoot, and carried their loads on their heads precisely like the former. As we passed these busy pedestrians, the blacks almost uniformly curtsied or spoke; but the whites did not appear to notice us . . . [another passenger travelling with the two men] inquired whether we were not struck with this difference in the conduct of the two people, remarking that he had always observed it. It is very seldom, said he, that I met a negro who does not speak to me politely; but this class of whites either pass along without looking up, or cast a half vacant, rude stare into one's face without opening their mouths. Yet this people, he added, despise the negroes, and consider it quite degrading to put themselves on terms of equality with them. They will beg of blacks more provident and industrious than themselves, or they will steal their poultry and rob their provision grounds at night; but they would disdain to associate with them. Doubtless these 'sans culottes' swell in their dangling rags in the haughty consciousness that they possess 'white skins'. What proud reflections they must have, as they pursue their barefoot way, thinking on their high lineage, and running back through the long line of their illustrious ancestry, whose notable badge was 'white skin'! No wonder they cannot stop to bow to the passing stranger . . ."

See Edward Stoute, "The Poor Whites of Barbados" (Part IV), *The Bajan,* February 1972, 30.

CHAPTER SEVEN

Prelude to the Storm

I heard my boss say one day: "You know what that blasted man Lewis has gone and done? He has just joined the BLP!" (Hammond Burke)

By the year 1948, Lewis had built up a formidable reputation for himself as an agitator on behalf of the underprivileged.

Clear evidence of this is contained in a letter he sent to the *Barbados Advocate* one year earlier protesting the sugar price levy that was to take place by the terms of a bill then before parliament. As far as he was concerned, at issue was not so much the size of the levy which would raise the export price of the 1947 crop by 25 percent. Nor even the fact that 90 percent of this levy would benefit the sugar industry while only 10 percent would go towards a Labour Welfare Fund. For Lewis, the real question appeared to be why the increased charge should apply also to sugar consumed locally, thereby hitting those who could ill afford the hike. Writing under the pseudonym "Consumer", Lewis accused the Legislative Council of being a "sugar-representing body". For giving consideration to such a bill, the House of Assembly, he said, was "composed of a majority of sugar barons . . . in all the parties." He continued:

It is common knowledge that the planters and sugar manufacturers have all made satisfactory profits during the war years, and in the case of the sugar factories that are limited liability companies, it is reasonable to assume that they have built up good reserves . . . The argument of these sugar producers is that even the very agricultural labourers should buy their sugar at the price for which it can be exported plus a merchant's profit . . . Is it too much to ask the sugar manufacturers of Barbados to be decent enough to make some sugar for the population and sell it to them at a price lower than that at which they can sell it outside the island? . . . For these sugar producers to claim that they should get their pound-and-a-half of flesh out of the people who keep them, and by the sweat of whose brow they live, move and have their being, should be an act impossible in a Christian community.[1]

Lewis' speech shows a consciousness of the role of labour as a fundamental force in the process of production. By openly expressing such socialist views it is not difficult to see why Lewis was set on a collision course with the existing plantocratic and business elite. One particular feature of the TT Lewis phenomenon irked them greatly:

The white establishment clearly viewed TT Lewis as a traitor and probably called him as much in their private conversations. A member of the merchant class once told me that TT was the most dangerous man in Barbados – not because of what he said – others were saying the same thing – but because it was a white man saying it. (Ronnie Hughes)

> ## A Businessman's Perspective
>
> A.R.E. "Bob" King: I could never have called myself a friend of TT's. TT took the line that everybody else was wrong and he was right. He wanted to go against all employers. I got the impression that he had had a rough deal at some time in the past and was taking it out on somebody. TT was the sort of person who liked to move from one political party to another and seemed happiest when he was in opposition to something. I was elected as a vestryman, and as part of the local government of the time I was a strong supporter of Ernest Deighton Mottley who didn't approve of TT either. In my view, TT would move from one issue to another if he felt that an interesting argument would soon develop around it. I especially didn't approve of what he was doing with the clerks.
>
> *Author: You mean his involvement with the Clerk's Union?*
>
> King: Yes. He was going way overboard – I would say he was being rather communistic in his ways.
>
> *Author: Could you say whether there was an argument for advancing the cause of the lower income groups in those days?*
>
> King: Of course there was. But TT didn't have any limitations. He wanted it so that the clerks could tell you when they were coming to work and what they would do and when . . . I found the approach of the Barbados Workers' Union and Grantley Adams much more reasonable.

Being a white man, his challenge to the established white business community in Bridgetown and to the colony's plantocracy would no doubt have been considered treacherous. However, as an employee, Lewis was at the mercy of anyone with the wherewithal to exercise influence over the firm with which he was employed. Lewis must have known this, but gambled that two things would work in his favour. First, he was an elected member of the House of Assembly and a prominent personality whom they would not wish to touch. Second, and probably more importantly, he may have calculated that since he was employed as a senior staff member of the Barbados branch of an overseas-based firm, he could consider himself immune to victimization at the hands of his local opponents. This, after all, was surely one of the reasons he had been able to express his anti-establishment views in the past. If these were his calculations, Lewis was wrong on both counts. According to Hoyos: "Most of us feared for TT much more than he feared for himself. He went his way caring naught for the fate that awaited him. While we hoped for the best, we had an abiding suspicion that the hour of doom would strike at the appointed time."[2]

THE 1948 ELECTION

The 1948 election was the last to be fought on a restricted franchise in Barbados. Ever since the issue of the "twelfth seat" in late 1947, Grantley Adams had been insisting that the Labour Movement was threatened by an "unholy conspiracy" between the BEA and the Congress Party. He alleged that a secret "agreement" had been hatched between the BEA and Congress to the extent that they differed only on the question of nationalization.[3]

As regards the BEA, the ever-looming dismantlement of the restricted franchise appeared to have had a sobering effect. Strengthened by the return of political strongman and strategist, E.K. Walcott, it was sitting up and paying more attention to the developmental needs of Barbados – promising major public works, an East coast road, rent restrictions, compulsory education, social security and even control of profit margins.[4]

Trailing the pack was Crawford's Congress party – by this time clearly on the way out of the political limelight. It had not even fielded enough candidates to form a government if successful. Crawford's pitch to the electorate centred on the highly popular question of opening up migration opportunities for Barbadian workers. But in the end it was Adams who would carry the day, buoyed up by the wave of popularity which followed his performance at the United Nations and the speech he made on his return to Barbados which tended to overshadow all other issues in the 1948 election.

Having joined the BLP just over a year earlier, Lewis was one of the twelve successful MCPs[5] who romped home on that party's ticket in the 1948 elections. Nomination day for the elections was 6 December. A couple of days later, Lewis wrote to his wife in Dominica, telling her of his straightened financial circumstances and of his jitters over the election that would take place five days later on Monday 13 December:

Marjorie, I am very sorry about all this delay and uncertainty about sending you money. And I wouldn't like you to get the impression that I am using my salary for Politics. I am not, most decidedly. Will have to spend a few dollars of it that way, but it is not much. I could borrow only a portion of my deposit this time, so I have to augment that but hope to get it back. I am not sending out any circulars this time and I hope to God it does not prevent me from getting in. These people so like a circular that it is a serious handicap, but I have been explaining the matter to the people and they seem to sympathize and understand. Grantley [Adams] came back on Saturday and there was a hell of a welcome for him.[6] I was allowed to open the proceedings in the Park as I had been out of the Island recently and the opportunity was given me to announce my return. Monday was Nomination Day and I made a one and a half hour speech which was well received. The Paper published only 1½ inches of it. Monday next is Polling Day and I'm not looking forward to it at all. The whole day on my feet, from 7 am to 6 pm. After the Elections I will be able to send you some money. It is very unlikely that I will be able to buy presents to send for the children . . . I really have nothing special to write about, but I hate a mail [ship] to go without even a line from me. When do the children get holidays? I was keeping at the back of my mind a Christmas trip to Dominica but this is not possible at the price I would be able to pay, so it's out of the question. And there are lots of unpaid bills to catch up with. TT

(A.E.S. Lewis, Letters, 8 December 1948)

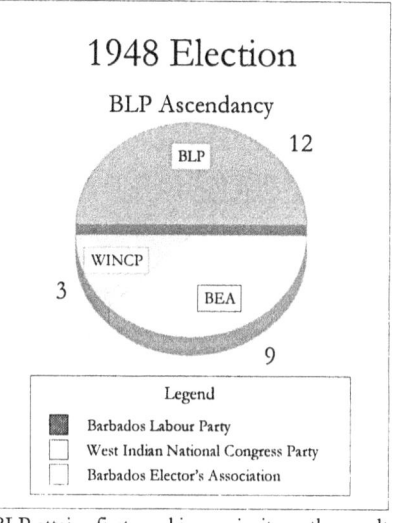

1948 Election

BLP Ascendancy

BLP 12
WINCP 3
BEA 9

Legend
■ Barbados Labour Party
□ West Indian National Congress Party
□ Barbados Elector's Association

BLP attains first working majority as the result of an election. Following the breakup of the first labour coalition in the previous parliament, Congress emerges badly damaged in this election. Its demise boosts the conservative BEA which gathers seats in its last impressive electoral showing. The 1948–51 parliament witnesses the appointment of the first black Speaker of the House, K.N.R. Husbands.

Even at this stage, there is no hint of the trouble that was brewing in Bridgetown on the subject of his continued political criticisms of the oligarchy. Or of his being the only white face in the BLP lineup for the election. Or of the trouble that would befall him upon the news of his winning a City seat for the fourth successive time.

The fact that Lewis, as a senior staff member of a reputable Bridgetown firm, would deign to join the ranks of the BLP, must have been seen by the merchants as a grave challenge. From Lewis' papers, we later discover that he was expecting his victory in the election to be contested although it is not clear on what grounds. On the 28 December, a *post scriptum* in a letter to his wife says: ". . . it is now 3:20 pm, and 4:00 pm is the last minute that petitions against my election can be filed. I've heard nothing further yet." After posting the letter, he would find out that a petition to controvert his election had, in fact, been filed in the Registration Office on that day at 3:55 pm. It had been lodged in the name of the solicitors Yearwood & Boyce.[7] The BLP's *Beacon* reported a few days later: "Elected Junior representative for the City on a Labour Party ticket at the recent elections, only 18 days ago, Mr Lewis has soon discovered that his fight against the forces of big business in this island would be made more difficult for him, and on Wednesday last a petition to controvert his election was filed."[8]

Although neither the newspapers nor Lewis' letters indicate on what grounds Lewis' victory was being challenged, the only reasonable guess, in the absence of any hint of electoral malpractice, is that he was being challenged on his property qualification. In his letters, Lewis reveals that Grantley Adams, his party leader, was hoping that those who filed the petition would carry through with it. The implication appears to have been that to do so would have damaged the initiators of the challenge more than Lewis. On 3 January, the petition was mysteriously withdrawn, without explanation.

Events that December, and indeed for the entire Christmas and New Year period were perhaps the most critical in Lewis' life. Utter desperation at being dismissed from the firm he had worked for was followed by elation at the level of public response to his plight. But although successful in securing an indemnity, Lewis was never really able to recover ground lost in this particular battle.

A Working Life at the Central Agency Ltd

By the end of 1948, Lewis had been employed at the Bridgetown firm called the Central Agency Ltd for a total of 28 years. The Central Agency Ltd was a subsidiary of the Scottish threadmaking firm called J.P. Coats, Clark and Co headquartered in Glasgow.[9] According to a memorandum submitted by Lewis to the Board of Enquiry set up to look into the causes of his dismissal, he had started work at the Central Agency in 1920 just before he turned 15 years old.

I was taken on to work in the Warehouse Department and can well remember the then Head Warehouseman remarking at the interview that I was rather young and small in statue [*sic*] for the job, but I soon allayed his fears in this respect. In a short time I was promoted to the office and put to do very responsible work. As I had a fairly good style of handwriting, I was put to post the Ledger and had to write their letters to their customers. At times this letter writing by hand involved all letters to customers and the various departments in the Head office in

Glasgow. The pre-typewriter days of the Barbados depot stretched down nearly to the end of the 1930s. After I had been with the firm for ten or twelve years [it was recommended] that if, through illness or otherwise, either of the two Attorneys had to be away from the office, I knew all about the business and could quite easily carry on. (A.E.S. Lewis, Memorandum to the Board of Enquiry, 2 Feb 1949)

In 1936, Lewis was appointed Assistant to Mr John Jack, the company's Manager-Attorney. His job then involved working for the company as a travelling salesman plying the Windward and Leeward Islands route, while Jack handled the company's more important thread markets in Trinidad & Tobago, British Guiana (now Guyana), Dutch Guiana (Suriname) and Curaçao. In early 1942, during the period of wartime emergency, Lewis acted in the place of Jack – a position that effectively meant he was acting manager of the Barbados depot.

> THE CENTRAL AGENCY
>
> According to the records of the Barbados Registrar of Companies, the Central Agency was incorporated in the UK on 24 December 1896. Soon afterwards, it established its cloth and thread wholesaling operations in Barbados, using T.S. Garraway as its agents. It is unclear when the depot itself was set up. The company would operate in the island until 29 February 1968. Following its closure, Central Agency's operations were carried out on its behalf by T. Geddes Grant. During its life in Barbados, the company was forced to move twice. First, after the fire that took place on 1 March 1944 and which destroyed over 90 per cent of the stock at its Hincks Street address. This necessitated a shift in location to High Street as a transitional measure. But space constraints required a second move, which could not be dated, to a bond, at the corner of Magazine Lane and Pinfold Street in the city. Interviews with former workers confirm that in the 1930s and 1940s, the depot would have employed between 10 and 15 people.

J.P. Coats, Clark & Co. threadworks outside Glasgow (photographed in the 1930s)

In August 1946, Lewis was made full-time travelling salesman and his bookkeeping tasks were assigned to a colleague. In the Notes of the Meeting with the Labour Commissioner, the Central Agency claimed that this move was an indication of the value which the firm attached to Lewis' services. Whether this move to shift Lewis' responsibility away from both travelling and accountancy work was intended to sideline Lewis, in career terms, remains unclear. By 1948, Lewis had been given responsibility for all the firm's routes in the eastern Caribbean, and the mainland South American territories.

However, several incidental references in Lewis' papers give the impression that the situation there was growing awkward. Lewis states, for instance, "my experiences at the Central Agency from [August 1948] to the time of the intimation of my dismissal I would prefer to relate orally in evidence."[10]

A glance at any of Lewis' travelling schedules for the years 1946, 1947 and 1948 shows that the man spent only about one-third of the year at home in Barbados. This, in large part, accounts for his long absences from the debates in the House of Assembly.

THE DISMISSAL

In his letter dated 30 December, Lewis' tone suggests that his dismissal by the Central Agency may have been caused by ongoing problems at the firm. He would later admit that during the previous four months his working environment had become extremely difficult. The fact that Lewis was only given one day's notice does not appear to have surprised him either, as this was a common practice at the time.

Marjorie, at last it has happened. Yesterday [Thursday, 29 December] evening after everybody else had left the office, Mr Thirian, the new Manager, called me and said he wanted to see me privately and he told me a whole lot of things like the Central Agency Ltd don't think they need a whole-time traveller like what I'm doing now, that he could do the travelling and manage the depot and all this meant that they wanted to cut down the staff here.[11] And the choice for this great event had fallen on me. I was to leave for good on Friday 31st and in addition to returning my Superannuation [pension] Fund Contributions with interest they would give me £1,000 by way of Conscience money. I told him I would not accept one brass farthing that I did not work for from anyone, and so he could rule that out. I told him that all he need do was give me a month's notice and let me try to make the best arrangements I could during the month. I know, and apparently he doesn't, or he's being smart, that they can't just return me my Pension Fund money after I've reached the age of 40. They have to give me a pension and this morning I'm reminding him of that . . . Yesterday seems to have been the worst, or best, day of my life . . .

I'm very sorry to have to send you this sort of New Year letter, but there is nothing else to do. Things could not be worse for us, but the facts have got to be faced and perhaps there will be some kind of help forthcoming after they are known. But at present, things are bleak and I really don't know which way to turn. The big question is money, and the immediate future would be OK if I were to accept the blood money offered me, but I can't stain my hands with that, not if I starve to death from today . . . (A.E.S. Lewis, Letters, 30 December 1948)

Lewis requested to be given one month's notice instead of just one day. The Central Agency obliged, and in a letter dated 31 December stated: "consequent upon the reorganization of staff at this depot your employment with this company will be terminated with effect from one month from this day's date, i.e. on the 31st January, 1949."

In his numerous letters, Lewis promised several times to write to his wife all the details of how he had come to be dismissed. This he never managed to do. However, firsthand evidence of what happened at the depot was uncovered in the course of the interviews by the only person then still alive who actually witnessed the events from within the firm's walls.

Shirland "Hawk" Medford: When I joined the Central Agency in 1945 as a job hand, Mr Lewis was already working there. I was put on the staff roll in October 1946 as a messenger . . .

Author: What happened around the time of the dismissal?

Medford: I remember that the manager, Mr Jack, could not bring himself to hand over the letter of dismissal to Mr Lewis, so the Central Agency had to have someone [Thirian] come down from Glasgow to do it. To my knowledge, Mr Lewis had not been warned that he would be dismissed. On the day of the dismissal, I remember hearing workmates saying that Mr Lewis stood up and told Mr Thirian that no one could stop him from going into politics – only God.

Shirland Medford (1992)

It is not difficult to imagine the thousands of confusing thoughts that would have been rushing through Lewis' mind. At the time of his dismissal, he was married – though separated – and the father of two children. These facts would weigh heavily on him during the next few weeks as he fought to reconcile his principles with the needs of his family to survive. All his letters, without exception, are replete with references to money: when it would run out; how much he could afford to send to Dominica; when he could send it; who he would have to borrow from and how much he owed away. He always talked in terms of small amounts of between $5, $10 and $20. But to a man of modest means, these sums must have seemed enormous. Although he probably felt he could rely on his wife's parents to cushion some of the financial blow caused by his dismissal,

Staff of the Central Agency photographed in 1946. Shirland Medford is pictured standing in the middle of the back row with Lewis standing at the extreme right.

he knew that by this time the citrus plantations her parents operated in Dominica were financially strapped. Their situation was unsustainable.

Causes of Dismissal

TT's dismissal would have at that time been acceptable to the establishment, as, in the mood of the times, there would have been many justifiable reasons to fire him. (Sir Hugh Springer)

Local representatives of the BWU and the BCU were suspicious about the circumstances of the dismissal and sought confirmation from the Central Agency's headquarters. When the response came, it was clear that the company's headquarters was standing behind its Barbados depot, as the following telegram exchange indicates:

```
DATE: 5 JANUARY 1949
TO: CENTRAL AGENCY, GLASGOW
MESSAGE: HAVE YOU APPROVED LEWIS' DISMISSAL FROM YOUR
BARBADOS DEPOT AND TERMS AND CONDITIONS THEREOF STOP IS
THIS DECISION IRREVOCABLE STOP IMMEDIATE REPLY ESSENTIAL
SIGNED: BARBADOS WORKERS' UNION AND BARBADOS CLERKS' UNION
```

```
DATE: 8 JANUARY 1949
TO: BARBADOS WORKERS' UNION AND BARBADOS CLERKS' UNION,
BARBADOS
MESSAGE: REFERRING YOUR TELEGRAM FIFTH OUR LOCAL MANAGER
HAS FULL AUTHORITY REGARDING LEWIS
SIGNED: CENTRAL AGENCY, GLASGOW
```

At the time of his dismissal, Lewis was the firm's most senior and most experienced locally recruited staff member. The stated grounds on which Lewis was being fired had nothing to do with either inefficiency or dishonesty. Notes from the meeting held at the request of the Labour Commissioner at the Labour Department on Monday 10 January, report that Mr Thirian stated "Mr Lewis' services were of the highest order". The justification used was rationalization. Their operations needed fewer staff. Simple as that. However, according to Lewis, this made very strange commercial sense, given that the increase in postwar consumer demand in the major metropolitan countries and their colonies, seemed to require at least the retention of all staff in view of the greater workload which had accompanied increased sales. It was noted at the meeting held by the Labour Commissioner that the thread business had significantly expanded in volume, and this appeared inconsistent with the firm's claim to wish to reduce staff. Lewis himself, in confidential notes scribbled as preparation for the Board of Enquiry meeting asks himself cynically "a wholetime traveller is not now necessary when competition is coming back, but was [deemed] necessary [during the war[12]] when there was no competition?"[13] The minutes of the enquiry do not state that the depot operations of J.P. Coats, Clark and Co in any of the other colonies were being streamlined too. As such, it is curious why the Barbados depot should have been singled out for retrenchment.

The January 1949 issue of the BLP organ, *The Beacon* asked sarcastically:

Has a man like Lewis, after 28 years of service with a firm which holds a monopoly and is strong, so little claim on its respect and indeed on its sense of gratitude that he should be treated with such disdain, indifference and discourtesy? How strange that it has only now been discovered, after all these years, that the business could be reorganized and could best be reshaped by getting rid of Mr Lewis, one of the topmost, ablest and most efficient of its employees![14]

In their presentation to the Board of Enquiry, the Central Agency Ltd never made the charge that Lewis was spending too much time in politics and that this was affecting his work. It is known that Lewis had sought, and obtained permission from his employers to take part in politics. But even assuming that this was a hollow gesture on the part of the Central Agency and that they really were concerned that he was neglecting his work for politics, the fact that Lewis' travel schedule permitted him so little time in Barbados makes it difficult to see how he could have been culpable in this regard. Most of those interviewed who expressed views on the subject saw the matter in an altogether more straightforward manner.

It was politics that got TT dismissed from his job. Upon hearing of the dismissal, Frank Walcott and I went to Central Agency to discuss with the manager the reasons for his dismissal.[15] We eventually managed to extract from Mr Thirian that the Barbados-born manager who had until recently been running that branch of the Central Agency had cleverly been transferred to Puerto Rico. Mr Thirian (who was formerly manager of Central Agency's operations in Puerto Rico) had been switched into Barbados possibly for the express purpose of dismissing TT. He had in fact been told to do so or he himself would be fired. I recall that the guy from Puerto Rico admitted to Walcott and me that TT was an excellent staff member. (Christie Smith)

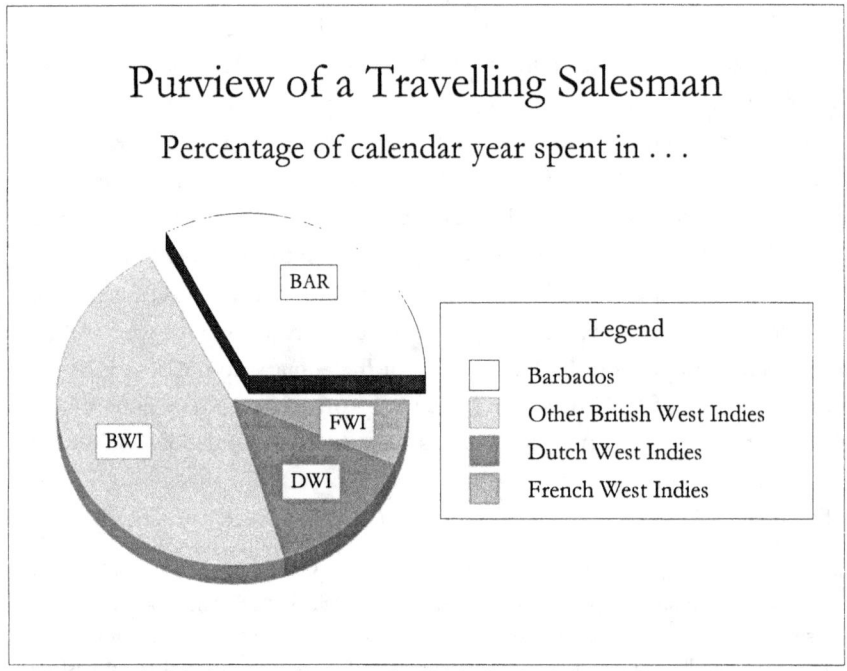

Lewis' travel schedule for an average year prior to his dismissal shows him spending two-thirds of his time outside the colony of Barbados. His travelling salesman's job took him to all corners of the eastern Caribbean and included visits to the British, Dutch and French South American territories. Typically visits to each island or territory would last between 1–2 weeks and some considerable time would have been spent getting to and from the markets since Lewis' principal mode of transport was by sea. Almost all of his travelling would have been undertaken aboard the white painted passenger steamers known as the Ladyboats of the Canadian National Steamships which provided regular services between the British West Indies and North America in the 1940s and 1950s.

If [Lewis] had watched his step, he could have been manager of Central Agency. But I think he was too much sold on the idea of becoming a politician. The day before I left Barbados in 1946, I told him to concentrate his energies on the Central Agency. He was often sent to the islands on the company's business and unfortunately he came to the conclusion that Central Agency was sending him to the islands to keep him out of politics here in Barbados. He also thought that the company was doing this at the behest of E.K. Walcott. (Andrew Christine)

It was common knowledge at the time that all the "big boys" got together and put pressure on Central Agency to fire TT otherwise they would discontinue their business. Keith Walcott, who was the then Attorney General, was the architect of firing – I don't care what anybody tells me. He hated TT. They [the Central Agency] used the excuse that TT was spending too much time in politics when they fired him. (Hammond Burke)

> ### AN EX-MANAGER ON LEWIS' POLITICAL VIEWS
>
>
>
> Andrew Christine (1992)
>
> After several attempts to locate one of Lewis' ex-managers whom the author had learnt was still alive, a meeting was arranged in the tiny flat which Andrew Christine occupied in Hastings on Barbados' south coast.
>
> *Author: What would you say were TT's political views?*
>
> Christine: He was touched by the condition of the people.
>
> *Author: Was that something needing attention in those days?*
>
> Christine: Oh yes, very much so.
>
> *Author: So were TT's views really all that "radical"?*
>
> Christine: I think for the times they were. But not in today's terms. His concern for the people's welfare was very justified at the time. So in today's judgement he would not be a radical.
>
> Christine pulls out a Benson & Hedges Light and offers the author. "Do you smoke?" Author declines. "Neither did TT. That was quite unusual in those days . . ."

It is the date of the dismissal which gives a clue to the major impetus behind it. In December 1948 Lewis had been elected again to the House of Assembly, this time on a BLP ticket. Alarm among the merchants over Lewis' success at the polls would have been considerable.

Although it is known that Lewis had received the manager's well wishes for the election as well as his congratulations upon having won, the dismissal occurred suspiciously close to Lewis' election victory, leading to the conclusion that termination had been suggested to his employing firm. Curiously, his victory had been contested by petition almost at the exact same time. Because this was still a time of the restricted franchise, members of the legislature were obliged to possess a certain amount of property or earn a certain amount in salary in order to be eligible to sit in the House. Thus there was one simple measure that could be taken to remove a member from the corridors of political power. Lewis himself recognized this in a letter to his wife: "Dismissal... will mean that I must resign the House of Assembly right away, and fancy that happening to me just as they are about to pay the members." (A.E.S. Lewis, Letters, 31 December 1948)

As noted above, Lewis later received the month's notice he had requested. This would allow him to remain employed until the end of January 1949.

This gives me the right to sit in the House of Assembly and try to make other arrangements before the end of the month... I will try to maintain my seat in the House and take any salary they give there, and try also to get a job outside so as to retain my qualification for the House. (A.E.S. Lewis, Letters, 3 January 1949)

The view that, disgruntled at Lewis' electoral victory, and wary of yet another legislative session with him as a thorn in their side, the oligarchy engineered his dismissal by putting pressure on the Central Agency is a perspective shared by several of Lewis' contemporaries who recall the dismissal.

Of course, the real point behind the dismissal was that the merchants didn't want TT in politics, and after he had won the 1948 elections just weeks before, they were trying to remove his eligibility to sit in the house by taking away his job. You see, at the time, the franchise was still property or income based. So if TT had no income he wouldn't be able to sit in the House. This was an attempt to force him to resign from the House. (Father Laurence Small)

TT would have had to relinquish his seat if he lost all his income, through losing his job. When you sat in the House on a property qualification, if you lost your income, you lost your right to sit in parliament. Before entering the race, you had to sign a statement saying that you made such and such a month (I can't remember what the figure would have been). The fact that this was their [the merchants'] way of getting him out of public life was the nastiest part of the whole thing. (Sir James Tudor)

There is therefore a considerable body of circumstantial evidence available to suggest that the Central Agency was pressured into terminating Lewis' employment. The pressure would have come from those in Bridgetown who saw him as a grave threat to their interests. The view that Lewis' dismissal was instigated by Bridgetown merchants gains added weight from pressure later reportedly brought against, but resisted by, the small Bridgetown firm which then dared to employ him years after his dismissal. One may assume that a similar or an even greater level of pressure was brought to bear on the Central Agency to fire Lewis in December 1948.

NOTES

1. *Barbados Advocate*, 1 June 1947.
2. F.A. Hoyos, *The Quiet Revolutionary*, Macmillan Caribbean, London, 1984, 103.
3. R.L. Cheltenham, "Constitutional and political development in Barbados 1946–66", PhD dissertation, University of Manchester, 1970, 52.
4. Cheltenham, 61.
5. Members of Colonial Parliament, as the title then read.
6. Adams had just returned to the island having attended a United Nations General Assembly meeting in Paris (September 1948) in the capacity of colonial representative in the United Kingdom delegation.
7. *The Beacon*, 31 December 1948, 1.
8. *The Beacon*, 31 December 1948, 1.
9. The firm's premises are still located outside Paisley near Glasgow. Its corporate offspring, having amalgamated with other European textile interests now goes by the name "Coats Viyella" and was cited by the *Economist* newspaper (18 February 1995) as Europe's biggest clothing and textile firm with sales of US$4.1 billion.
10. A.E.S. Lewis, Memorandum to the Board of Enquiry, 2 February 1949.
11. The simultaneous dismissal of another office member, a typist, can be interpreted either as a related part of an overall restructuring effort of which Lewis' dismissal was only a part, or as a smokescreen intended merely to convey this impression.
12. Recorded trade patterns confirm the fact that Barbados witnessed a decline in trade volume during the early war years (1939–42) but that this trend was reversed for the remaining years of the war 1943–45 and trade volumes expanded significantly thereafter. See Frank Long, "Aspects of external trade and the Barbadian economy during the 1939–45 war: some preliminary observations" in *The Journal of the Barbados Museum and Historical Society*, Vol XXXVII, No. 1, 1983, 57–67.
13. A.E.S. Lewis, Letters (Memorandum Notes), undated.
14. *The Beacon*, January 1949.
15. Confirmed in letter from A.E.S. Lewis to Grantley Adams, Adams Collection, Barbados Department of Archives (Reference Z17/4/10).

CHAPTER EIGHT

The Lewis Demonstration

On Thursday 6 January 1949 there took place a spectacle which shook the humdrum lifestyle of sleepy colonial Barbados. Thousands upon thousands of black workers downed tools and descended on Bridgetown to begin what would turn out to be two days of protest marching through its streets. At their head, beside Grantley Adams, leader of the labour party and its affiliated union, walked the solitary white figure of TT Lewis.

Whatever else the interviews conducted for this book may have unearthed about Lewis and his times, this image is the one emblazoned upon the minds of countless Barbadians of that era. The act was classic for its sheer audacity and irreverence in rigidly hierarchical Barbadian society.

THE MERCHANTS GOT THE MONEY BUT THE UNION GOT THE MEN

Interestingly, this was the first union-based march in Barbadian history against the alleged unfair dismissal of an employee. On the last day of 1948, the flagship publication of the BLP and the BWU, *The Beacon*, blasted Lewis' employers the Central Agency in its lead story: "With brutal and stunning suddenness, Mr Lewis has been given the push, in a manner which makes the Pearl Harbour sneak attack look like child's play. If this is an example of the benevolent manner adopted by private enterprise in the twentieth century, then heaven help us!" And in a clear exhortation to public action on the matter, it continued: "... for when such treatment can be meted out to an employee who has served his employers long and faithfully and one who has attained a high and responsible position, it is time that the public sit up, take notice and guard against such [an] infringement of justice and fair play."[1]

When the news of Lewis' firing broke, contemporary accounts from the BLP/BWU side indicate both a sense of consternation coupled with a determination to meet the challenge being laid down by big business. If Lewis was fired on account of his worrisome connections to the BLP, that fact also proved to be his salvation. Adams quickly rallied behind him and visibly sought to make out of the dismissal an issue of the utmost political significance. Adams would galvanize the response and demonstrate – through the physical presence of thousands of marchers – that the establishment could no longer pursue, unchallenged, what he considered to be a policy of intimidation.

The first step was to stage a torchlight demonstration in Queen's Park, the place where most major political rallies were held in those days. In the Queen's Park meeting on the night of Wednesday 5 January, Adams threatened to halt not only business activities in Bridgetown but also the harvesting of the sugar crop which was just about to start. The latter threat would have caused considerable anxiety since at the time Barbados was a one-crop economy, and that crop was sugar cane.

The next day, Thursday, Adams bid the workers march:

That march on behalf of TT up Broad Street was something that you wouldn't see in any other part of the world. In one section of the march there was a flag belonging to the BWU with a hammer and sickle flying on it. In another part, do you know what they were singing? You'll never guess . . . It was "Onward Christian soldiers!" It was quite an expression on behalf of TT. (Seymour Beckles)

Carrying banners and bearing slogans 'Lewis

Big Torch Light Demonstration
AND
THANKSGIVING MEETING
will be held
under the Auspices of the
BARBADOS LABOUR PARTY
and
THE BARBADOS WORKERS' UNION
at
QUEEN'S PARK
on
WEDNESDAY NIGHT

5th January, 1949 at 7.30 o'clock
The Labour Party will inform the public of the recent dismissal of **Mr. A. E. S. LEWIS**, and the proposed Controversion of his seat for the City of Bridgetown.
Speakers :
Mr. G. H. ADAMS
Mr. M. E. COX
Mr. A. E. S. LEWIS
Mr. F. L. WALCOTT
Mr. T. O. BRYAN
and other members of the Party.
1.1.49.—3n.

will not be butchered'; 'Lewis victimized, who is next'; 'Hitler is dead, kill local fascism', the workers left their headquarters yesterday at 11am and assembled at the open pasture opposite the Empire Theatre . . .[2]

Lewis (left) and Adams (right) during the march

Here is how Hoyos, who witnessed the march, describes the events and the mood of the moment:

I well remember the day in January 1949 when I was driving from St John to Bridgetown. I was flagged down by a mutual friend as I was passing through the parish of St George and told that TT had been dismissed from the job he had held for nearly 30 years. There were tears in the eyes of [my friend] when he gave me the news. After leaving [him], I drove into the city to find it in a state of turmoil and confusion. Thousands of people were marching in demonstration through the streets led by Grantley Adams and Frank Walcott. Without hesitation I joined in the march of protest against what seemed to be a flagrant injustice. My impression then was the same as that of columnist Gladstone Holder, expressed many years later. If Grantley had lifted a little finger, the whole of Bridgetown would have been burnt down that day.[3]

I was . . . standing on Broad Street. The march was light hearted, almost comical until the Barbados Labour Party top brass came in sight. Orrie Bryan, Cummins, TT Lewis, Mencea Cox were there but they were all dwarfed by Grantley Adams,

Marchers passing along the wharf towards Hincks Street

The Lewis Demonstration

looking grim and implacable. It was a moment in local politics that I will never forget. In the hot sun I shivered. As I saw it, Adams held that crowd in the palm of his hand and they would have done anything he ordered them to do. On that morning I saw naked power for the first time. I have abhorred it ever since. No human being should have so much control over his fellows. I've seen no one since possess it in that degree. (Gladstone Holder[4])

Sir Frank Walcott: That [march] was something massive. In my time, the TT Lewis demonstration was the biggest thing I'd ever experienced. At that time I was very young in politics and TT was a popular person. Colour did not seem to make a difference. As a sportsman he had played cricket and had entreated himself to a mass audience on the cricketing grounds. People therefore saw him not as a white man, but as TT.

Author: Did you lead the demonstration?

Sir Frank: No. In Adams' time there couldn't be any other leadership. As I said, at the time of the demonstration I was very young – 32 in fact.[5]

One of the reasons for TT's popularity was that he wasn't wealthy. In those days some white people really did suffer as bad as the blacks. In fact, there were a whole string of tiny shops all the way along Roebuck Street which were nearly all owned and operated by the small white community . . . Basically all the lower class people suffered the same fate. The Clerks' Union was just half a step above the ordinary porters and workers. Any whites who came out in support of the workers marching for TT would have lost their jobs. But the blacks really didn't have anything to lose. And that is why they marched. (Owen T. Allder)

The preplanned route took the marchers through the heart of commercial Bridgetown. It started from the Labour Party and Union headquarters at the corner of Nelson and Fairchild Streets. It then crossed the Chamberlain Bridge

"Adams walked all round Bridgetown in the hot boiling sun for TT. And once Adams was there, you know everybody would be turning out to support TT too." (Owen T. Allder)

"Man, you should have seen the stream of people . . . all the workers were there . . . hundreds upon hundreds of black people marching in support of this one white man. Even people who used to lift sacks of sugar on the wharf marched . . ." (Hammond Burke) This photograph, taken on upper Broad Street, depicts Grantley Adams (head circled on original print), Lewis (with white suit and hat) and Frank Walcott in line abreast at bottom centre.

The Lewis Demonstration

and continued down along the wharf, turned inwards and back up through Broad Street, the main centre of business. The photographs of that occasion depict a solemn faced Adams walking next to Lewis. Businessmen and others peer down from the windows of their stores onto the multitude assembled and moving slowly in an orderly manner. With a few additional detours, the marchers then turned and headed back to where they started out at the party and union headquarters.

Then they did it all over again on the following day. For two days in a row, traffic and commercial business was brought to a halt in Bridgetown by the combined force of marching workers. Unverified but credible reports put at 7,000 the number of marchers involved. That evening, Lewis penned a quick note to his wife in Dominica. "Marjorie, am sending you an *Advocate* newspaper which will show you something of the march we had in the City yesterday. It was very, very big and grand, and the behaviour superb. Today we had a much, much bigger and better one and we are awaiting results . . . (A.E.S. Lewis, Letters, 7 January 1949)

Later that night, Adams again rallied his forces in Queen's Park and laid down his ultimatum: either Lewis was paid out in an appropriate manner, or there would be trouble. In throwing down the gauntlet to the merchants, Adams threatened to call a general strike. Judging from the surprisingly large turnout on behalf of Lewis, composed both of union members and thousands of sympathizers who either joined the march or lined the route to cheer it on, there would have been no doubt in the minds of the Bridgetown establishment that Adams could pull it off. Adams probably reckoned that he could count on at least twice that number to strike if called upon to do so.

The march spanned two days and the main person organizing it was Freddie Miller [a BLP member of the House]. It took place during business hours, and on the night of the second march, Grantley Adams convened a meeting in what is now the [Queen's Park] Steel Shed where I remember him saying, 'Tonight I am driving without any brakes, and no one had better get in my way or they will be run over', or words to that effect. His basic point was that TT should be paid out or be re-instated. E.K. Walcott was one of those rumoured to have engineered TT's dismissal, but I don't know if it was him alone. Grantley certainly mentioned

Laurence Small (left) in 1945, marcher for Lewis, and Father Small (above) in 1992

his name at the meeting. Grantley also said that he was holding out an olive branch to the merchants, but that if they wished to live by the sword then they would die by the sword. (Father Laurence Small)

At that meeting in the park following the march, Adams implied that unless compensation were paid to TT Lewis, [the union's control over the sugar workers would mean that] the country would find it difficult to harvest the [soon to commence 1949] sugar crop. (Christie Smith)

I think that at that steel shed meeting, Adams actually tried to intimidate the merchants. In effect he was saying: you dare not fire any of these men who have marched on TT's behalf. (Father Laurence Small)

Hoyos confirms the threat of a general strike over the issue:

"I can remember vividly the march. The song was: 'The merchants got the money, but the union got the men.' It was sung to the tune of *John Brown's Body*." (G. Vernon Marshall)

He threatened a boycott of the goods consigned to [the Central Agency] and declared that he would call out all the workers in the Island in a general strike. "Big business", he thundered to the assembled multitude, though he had to stop every now and again to be heard amid the roars of approval, "has been foolish enough to declare war, but the workers will dictate the peace, and peace on their own terms. I have not denounced totalitarianism in Paris to tolerate or condone it here at home."[6]

The spectacle of such a massive show of support for Lewis plus the attendant threats to carry out further industrial action, must have struck fear into the white oligarchy. All the more because it was so organized and disciplined. The city had come to a standstill. Further action was threatened unless the white merchants, now visible in the embodiment of Lewis' employers, were prepared to talk terms.

The Lewis Demonstration

TERMS OF THE SETTLEMENT

The enormous political pressure that had by now built up behind the Lewis issue, owing in large measure to the solid support for him by the BLP/BWU, ensured that the terms of his separation received a considerable amount of attention. Barbados had never seen such a flurry of activity surrounding a single dismissal. Such a thing as a dismissal had been commonplace before. This time, however, the circumstances leading up to Lewis' firing would first be reviewed before the Labour Commissioner and then an independent Board of Enquiry.

In a letter dated 31 December 1948, the Central Agency had offered to pay Lewis out. There were two elements: first the "conscience money" – as Lewis had derisively called it, and second a return of pension fund contributions made by Lewis over the previous twenty-five years. As far as "conscience money" was concerned, the first of a series of offers made by the Central Agency came to the sum of £1,000: £400 immediately and £50 per month for the twelve months of 1949. Lewis at first rejected both options. This reaction would probably have been fuelled out of the feeling that he had been wronged, and this would in effect be, as he himself put it, "blood money". No doubt he reckoned that by taking it he would effectively rule out the option of reinstatement at the firm, which his letters claim he would have preferred, despite all that had happened.

Freddie Miller (1940s), organizer of the Lewis Demonstration in 1949

The impetus of the demonstration no doubt added a degree of urgency to the need to get things moving. Documentary evidence would appear to support this. According to Lewis, at the meeting organized in the presence of the labour commissioner on 10 January, the latter:

> ... started off by saying that it was an important meeting and a difficult one and he hoped we would all approach it in a spirit to reach a settlement; he made some reference also to the bumper sugar crop and the prospects of losing it, why he did this I do not know, but it follows on a broadcast we made last night about the same matter.[7]

At that meeting, the option of reinstatement was ruled out once and for all by the Central Agency. The representative of the Central Agency, although claiming to come to negotiate, had in fact brought along a cheque in the amount of £1,500 which represented a large increase on its first offer of "conscience money". The meeting ended with neither side comfortable with the position taken by the other. The labour commissioner then decided to recommend to the governor that an independent board of enquiry be set up to investigate the matter. But this too posed problems:

> Marjorie, . . . The great trouble now is the personnel of the Board of Enquiry. It is so hard in a small place to find someone who is not a near relative or a distant relative of somebody else. Although the case is a very simple one in many respects, it is not a simple matter to find someone who is so disinterested, not to say actually biased, as to give everyone a fair trial . . . (A.E.S. Lewis, Letters, 12 January 1949)

On 18 January 1949 the House of Assembly passed a resolution proposed by Dr H.G. Cummings for £100 to be placed at the disposal of the governor-in-executive committee to meet the costs of a board of enquiry. This body was mandated to deal with the dismissal of Mr A.E.S. Lewis, MCP, Junior Member for the City of Bridgetown from the local branch of the Central Agency Ltd. An arbitrator to sit on the board was to come from abroad. The measure was passed by the Legislative Council on 25 January.[8]

In the meantime, Lewis was hit from another angle. On 24 January, the Central Agency wrote informing him that unless he accepted their offer, it would be withdrawn on 31 January, the deferred expiry date of their notice. To a man boxed into a corner and trying to balance his dignity with his need to retain a livelihood this must have come as a mighty blow. Could they be bluffing? Lewis decided to

Lewis (dark hat) flanked by Adams (to his right) and Walcott (to his left) during the march

call their bluff, if that was what it was, by responding crisply the next day: "I had thought that the whole matter of my dismissal having been referred with the consent of all sides to a board of enquiry, all offers etc., made in connection therewith would be in abeyance until the report was made."[9] The Central Agency threat subsided.

The board of enquiry was set up under Section 8 of the Trade Disputes (Arbitration and Enquiry) Act of 1939 (subsection 6). It was presided over by the prominent Trinidadian jurist, Mr Justice S.E. Gomes and had the following terms of reference: "To enquire into and report on the following matter, namely, the circumstances connected with or relevant to the non-employment of Mr A.E.S. Lewis, MCP, by the Central Agency Limited after the 31st of January, 1949." The Board met first on Wednesday 2 February in the Social Welfare Office at the Garrison. It brought together the Central Agency Ltd (on whose behalf the new manager of the local branch, E.M. Thirian appeared) and Lewis who would be represented by Adams. Interestingly, the man chosen to represent the Central Agency was E.K. Walcott, one of the rumoured protagonists in the struggle to dismiss Lewis, and also himself a determined opponent of Adams.

It would take three meetings before a settlement was reached. The Central Agency did not budge from its position. It categorically refused Lewis' claims either for reinstatement or the payment of a pension in lieu of his twenty-eight years' service. What was eventually arrived at represented a settlement reported in the press as "amicable". While not being forced to give in on its opposition to reinstatement or pension, the Central Agency would end up paying out a much larger amount of money. The basis for the calculation would be one month's salary for every completed year of service plus the return of Lewis' contributions to the Central Agency Ltd's Superannuation (or pension) Fund, with all interest accrued to date.[10] Lewis had, at first, been reluctant to take the "conscience money". However, he must have felt caught on the horns of a dilemma: should he make a principled stand and face the prospect of having his wife and children live a life of penury, or should he take the money which, by virtue of the considerable increase arrived at, in effect represented a climb down for the Central Agency.

In the end, Lewis opted to take the gratuity. However, at this stage he appears to have struck what he considered to be a principled deal with his own conscience. He determined not to keep the gratuity for himself. From the settlement he would hold onto only the returned pension fund contribution. In eventually accepting the gratuity on behalf of his family for forwarding on to them (plus a couple of thank you contributions to the BWU), Lewis seems to have made the rather unclear moral distinction between his refusal to accept the money and his agreement in principle, that if his wife wished to accept the money on behalf of herself and the children, she could do so.

Effectively, the Lewis settlement witnessed the first case of severance payment in Barbados, though this is not what it was officially called at the time since there was then no provision for severance payment on the statute books. The eventual sum paid out to Lewis was £2,250 (B$10,806). Roughly 70 percent was sent to his wife; 10 percent was given to the BWU; and the 20 percent comprising his returned pension contribution, he kept. "TT gave the bulk of the money to his wife for the upkeep of his daughters. He himself is supposed to have kept only a small amount. I remember thinking at the time that to keep only so little was asinine." (Wynter Crawford)

Lewis always intended to keep the money refunded to him from the pension fund, as he regarded this as his money anyway. Clearly a pension, to which he felt he was entitled after so many years service, would have been financially more attractive, but this was not to be. Interestingly, Lewis considered it important to make a contribution to the BWU, presumably on account of the support that the party and the union had shown during the marches. It is possible that this support had pushed the Central Agency towards increasing its offer of a gratuity from £1,000 to £1,500, while Adams' interventions would have most likely driven up the Central Agency's final offer from £1,500 to £2,250. To ensure that he was not seen to be touching any of the gratuity money, Lewis asked his wife to agree to make a gift to the BWU and a separate investment in the union's Building Fund. He wrote to his wife that he also wanted to make a tangible offer of appreciation to Adams who must have seemed, in this desperate period, to have been a tower of authority and strength. But Adams declined the offer: "I was thinking too that I should make Grantley a gift of something, but when I hinted about this to him, he told me to regard it as part of what I give to the Union."[11]

While the Lewis dismissal crisis appeared to have been settled in an agreeable manner through the board of enquiry's intervention and the resulting compromise settlement, the after effects of the incident were immense. The power of the union was in the ascendant. The BLP was seen as the workers' champion and Adams had further indelibly imprinted his absolute command over the Barbadian rank and file on the minds of all who cared to take note.

The Lewis Demonstration

The Lewis episode of 1949 – in which 'TT' Lewis, the generally beloved white Barbadian socialist, was victimized for his radical views, and received full retribution only after a mass demonstration of both union and party provoked an official inquiry – finally served notice on the Bridgetown mercantile oligarchs that the days of easy victimization were over once and for all.[12]

The Dust Settles

That amount remaining after the various transfers to Dominica and contributions to the union was sufficient to allow Lewis to retain his seat in the House. But in terms of sustaining him financially it would probably not have been sufficient to keep him going for more than two years. He still needed a job. But following the tumultuous events of January 1949, Lewis was now more than ever a marked man. No Bridgetown firm would hire him. Lewis recognized this immediately, as he wrote to his wife in February 1949: " . . . the fact remains that I must find a job that will give me sufficient to live on half decently and send something for you and the children, and so far such a job is nowhere in sight." (A.E.S. Lewis, Letters, 10 February 1949)

Of his treatment at the hands of the Bridgetown mercantile community, Lewis' old friend, E.L. Cozier, writing in 1981, had this to say:

Unhappily, TT did not escape martyrdom, and the fact that he underwent such victimization is a sad, sad reflection upon the business community of that time. He believed, as I believed, that his treatment was suggested to his employing firm. But whether this was so or not, the fact that no big Bridgetown firm offered to employ him afterward was an eternal disgrace.[13]

Lewis' papers during this period contain a trail of depressing correspondence – letters of reference written on his behalf by colleagues and responses by businesses declining offer of employment. It would take five years before Lewis located a job. Employment would come in the form of a low profile backroom operation in a small, newly established stationery firm run by Cecil Jordan and H.N. "Turk" Rogers. The latter had ironically served under Lewis at the Central Agency in the 1940s. In the interviews, Rogers related his discomfiture at not being able to do more to help out a former boss whom he clearly held in high esteem.

[Sometime] after he was fired by Central Agency, TT was taken on by our stationery company. At the time there was immense psychological pressure put on any firm known to be considering hiring TT. We received veiled threats that our business contacts would stop doing business with us if we took on TT. But we took him on nevertheless, and found that none of the threats were

H.N. "Turk" Rogers (1993)

ever carried out. I accepted, however, that as a quid pro quo for their not carrying out the threat, TT's role in our firm would not be one where he was prominent in the front desk area. So we put him in the back office. (H.N. "Turk" Rogers)

Lewis' job was to keep the office books in order. For this, the young firm could pay him no more than a subsistence wage. There is no evidence of how Lewis managed financially in the period 1949–54. It can only be assumed that during these years he lived off the declining bank balance from his pension fund payout plus the regular $80 cheque which he earned every month as a sitting member of the House of Assembly from 1950 onwards.

NOTES

1. *The Beacon*, 31 December 1948, 1.
2. *Barbados Advocate*, 7 January 1949, 1.
3. F.A. Hoyos, *The Quiet Revolutionary*, Macmillan Caribbean, London, 1984, 103.
4. Reflecting in the *Daily Nation*, 28 October 1989.
5. For a contrasting account of who was the prime mover behind the Lewis demonstration, see Hilary Beckles "Ethics solidarity vs nationalism", *Daily Nation*, 21 May 1989.
6. See F.A. Hoyos, *Grantley Adams and the Social Revolution*, Macmillan Caribbean, London, 1974 (1988), 151. The "Paris" remark refers to comments he made as a colonial representative in the UK delegation to the United Nations General Assembly meeting in September 1948. At that meeting, according to Hoyos, the Ukranian representative accused Adams of being the mouthpiece of his colonial masters and a traitor to his people. Ukraine, by a historical oddity, possessed its own seat at the UN even though it was then an integral part of the Soviet Union. Adams is reported to have upbraided the latter as someone who, coming from a totalitarian system, would be incapable of understanding the real meaning of democracy.
7. Letter from A.E.S. Lewis to Grantley Adams, Adams Collection, Barbados Department of Archives (Reference Z17/4/10).
8. *Barbados Annual Review* (1948–49), 16.
9. A.E.S. Lewis, Letters, 26 January 1949.
10. *Barbados Annual Review* (1948–49), 53.
11. A.E.S. Lewis, Letters, 10 February 1949.
12. G.K. Lewis, *The Growth of the Modern West Indies*, Modern Research Papers, New York, 1968, 242.
13. E.L. Cozier, *Barbados Advocate*, 2 March 1981.

CHAPTER NINE

Later Years with the Barbados Labour Party

Even though Lewis drew nothing more than a pyrrhic victory from his battle with the local establishment, his spirit appears not to have been tamed. For the first five of his eight years with the BLP, Lewis' views pepper the pages of the House records. His observations recall what were then the hotly discussed issues of the day: payment of salaries to House members, the BLP's electoral strategy for the island's first genuinely free election in 1951, the subsequent dispute over revenue equalization which showed the cracks that were starting to appear within the BLP, the introduction of ministerial government and the idea of a federation of the West Indies.

In the following extract, he is heard speaking on the question of payment to members of the House, a measure which he had championed during his very first campaign. Lewis' bitter, though unstated, experience in being fired for speaking his mind make the following remarks especially poignant:

Unless we, as taxpayers, are prepared to pay members of the House, we are not likely to get as wide a choice of those who are capable of taking part in the government of their country. Barbados of all places, should pay its legislators. This is a small place. The economic setup is such that independent minded persons coming into politics or expressing political opinions are likely to suffer thereby.[1]

In the following full bodied, pithy exchange with protagonist E.K. Walcott on the same subject Lewis sought to drive the point home:

MR LEWIS: From time immemorial, it has been the habit for people in this country to go to members of the House for all sorts of advice and to do all sorts of things for them. The honourable members of the past have been quite willing to assume those roles for no direct payment. This country, in those days, was run by boards. A member would come into this House; he would be appointed a member of a particular board. Let anyone go into the auditor General's office and find out the amount of taxes that go into the coffers of firms in the City of Bridgetown for supplying the government with goods. Would it not be a good thing to be on the Housing Board and know that a Housing Scheme is to be put in operation? You may be able to import shingles, lumber and things of that sort in advance. Would it not be advantageous to be on the Road Board when you have a lot of 'Colas' [2] and a lot of cement for gutters and things of that sort to sell? Don't you think it would be a nice thing to buy them from the company that concerns a particular member of the Board? Those are things that used to happen. [Members] never used to get direct payment but look at the amount of taxes that went into their pockets for supplying goods to the various government departments. Go and look up the records and see, apart from administrative expenses, where the amount raised from taxes goes. There are many people in business in this community who thought at one time that it was a good thing to get into the House of Assembly and get on Boards because it would tend to have an influence on their businesses. Those days are gone . . . Mr Speaker, it may not be an honour to accept payment for your services in this House, but is it not an advantage if you are the managing director of a limited liability company to have sufficient of your kind in here not to raise the Companies' Tax? The entire membership of this House as we heard tonight, will cost the country $37,000 if members are paid. By one single vote in this House a particular company would not have to pay $37,000 in taxes. One member in this House, by voting no, can pay himself $37,000.

MR E.K. WALCOTT: On a point of order. According to the Rules of the House a member who is interested financially in a measure before the House cannot vote on it.

MR LEWIS: I understand what the honourable member has said, but has he ever seen a vote on the Companies Tax synchronize with the walking out of directors or shareholders of companies in this House?

MR E.K. WALCOTT: The suggestion was not that. The honourable member suggested that the reason why certain persons wanted to be members of the House is because, by reason of that, they would be able to vote for paying themselves $37,000.

MR LEWIS: The honourable member is a little wrong. I am glad he is remembering all the points I am making, but he has got confused over them. I will put it this way: . . . it is an attempt to fool the people of this country to tell them that they should not pay members of the House for the work they do because if they continue to swallow a pill like that it means that they would have to look, for their representation, to a certain type of individual only – the successful businessman or the man who has been successful without doing any business . . . Mr Speaker, for an honourable member to get up in this House today and say that $37,000 a year is too much to pay for the legislative work of this country, and that representation of the people is a sacrifice that has to be made by the members who come into this House today, is, to my way of thinking, ridiculous. Will that same honourable member, with the financial statement of a particular political organization [the BEA] in his possession, say how much money they spent to get back in the House! If $37,000 a year is too much to pay for doing this work, is more than $37,000 too much to pay to try to get in to do the work for nothing?[3]

Later Years with the Barbados Labour Party

Members of the Barbados House of Assembly first received a cheque made out by the treasury in 1950.

E.K. WALCOTT

Edward Keith Walcott was a great foil of Lewis during the years when they faced each other across the floor of the House of Assembly. A diminutive white man twelve years Lewis' senior, he appears to history as an impressive but curious figure. Socially, his family were small planters – linking him to the white middle class described in chapter 1. His was not of one of the landed white elite families, but they were in a position sufficiently comfortable to enable him to be educated at Harrison College in the days when there was no free secondary education. He also travelled abroad and served in the officer ranks of the British Armed Forces, fighting the Germans in what was then Tanganyika (now Tanzania) during the First World War. Walcott, a solicitor trained in Britain, is described by those who knew him as being very bright: 'sharp as a tack' one elderly black Barbadian recalled, and greatly feared with a record 23 convictions in the 24 murder cases he tried.

E.K. Walcott (1930s). During his heyday as Attorney General of Barbados (1936–46) he was in practice probably the most powerful man on the island and was consequently dubbed the "Eternal General".

In the political arena, there appears to have been no love lost between Lewis and Walcott. Here were two white men representing the different interests of the time locked in battle. Perhaps what made them so unforgiving of each other was the fact that they were both men of great resolve who possessed an uncompromising attitude on matters of principle.

Walcott himself is often described as the last and foremost example of the "Great Attorneys General". The powers available to him in his heyday were awesome in an island so small. In practice, he was the colony's principal policy maker. As a member of the Executive Committee, Walcott was the chief expounder of government policy in parliament, but – wearing his cap as a sitting member of the House – he could turn and criticize that very same policy. As attorney general he was also de facto head of the judiciary. He thus occupied a grey area encompassing executive, legislative and judicial arenas. No Barbadian premier or prime minister has ever held such unchallenged authority in public affairs. And to those espousing the need for a separation of powers and the imposition of checks-and-balances in the colony, the role of attorney general unhealthily smacked of too many conflicts of interest.

There is no doubt that he was the principal mover in the land during the period 1936–46. This time span encompassed both the Riots, where Walcott appears a reactionary figure, and the Second World War where he essentially ran the country on a very small budget and organized production in such a way that the inhabitants did not starve when the German submarine fleet had effectively choked off the colony. His tenure on power continued until the Bushe Experiment which many of his supporters saw as an exercise manipulatively aimed at removing him from power.

> The so-called Bushe Experiment [wrote J.C. Tudor in an obituary] . . . required the office of Attorney General to be a civil service post. It further required those members of the assembly who sat on the Governor's Executive Committee to be of the same political persuasion. Thus was Walcott's power broken by those who could not get the better of him.[4]

Despite his war record, Walcott was notorious for his great dislike of the British – a perspective commonplace among many Barbadian whites. Irksomely, the British tended to be seen by such whites as meddlesome reminders of the fact that they were living in a British colony after all. The story goes that governors were warned, on coming to Barbados, not to upset "that little nuisance Walcott".

His bitter struggle with Grantley Adams is probably reflective of a man – patriotic in his own way – whose innate conservatism caused him to resist the forces of change. Walcott was, for example, a founder member of the BEA.

Walcott's power derived from his broad knowledge of the workings of Barbados. Yet, he was observed to have limitations. A representative of the Colonial Office who accompanied him to the Montego Bay conference in 1947 where the idea of a West Indies Federation was being promoted, recalled that Walcott seemed uneasy, out of his depth and dying to get back to Barbados where he was 'kingpin'.

Walcott was a man you either loved or hated. Even after the Bushe Experiment removed much of his power as attorney general, he was able to capitalize on the immense popularity he enjoyed in his relatively affluent St James constituency to gain the highest winning percentage in any constituency in the island in the 1948 election. But his electoral support was not drawn exclusively from society's upper tier, for he was returned to the House in his final electoral contest in 1951 by a population which had just received full adult suffrage.

Mr Deputy Speaker

As a tribute to his commitment to the cause for which his party stood, on 21 June 1949, Lewis was nominated by the BLP for the post of Deputy Speaker in the Barbados House of Assembly. It was a post he would occupy until his departure from the legislature following his electoral defeat in 1956 and for which Lewis appeared well suited.

TT was a master of the Rules of the House of Assembly and was punctilious in seeing that they were not breached. Apparently he had read the rule book by May[5] and became the acknowledged authority on the procedures. Whenever there was uncertainty over any points of procedure the question was often asked: "And what is the view of the honourable member for the City on this particular point?" (Sir Donald Wiles)

TT knew the rules of parliamentary procedure perfectly. If he had been elected Speaker he would easily have been the best the Commonwealth had ever seen. When he sat in the chair, he did two things that helped improve the quality of debate. First, he never deviated from the point at issue. Secondly, he always took the opportunity to impartially improve the presentation of the ideas submitted by MPs during the course of debate. He would do it, for example, like this: "It really isn't for me to put words in the mouth of the honourable member, but perhaps the honourable member might like to have his position expressed thus . . ." By doing this he not only improved the quality of debate, but illustrated the quality of his own thinking. (Sir James Tudor)

The years 1949–51 find Lewis at the peak of his political career. He was a member of the governing party, though not himself a "minister" in the Executive Committee. As a relatively new member of the BLP he could not have expected to claim a seat on the Executive Committee at the expense of such "old brigade" stalwarts as Cummins, Cox and Walcott. Still, the deputy speakership would have been quite an honour. Soon, the assets which had qualified him to sit in the chair of the House – experience, knowledge of the political process, ability to penetrate to the core of an issue – would land him on the task force set up to plan the party's strategy for the monumental 1951 elections and the era of the full adult franchise.

First, though, something which for him must have come as a personal achievement: the passage of legislation which abolished the Occupancy Tax. Although Lewis was to play a central role in bringing about free secondary education, this would be the only legislative triumph he witnessed in his lifetime. Despite having witnessed delays on the matter for more than three years, the amendment to the Vestries Act of 1911 was passed by the governor on 26 November 1949. In the final debate on the subject, Lewis vented his traditional

Undated when discovered among Lewis' few personal possessions, this historic photograph is likely to have been taken during the parliamentary session 1948-51, when K.N.R. Husbands was Speaker and J.H. Wilkinson (extreme left in background) was still a member. The three members of the Barbados Electors' Association visible in the distance on the left of the picture are (left to right) J.H. Wilkinson, E.L. Ward and W.W. Reece. The BLP members in the foreground are (left to right moving anticlockwise around the horseshoe table): G.H. Adams, Dr H.G. Cummins, F.L. Walcott (looking back at camera), M.E. Cox, T.O. ("Orrie") Bryan, A.E.S. ("TT") Lewis, R.G. Mapp, F.E. ("Freddie") Miller, D.A. Foster and L.E. ("Boychild") Smith. The political weight of the BLP politicians can be gauged by their proximity to Adams, the party leader. Husbands, the first black speaker of the House, sits in the high chair presiding over proceedings. In front of him sit Dudley Sergeant (Clerk of the House on the left) and Lisle Thomas (Deputy Clerk of the House on the right).

Later Years with the Barbados Labour Party

objections to the tax based on the notion of social equity. The bill received the governor's assent on 26 November 1949.

Soon the island was gripped by the prospect of universal adult suffrage. Long and arduous debates took place on the subject. But by now there was every prospect that Barbados would become the very first British West Indian colony where all adults could vote. This was a matter on which Lewis had, years earlier, expressed himself. By this stage, he had turned to focus on the island's political structure as organized under the Bushe Experiment. Although only three years had passed since the Experiment was introduced in 1946, Lewis felt that the colony had outgrown it and was ready for more devolution of political power to the elected representatives. His views anticipated the advent, five years later, of a system of full ministerial government in the colony. When it came in 1954, the introduction of ministerial status would bestow upon Barbados the most advanced system of self-government to be found in any British colony in the world. In the following excerpt from the House records, Lewis' views on what he viewed as the half-hearted nature of the Bushe Experiment display a characteristic impatience to let the islanders get on with the business of governing themselves and determining their own future.

We have at present, Sir, what is known as an experiment. In my opinion, our political status in the British West Indies is such that the use of the word 'experiment' is nothing more than an insult. In my opinion, it is an experiment without responsibility at all . . . It is an experiment, not saying whether we are fit for responsibility. The experiment should have gone far enough to entrust our ministers with responsibility and see how they use or misuse it, otherwise it is not an experiment for the granting of responsibility. This experiment has not given members of this House the opportunity of making important decisions and of being held responsible to their fellow members and the electorate for the political progress of this colony. We have it from the mouth of the governor that he considers that the experiment has worked well. Well, we are taking the time from him; he agrees that it has worked well and we are saying that it is time for it to go a step further. The members of this House who are not on the Executive Committee, when a question affecting the administration of this colony gives rise to public discussion and outrages public feeling, would prefer to discuss the matter with the minister who is responsible; discuss it with that minister who will have to take his responsibility seriously and, who will be obliged to give us the answers to the questions that I know he will be asked.[6]

Leaving aside his success with the Occupancy Tax, and the major conceptual contribution he was to make on the question of free secondary education, this extract, one of many quotable opinions, demonstrates Lewis' major asset: his flair as a social critic – in the positive sense of that term. Owing to his earlier long absences from the island, he had introduced few bills, members' questions, petitions or even simple messages. In the period before 1949, this would have been explained away by the demands of his job. But after he was dismissed, all he had left was his politics.

This period allows us to see both the strengths and limitations of TT Lewis as a legislator, for while his contributions to the debates of the House attest to his skills and clarity of thought in the role of reformer and improver, most of his contributions were made in response to some measure or other. In addition, he seems to have been unable or unwilling to broaden his scope beyond the Barbados shoreline and develop the qualities of statesmanship which were admittedly manifest in only a few House members at the time. Such qualities, to the extent that he ever sought to develop them, would forever elude him.

Competing Under Universal Adult Suffrage

Hoyos, biographer of Grantley Adams and himself a staunch BLP supporter, recalls the run up to the 1951 election. It was both groundbreaking and immensely symbolic. In this election the BLP would go to the country with a manifesto chronicling past achievements and promising future exploits. That manifesto, Hoyos claims was the work of only a few, among whom Lewis played the key coordinating role.

Alexander Hoyos in the 1940s (left) and Sir Alexander Hoyos in 1993 (above)

In 1951, three or four party stalwarts were appointed to the committee to write the party manifesto that would lead us to the New Jerusalem. Barrow was on that committee. So was Frank Walcott. TT and I were the two others. I can't be sure of Frank Walcott, but for sure Errol Barrow never attended any of the meetings. TT and I wrote that manifesto – TT would put forward the ideas. I would put these ideas into better order. Looking back, Barrow eventually convinced himself that he had written the manifesto for he went about telling everyone this. Even the day after he died, I heard the radio playing one of his speeches and there he was saying that Hoyos had got it wrong and that he had done the manifesto. I remember TT saying "We'll waste more time waiting for these [fellows] than it would take to write the damn thing". (Sir Alexander Hoyos)

Hoyos states that the manifesto was later claimed as the best the BLP had produced to date and was fully in keeping with the importance of the election.

The central role he played in organizing the content and writing of that document allowed Lewis again to bring to the fore his long cherished idea that all secondary school students in the island should be entitled to an education free of charge.

Again, we are talking late 40s and 50s – a period when Barbados was still a colony. Not a lot of revenue was generated. Everyone tended to think that if you're going to do anything you had to wait for the Colonial Office to make a decision. It was about this time that TT, Errol Barrow, Ronald Mapp and I were asked to prepare and write the BLP manifesto for the 1951 election. We put in it the concept of the school meals programme and the concept of free secondary education. The school meals programme belonged to Barrow. Free secondary education belonged to TT Lewis. Both were advanced concepts for that era and both helped the BLP to win the 1951 election. (Sir James Tudor)

Once the campaigning got underway, it was immediately clear that the poll would be a two horse race. With Congress now consigned to political oblivion, it was a straight fight between Adams' BLP and the BEA with the BLP having the upper hand from the outset. Aside from the overwhelming force of demographics on the side of the BLP under the new "one person one vote" system, Adams could point to significant achievements since the previous election: his role in negotiations between BWU and Sugar Producers Federation giving workers more benefits; holidays with pay; greater security on factory floor; and finally the presence of a group of young professionals (soon to be dubbed the "Young Turks") among its ranks who would give the party an extra element of flair and sophistication.

Lewis was again one of the successful BLP candidates swept to victory by the newly enfranchised electorate on 13 December.

Revenue Equalization and the South African Debate

With the electoral victory of 1951 Adams got the majority in the House he had always sought. And it was a comfortable one. The opposition was splintered. The future probably seemed clear. It would certainly be easier than the recent past, with its cobbled coalitions, and its deals struck to ensure continuous voting strength in the House. Adams now had a comfortable 16 seats in the House.

Perhaps, as historically happens, it was his new political supremacy that bred complacency. Perhaps it was the arrival of bright, new members among Adams' own ranks who thought they could do better. But following the election there soon developed a sense that the party could no longer contain all the divergent views that were welling up within its ranks. The first real instance of this came over the issue of what was then dubbed the Revenue Equalization Debate. At issue was the government's proposal to establish a Revenue Equalization Fund for which it introduced a bill into the House in 1952. The fund's purpose was to lay aside surplus taxation revenue in any particular fiscal year for the proverbial rainy day.

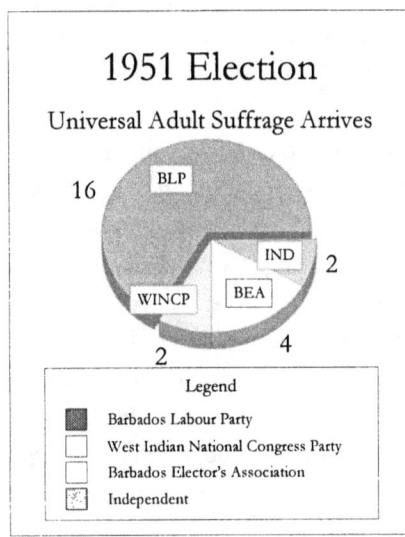

The 1951 election feels the full effect of newly enfranchised black voting power under the one-person-one-vote system. The BLP sweeps to victory on the strength both of full adult franchise and its record of legislative reforms during the previous three years. The island witnesses its first woman representative in the House of Assembly as well as a BLP victory in the St James constituency – long regarded as a conservative stronghold.

On the surface, the argument which developed was simply over a difference of opinion on national financial housekeeping. At root, however, the divergence of opinion between Adams and some of his backbenchers betrayed a chasm separating Adams' more conservative instincts from the ideas of those who sought a more immediate developmental response to the visible problems of the day.

This would develop into a fundamental divergence of ideological outlook within the party. R.L. Cheltenham, the author of what is to date the most detailed account of political developments during the immediate pre-independence period has identified the year 1950 as the "point at which the BLP abandoned its commitment to wholesale nationalization and set the Barbadian economy on a course of controlled capitalism in the private sector."[7] Cheltenham concludes that since 1949 Adams had been willing to seek a *modus vivendi* with the planters.[8]

Lewis counted himself among those who argued that any surplus money ought to be ploughed back into the country for developmental purposes rather than be put aside for the proverbial rainy day. In doing so, he displayed views on the subject which were typically socialist.

Later Years with the Barbados Labour Party

In 1952 or thereabouts, when TT was still with the BLP, he made a speech in Queen's Park denouncing the use of the Barbados Government's surplus for investment by the Crown Agents in the Republic of South Africa. This, as far as I know, is the first recorded instance of someone denouncing the use of these funds in this way in Barbados. (Ronnie Hughes)

Quite a few people were against it – not only TT. In fact the money saved was to be invested in other countries as well as South Africa. The Adams government was making out that they were putting money by for a rainy day. (Owen T. Allder)

I was at that meeting. The central issue was not so much the South African question, however. It was a financial matter of what to do with excess government receipts. The Adams government was sponsoring – possibly at the behest of the Colonial Office, but I'm not sure so I shouldn't say – a Revenue Equalization Act in Barbados. Its basic design was to put money aside for a rainy day. It stated that if, in any one year, government's revenues were in excess of expenditure, then you could not, by law, carry forward that income into new projects. Instead, you were obliged to put the money aside for that rainy day. That way you had revenue equalization. The South African angle came about because the Colonial Office would tend to draw your attention to countries where they thought you would get a good return on your money. Some of the money was supposed to be invested via intermediaries like the Crown Agents in South Africa and Rhodesia [now Zimbabwe]. But TT and others of us wondered how you could take surplus revenue from a country in which there was a black majority of the population and invest it in countries where blacks suffered gross indignities through racial policies. There would probably have been no objection to investing the money in the British coal mining industry or in a Canadian silver mine . . . but what was being proposed was just too much to be contemplated. Despite the fact that the legislation was put through by his own party, TT fought the idea tooth and nail. Aside from the South African aspect to the debate, he objected to the whole 'putting aside the money for a rainy day' idea. His ideas were developmental. He felt that since the money came from the people in the first place it should be spent back on them. At the meeting you refer to, which was held in the [Queen's Park] Steel Shed, he outlined his ideas on the matter and went for his own party hammer and tong. (Sir James Tudor)

The revenue equalization debate was to spark another more serious crisis within the BLP and one that would have disastrous effects for Lewis' future political career.

THE SPLIT WITH ADAMS

Lewis is on record as having once stated: "In Barbados, the sincerity of a white man's behaviour is rarely taken for granted."[9] Taken in the context of the times these words do not appear to be out of place. Not even if spoken by a white man like Lewis. The supreme irony came when Lewis himself was held up as that white man whose sincerity was being doubted.

The Revenue Equalization debate had drawn attention to discontent among a group of rebel backbenchers within the ranks of the BLP. Adams, claimed the rebels, was refusing to discuss government measures fully with the members of his own party. The Adams side of the story was that by bringing members of the House into the picture on proposed legislative measures he repeatedly opened himself up to attack from dissenters within his own ranks. Errol Barrow appeared to be the most prominent member of the rebel group but there were others. It was this episode that set in train Lewis' eventual downfall within the BLP.

At the heart of the issue was a perception that the government was not representative of the wider views of members of the House. Politicians of the time who were interviewed expressed the view that on several occasions, but especially on the revenue equalization issue, the policies of the governor as directed by the Colonial Office were wielding more influence in the affairs of the country than the opinions of elected members of the House of Assembly. Proper cabinet government was still another six years away. And there arose a feeling that the members of the Executive Committee (the so-called 'cabinet') were not taking into account the wider views of their party colleagues in the House. This worsened the ever present tension between the members of the House who were outside the Executive Committee and the 'insiders'.

But there was another angle to it. Views expressed in the anti-Adams newspaper, the *Torch*, claimed that the criticism mounting against Adams derived ultimately from his selection of members for the post 1951 election 'cabinet'. Bickering within the BLP had prompted Adams earlier in 1952 to bring the rebels to heel on at least two occasions. Barrow's objections to the revenue equalization proposal were considerable. And despite having only been with the BLP for two years, he may have been using the debate to test the waters for his own eventual bid either for leadership of the BLP or a breakaway party. Barrow duelled directly with Adams on the floor of the House over the subject, and the dialogue soon turned to threats and allegations of disloyalty. All this amid rumours that Adams would call early elections to refresh his mandate.

Lewis, however, appears not to have wanted to break with Adams and the BLP. The evidence indicates that he was looking for a way in which the party could indeed escape the web of suspicion and intrigue that was entrapping it. According to the minutes of the BLP Executive Committee, a meeting which took place on 18 October 1952 was called at the insistence of Lewis to discuss what he called the "crises of suspicion, distrust and disunity" in the ranks of the party. Lewis was the first speaker and dealt with the main causes of what he considered to be the "drift everywhere". These were: first, the lack of internal party organization which he considered was working to the detriment of the party. Secondly, he was appalled at the frequent clashes on the floor of the House between Adams, Walcott and Barrow. Thirdly, he cited Adams' lack of consultation on the Five Year Plan and on the proposals submitted for Ministerial Status.[10]

Another report gives Lewis credit for playing the role of honest broker in organizing this meeting of senior BLP members in order to arrive at a *modus vivendi* among the belligerents:

Every member [of the BLP] admitted . . . sensing that things were radically wrong, yet even the leaders left it to poor "TT" Lewis to ask for a meeting to put matters fair and square before "de Leader" [Adams] . . . Lewis led off . . . with a recital of the sins of omission and commission of the party leaders and then member after member followed, confirming what had been said and enlarging upon it.[11]

By all accounts, Lewis certainly associated himself with the left wing of the party. For example, despite a threat from Adams that the way party members voted during the debate over the island's first Five Year Plan – then under consideration by the House – would be seen as a vote of confidence in his government, Lewis plucked up the courage to abstain from voting. Barrow and Lorenzo Williams did likewise claiming that the plan had been produced and introduced into the House with little discussion. At the time, Lewis expressed regret that the Plan, which involved a capital programme costing $16.5 million, did not go far enough in easing the plight of the island's working population.[12]

The Five Year Plan was passed into law, but at one stage during the debate Adams said of Lewis and others: "Our friends on the extreme left are hardly likely to quarrel with the government for following Marshal Stalin's example in Soviet Russia of a Five Year Plan."[13] This sort of calculated political invective would have been carefully crafted to prey upon the minds of those in the island who were then much preoccupied with "McCarthyite" witch hunting in the USA. The communist bogey was used repeatedly in local politics during this period. Immediately prior to Barrow's abandonment of the BLP to form the rival DLP, for example, Adams claimed to be in possession of definite information that a communist cell existed in Barbados and that an unidentified member of the House of Assembly was engaged in the activities of this cell. In the resulting uproar Adams was forced to withdraw the statement.[14]

The oral evidence of the interviewees supports the view that Lewis was trying to foster open government and that it was his pursuit of this conviction that led him to walk into the crossfire developing between Adams and Barrow. Adams saw Lewis' interventions as a direct challenge to his authority. Against the wrath of Adams, Lewis stood no chance. His fall from grace within the ranks of the BLP was thus assured.

Following the vote on the Five Year Plan and the October meeting, Lewis blindly continued to play honest broker by arranging pre-debate meetings in his own flat. What was formed at Lewis' prompting was a so-called Study Group. Although membership of the group was nothing formal, and certainly varied, specific names crop up routinely in its context. Prominent among them were: Errol Barrow, Ronald Mapp, Cameron Tudor, F.T.G. "Sleepy" Smith and of course Lewis himself.

Ronald Mapp in the 1940s (left) and Sir Ronald Mapp in 1992 (above)

Sir Ronald Mapp: TT was basically pushed out of Labour and into the arms of the Dems [Errol Barrow's DLP] by Grantley [Adams]. Prior to ministerial government, the BLP formed a majority in the House. But the government was not a cabinet government. Errol Barrow would go to party meetings and hear the legislative measures being discussed. He would then go to the House armed and be critical of the government. Soon after Barrow started attacking measures in the House, Adams stopped holding the pre-assembly party meetings at Union and Party Headquarters. Adams claimed that Barrow would attend these meetings as a BLP member, say nothing during the meetings and then spring on the measures and attack them in the House. But loyal party members were very unhappy about having to vote on measures in the House which had not been discussed beforehand. So TT had the courage to volunteer to hold the discussion meetings at his house in Bay Street. Barrow of course used to attend these as well. So did I. But never once did we discuss breaking away from the BLP. In all the meetings that were held, I never suspected that TT was manoeuvring to leave the party.

Sir James Tudor: The members of the group that Adams was criticizing were in effect saying: 'Look, give us an opportunity work with you on the policies that you, in the Executive Committee, will be recommending to the Governor.' But Adams didn't seem interested. So we formed what we called the 'Study Group' and met separately to discuss the matters of the day without Adams. Somehow he came to regard TT as the most articulate member of the group which was urging policies on him which he was resisting.

Author: Who were the members of that group?

Sir James: Lorenzo Williams, Errol Barrow, TT, myself and probably also Ronald Mapp. But Mapp was not identified with the serious criticism of the Adams policies although he disagreed with them in some instances.

Sir Ronald Mapp: The meetings we held in TT's place weren't part of any formal arrangement. For these meetings, TT would call you up and say, 'As far as I'm aware, Grantley has not called any meeting to discuss what the Government has sent down to the House. Could you come over?' Adams heard that the meetings were taking place in TT's house and charged him with disloyalty and planning to form a new party. I denied that. Said that it had never been discussed . . .

But by now, Adams suspected that Lewis was attempting to mount a challenge against him. After this point, events unfolded rapidly. Adams is reported to have been warned that Lewis was about to leave the party to form another one in opposition to the BLP. Although the perception that Lewis could actually pose a challenge to Adams was a considerable unintended compliment, there is no evidence to support the view that Lewis wanted to do anything of the sort. Given that Adams is reported to have offered Lewis a seat on the Executive Committee on some unspecified occasion, cynics could argue that it was Lewis' disgruntlement at not actually receiving such a post that led him to rally the forces of discontent. But this hypothesis is unsupported by the oral evidence.

Adams remained convinced of Lewis' guilt. And on 14 November 1952, the inevitable happened, precipitating the demise of Lewis' political career. When the axe fell, Adams would show no mercy. The technique used would be public denouncement. Although none of Hoyos' books on Adams details the split between Lewis and the latter, Adams' biographer described the episode to the author.

Barbados' first cabinet: Edwy Talma, Grantley Adams (premier), Mencea Cox, Ronald Mapp, (absent: Dr H.G. Cummins). (Photograph taken in the Bridgetown Parliament Buildings, probably in 1954)

Sir Alexander Hoyos: Grantley [Adams] made a bad mistake with TT that caused him to leave the party. TT used to hold pre-parliamentary meetings in his living room where black and coloured men would come to discuss politics. Some of them would be well dressed, some would be barefoot. For a white man to do this in Barbados was unheard of. Someone left one of these meetings and told Grantley that TT was attempting to build up a following and launch another party or challenge him for the leadership.

Sir Alexander: Grantley was always particularly vicious to potential challengers. When he let loose against you on the platform even good men had to run for cover, as you would feel the crowd would run after you: I remember this happening to one poor fellow at a political meeting in the early days. Anyway, he waited until he was on the platform to denounce TT. However, as a sign of TT's strength of character he said nothing. When the meeting was over, and the crowd had dispersed, [someone said] "Man, this is a damned disgrace. That man Lewis has made a sacrifice and this is no way to treat him."

Hoyos never indicated whether Adams had had second thoughts about his treatment of Lewis back in November 1952. Seated on the platform next to Lewis at that meeting was a young J. Cameron Tudor who recalls the speech vividly:

J. Cameron Tudor in the 1940s (left) and Sir James Tudor in 1992 (above)

In that speech in Queen's Park – it would have been in November 1952 – Grantley accused TT of disloyalty and treachery. Adams tore TT to pieces. It was the most appalling example of a platform performance by any politician that I have known. All of us had been invited to the meeting on the grounds that it was being held to discuss the party policies on the current issues, and TT came along in good faith. He sat between myself and Adams who was the last to speak. When Adams' turn came, after a few minutes' introduction, he launched into TT with a personal excoriation of the man. Saying things like "I will never again ask the people of Bridgetown to support this man (pointing at TT) in an election . . . We marched for him and now look at what he has turned around and done." Things like that. The meeting was clearly designed to arouse his constituents against him.

Sir James Tudor: It was a very bitter personal attack, and I regret to say that there were racial overtones. The whole tenor of the speech was this: here is a man who looks different from us, whom we have nurtured and taken under our wing and now look at how he has betrayed his party. The crowd, which was composed mainly of agricultural workers and waterfront men was very much with Adams. I was on the platform, and could hear nasty comments and veiled threats coming from the Adams loyalists in the crowd at the side of the platform. Things like: "Yuh going against Adams? White son-of-a-bitch. He want something doin' to him!" I have always felt that this was the high point of TT's decency and aplomb. He sat through the entire diatribe and didn't utter a word. After the meeting ended, TT stood up and walked through the massive crowd towards the car of whoever had given him a ride – he never had a car himself. And no one touched him. Personally, it was that meeting that made me decide that I could no longer stay in the BLP. TT stayed on for quite a while longer though. I don't think he left until 1955, a short time before the election which he fought for our newly formed Democratic Labour Party.

Sir Frank Walcott: TT was frank and outspoken to all – not just to some. I remember when TT had that big break with Adams. At the time, that was seen as sacrilegious – to have a difference with Adams. Adams was regarded like a king or a godhead and TT was the only white man in the Labour Party. When he split with Adams some Labourites may have taken against TT simply because he was against Adams, and was white. But TT wasn't a racialist. You see, at the time Adams was fighting against the white oligarchy and probably felt TT was betraying him. The whole thing was then portrayed as a case of a white man fighting against not just *a* black leader, but *the* black leader. I personally believe that some of the slurs thrown against him as a white man would have strengthened his resolve to pursue his path and leave the BLP. But it may have also had a side effect on his health. At that time, society was more narrow. After TT broke with Adams, because of Adams' popularity, a lot of harsh things would have been said to him.

Lewis never recovered from the stigma of alleged disloyalty to the party. Towards the end of his political life, the BLP as a whole appears to have viewed him with great bitterness. His old electioneering ally, E.L. Cozier claims that his disagreements with the upper echelons of the BLP had brought him the undying hatred of many people, so that "even when his health was completely broken and he was deserving of sympathy, his political enemies could not find it in their hearts to forgive him."[15] According to another source: "The thing I seem to remember most about TT Lewis was that at some point he seemed to fall out with his own people." (Herbert Dowding)

Adams' denouncement of Lewis had the unsurprising effect of dampening the latter's keenness for the political fray. In 1953 and 1954, little is heard from Lewis on any subject. He would stay within the BLP until 1955, embarking upon the final part of his political pilgrimage to join the DLP with whom he would also fight his last election.

In contrast to his treatment by the Central Agency, Lewis must have certainly felt particularly misunderstood, and possibly betrayed by Adams, a man in whom he had placed a large measure of his trust and the intellectual health of whose party he had tried to salvage by playing honest broker and promoter of open dialogue. Betrayed too, by those Barbadians who had turned on him, and had instinctively used the badge of race as a target. All this on the basis of unproven claims of disloyalty to Adams. As a man who had sacrificed first his marriage, then his job to politics in the search for improving the quality of life for his fellow citizens, it is not unreasonable to imagine Lewis asking himself whether the various sacrifices made over the years had been worth it after all.

"TT was an enlightened liberal and an alert politician. TT was for the people as distinct from the aristocracy. Interestingly, he was perhaps the only member of the House who used to ride a pedal cycle. The majority of the other members at the time would have had motor cars." (Sir Theodore Brancker)

In retrospect, and at the level of high politics, the BLP's internal convulsions immediately preceding the formation of the breakaway DLP was indicative of a set of gradually declining political fortunes. They were the first warning signs portending the eclipse of an accomplished party and its extraordinary leader. Adams had by then been in politics for 21 years and in a leadership position for almost ten of those years. During that period, he had battled vigorously to keep his parliamentary power base together, but in the legislative session following his first outright triumph in 1951, he had allowed splits to develop within his party. The departures of such figures as Walcott, Barrow and Lewis within the space of merely a year reveal much about Adams' lack of control in the management of his party at this stage. Defeat in 1956 was staved off through the electoral inexperience of the youthful challengers in the DLP, which had been formed one year earlier. But this victory would turn out to be the BLP's last for a generation.

NOTES

1. *Hansard*, 7 June 1949, 529.
2. Pronounced "Cole-ass". Essentially it was a form of imported bitumen used in road construction. It would be heated and spread manually over the road surface and then sprinkled with gravel and rolled.
3. *Hansard*, 7 June 1949, 530.
4. J. Cameron Tudor, *Daily Nation*, 17 March 1981.
5. Sir Thomas May's *Parliamentary Practice*.
6. *Hansard*, 30 August 1949, 718.
7. R.L. Cheltenham, "Constitutional and political developments in Barbados 1946–66", PhD dissertation, University of Manchester, 1970, 75.

8. See Cheltenham, 77.
9. Quoted in G.K. Lewis, *The Growth of the Modern West Indies*, Modern Reader Paperbacks, New York, 1968, 255.
10. Cited from the Minute Book of the BLP Executive for 1952, Party Headquarters, Roebuck Street, Bridgetown. See R.L. Cheltenham, 89.
11. *The Torch*, 25 October 1952.
12. Norman Faria, "The Man 'TT' Lewis", *Barbados Advocate*, 28 February 1981.
13. F.A. Hoyos, *Grantley Adams and the Social Revolution*, Macmillan Caribbean, London, 1974 (reprint 1988), 193.
14. *Barbados Annual Review*, 1954–55, 33.
15. E.L. Cozier, *Caribbean Newspaperman: The Life and Times of Jimmy Cozier*, Coles Printery Ltd., Bridgetown, 1985, 54.

CHAPTER TEN

Life and Death with the Democratic Labour Party

It was schism within the BLP that led to the breakaway in 1944 of Wynter Crawford and his Congress Party. Discontent within the ranks of the BLP had been welling up for some time, but it was not until 1955 that Errol Barrow decided to break with Adams' party. He and three other sitting BLP MCPs were among those who formed a new party called the Democratic Labour Party. Lewis was one of the three.[1] Aside from the customary platform platitudes of wishing to work for democracy, honesty and responsibility and so on, the DLP aimed to "foster and support all politics on a federal basis, designed to raise the living standard of the people within the Caribbean area, and to hasten their independence."[2] Of passing interest, another of Adams' lieutenants, union organizer Frank Walcott, had quit the BLP a year earlier most likely on account of a dispute with Adams over the allocation of ministerial portfolios.

Lewis probably never envisioned leaving the BLP until he was forced to do so through Adams' withering denouncement. But the formation of the DLP would now offer him an opportunity to move to a less hostile home base. It is inconceivable that Lewis would have had an easy time in the ranks of the BLP during the years 1953–55. One author, writing about the state of the BLP in the years preceding the formation of the rival DLP states that paradoxically while the former was a political party claiming to be champion in the cause of wider social democracy, internally, it had come to resemble a sort of political plantation[3] with all that this implied in terms of governance and accountability.

A DLP publication which recorded the party's progress during its first ten years cites dissatisfaction with the leadership style of Grantley Adams and the BLP as what caused the DLP to split off. Foremost among these was the claim, allegedly made shortly after the 1951 victory, that Adams had said that if he were asked to choose between the advice of his party members and that of the governor, he would choose the governor's.[4] The new political party was formed on 27 April 1955 at a meeting in Fontabelle, St Michael. The meeting was attended by about two dozen persons including Lewis.

The DLP's goals were not significantly different from those of the BLP. At the time, they each shared a commitment to a West Indies federation. They each believed strongly in the role of trade unions and cooperatives and in raising the standard of living of the poor. The difference, as the DLP saw it, was more one of style. Organizationally, the new DLP structure provided for annual conferences and made a distinction between the party chairman and the party leader – the sorts of features which they claimed had fallen by the wayside in the inner workings of the BLP. "Decision making was collectivized and an opportunity was created for the accountability of leaders. In theory at any rate, there was all the appearance of a democratically constituted party, features which contrasted sharply with the BLP, where the institution of the Annual Conference had fallen into disuse, where the Executive of the party met irregularly and where Adams was *the* decision maker."[5] One of the founder members was Frederick Smith: "Three of us young professionals – Barrow, Tudor and myself – returned and joined Adams to fight against the entrenched interests. They called us the 'Young Turks'. But in those days, the BLP had no annual conference, hardly any internal party organization. It was only Adams and his word went."

Frederick Smith in the 1950s (left) and Sir Frederick Smith in 1995 (above)

Reading through the Barbados journals and newspapers of those days, one is imbued with a sense of cold war rhetoric and the very strong ripple effect that this war of ideas was having in the Caribbean. The signals and signs of the new international polarization were everywhere present. Having now to contend with a competitor party which also subscribed to its stated policy of democratic socialism, the old political master developed the tactic of labeling the DLP as a subversive organization supported by Moscow, even as the BLP had been similarly categorized by the conservatives a few years earlier.

The arrival of the DLP on the political scene meant that this new force attracted considerable attention in the pre-election debates in 1956. The elections were fought mainly on the question of the evolving structure of Barbados' political apparatus in the run up to cabinet government and eventual independence. It also centred on the topical issues of the day in Caribbean politics such as the proposed federation which now appeared inevitable. The election produced a similar result compared to what had emerged in 1951 between the governing party and its fragmented opposition, except that this time the opposition was now fragmented along different lines. The BLP was yet again triumphant, winning 15 of the 24 seats. The DLP and the former BEA (now renamed the Progressive Conservative Party) shared most of the remaining seats. Importantly, union leader Frank Walcott campaigned and won as an independent.

1956: The Final Campaign for the City

Lewis failed in what would turn out to be his last attempt to take the City seat. Those who remember the campaign in 1956 say that he had two things going against him. First was the political environment. Many of the voters who would sweep the BLP to victory in the campaign still remembered Lewis as the man who had broken with Adams four years earlier. They would not vote for someone who appeared to have sold out the cause. Moreover, the party which Lewis had joined was new and untested. That unfavourable combination made it virtually impossible for Lewis to recapture the hearts of many who had been his supporters in the past.

Secondly, there was the matter of his health. Among Lewis' documents are papers relating to medical treatment he received for his heart condition from a hospital in New York in September 1956. A medical certificate attached to

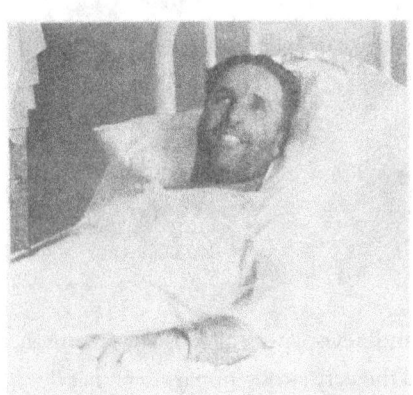

"TT took ill and couldn't do much campaigning. His opponents would ask: 'Yuh goin' vote fuh a dead man? TT dying . . .'" (Hammond Burke)

his passport also dated 1956 states that Lewis was suffering from "congestive heart failure". The certificate implied that his general physical state was not well. This condition hampered his ability to campaign effectively.

Lewis' brief and direct letter to the electors of the City of Bridgetown confirms that he was aware of the rumours circulating about the state of his health:

Dear Sir / Madam,

First of all, let me assure you that I am both willing and able to represent you as I have done in the past. I have never spoken or voted against any measure properly brought forward for your benefit or for the good of our Island community as a whole. On the contrary, many of my suggestions for better legislation have been turned down through sheer obstinacy only to be accepted later as amendments, and I am sure that many more will in time find favour with any government interested in the welfare of the people.

I have not the wherewithal to send you individual circulars, and I am hoping that, as on the previous occasion, you will accept this general communication as in some measure proof of my desire to continue to serve you in the House of Assembly, and when you go to the Polls on Thursday next you will honour me with your support.

You have had ample time to make up your minds for whom you are going to vote without my pestering you, 'blowing my own trumpet' or having one blown for me. I therefore rely on your letting your conscience be your guide, knowing full well that the heart of the people is still sound. Mine is doing fine. (A.E.S. Lewis, Letters, 3 December 1956)

1956 Election
Emergence of the DLP

- BLP: 15
- DLP: 4
- PCP: 3
- IND: 2

Legend:
- Barbados Labour Party
- Democratic Labour Party
- Progressive Conservative Party
- Independent

Following his split with Adams, Errol Barrow forms the DLP in 1955; his "Young Turks" contest the 1956 election but do not manage to oust the established Barbados Labour Party. Barrow himself loses his seat. By 1956, the Congress Party is defunct with Crawford, its erstwhile leader, running on a DLP ticket. The diminishing success of the BEA (now renamed the Progressive Conservative Party and led, paradoxically, by the popular black politician E.D. Mottley) reflects the eclipse of white political power.

First place in the contest for the two-member constituency would have in all likelihood been ceded even before campaigning started, to Lewis' old rival E.D. Mottley, who had by then risen to become the "power behind the throne"[6] in the Progressive Conservative Party and who entered the contest a seasoned, powerful and respected politician in his own right. Lewis' main rival was therefore the BLP's Tommy Miller – brother of his old friend, Freddie Miller. One source reported a saucy play on words used in connection with these two candidates which would doubtless have caused much amusement when pronounced with the intended emphasis. The joke of the campaign thus became the following slogan: "de people don't want TT [pronounced "titty"] they want the Tommy [Barbadian colloquialism for penis]."

Like Errol Barrow, although far less surprisingly so, Lewis lost his seat in the 1956 election. The DLP publication cited above claims:

Errol Barrow (1950s)

> By far the sharpest and most disappointing reverse for the party was the defeat of Mr Lewis in Bridgetown, and of Mr Barrow in St George. Mr Lewis, "TT", as he was affectionately known, had made an outstanding contribution to the politics of the island. His firm grasp of public affairs, of legislative procedure, of the world of commerce, coupled with his deep human sympathy, had together united to produce a statesman of formidable stature. Unfortunately for him, persistent ill health sapped his physical powers and this, strengthened by a subtle, undercover, rumour early on Polling Day that he was dying, made his defeat certain.[7]

LEWIS AND THE WEST INDIES FEDERATION

Very little reference is now customarily made to the West Indies Federation except that commentators and works of history routinely describe it as "failed". But hopes ran high in the decade immediately following the 1947 Montego Bay conference set up to explore the details of a possible federation among ten British West Indian island territories – Antigua, Barbados, Dominica, Grenada, Jamaica, Montserrat, St Kitts-Nevis-Anguilla, St Lucia, St Vincent and Trinidad & Tobago.[8] This push for political evolution coincided with the spirit of the times which, immediately following the conclusion of the Second World War, had witnessed a growth in the demand for national self-determination following the process of decolonization that had begun with the independence of British colonies in south Asia in 1947. Barbados along with others in the West Indies saw the goal of independence as attainable only through federation.

In the preliminary deliberations that took place principally through a series of standing committees, the view emerged that federation would provide a mechanism for the shortest path to self-government in the West Indies. Arriving at independence separately in the context of the ongoing cold war was not deemed feasible.

The federal elections would offer Lewis his final opportunity to seek a mandate in the political arena. The few papers he left behind on the subject demonstrate that he had been following the development of the federal question keenly. Although in Lewis' writings on the federation the reader finds nothing particularly remarkable, they do contain an essential optimism about the future of the proposed federal arrangements. But in typically critical style they repeatedly bring to public attention (most were published in the *Barbados Advocate*) the various gaps in the reasoning of the decision makers on such matters as the customs union and the hotly debated and ultimately crucial issue of federal taxation.

The federal election took place near the end of March 1958, and for the purposes of voting, Barbados became a single federal constituency with 4 electoral seats (by way of comparison, Jamaica, the largest and most populous island, boasted 17 seats). Lewis was then, and continuing up until the time of his death, in the forefront of the DLP shadow government. In the campaign, the DLP's party executive selected Lewis along with E.W. Barrow, C.E. Talma and J.C. Tudor to run for the House of Representatives. On polling day, only a quarter of registered Barbadians turned out to vote. None of the DLP lineup was returned.

As it turned out, Grantley Adams became the first Federal prime minister at the head of a party[9] which, after the election, found itself deriving its main political support base from among the smaller, poorer, Windward and Leeward territories. For this reason, among others, the Adams federal government was condemned to rule a federation, isolated in its Trinidad headquarters, that was by design weakly constituted and which would soon come to be seen by the larger, richer islands as an obstacle to their own economic development and aspirations for political independence. Ironically, in assuming the doomed federal mantle, Adams had abdicated direct leadership of the colony with the most advanced constitutional status in the British West Indies. In the end, after numerous squabbles and endless insular bickering, the lacklustre and impoverished federal government structure was dissolved following Jamaica's decision to go its own way to political independence in 1962.

Although a latent yearning for some form of closer union persists throughout the English-speaking Caribbean, the failure of the West Indies Federation in 1962 seems to have signalled to Caribbean leaders that regional integration might better be accomplished by means of the economic rather than the political route. Thus, with the exception of unconsummated flutterings over political union among the eastern Caribbean islands, this has been the avenue pursued ever since.

Laying the Groundwork for Free Secondary Education[10]

Education [continues to be] by the method of scholarships and this form of patronage should long ago have been abolished by the introduction of free secondary education. (A.E.S. Lewis, Letters, undated)

It is impossible to underestimate the importance which Barbados as a society has attached to building its social capital through educational attainment, especially in the latter half of this century. It has underpinned the country's development and its international profile. Since independence, the island's alternating governments have routinely given the lion's share of public spending, typically one-fifth of the government's total budget, to educating its citizens. The effect such intervention has had on economic output has been debated for years, but the correlation between such relatively high levels of social spending and the country's high ranking in terms of human development is surely striking.[11] The country still devotes a larger proportion of total annual income to education than any other country in the Western hemisphere.

The incremental evolution of improved schooling in Barbados gained considerable momentum in the generation immediately prior to independence. One significant reason for this improvement was the election, following the extension of the franchise, of public representatives with stronger links to the disadvantaged sections of society. Such persons were more disposed towards increasing social spending to buttress the essential link between improved public services – especially education and health – and social development as a whole. Two considerable results of this push were the availability of free secondary education in 1962 and the introduction of the school meals programme in 1963. The construction of new secondary schools, increased access to tertiary level education and the availability of virtually free school textbooks at secondary school followed a few years later. For the first 20 years following the attainment of independence, Barbados could boast of having one of the most eminent educational systems among all developing countries.

Ironic, then, that the legislative basis for such a system should emanate from the mind of a self-taught man when there were so many formally-trained minds in the House of Assembly. Free secondary education, the foundation for the intellectual enfranchisement of post independence Barbadians was attained in 1962. It had by then been a subject long on the political agenda. Though the DLP government introduced the measure following its first election victory in 1961, the measure's conceptual underpinnings can be traced back to utterances made over the previous generation by one legislator in particular.

"TT was the first to put forward officially the idea that there should be free secondary education in Barbados, even though the actual legislation eventually came to fruition under the Errol Barrow administration." (Sir Donald Wiles)

The greatest detail on Lewis' involvement in the free secondary school education debate is provided by J.C. (now the late Sir James) Tudor, who became minister of education after the DLP first gained office in 1961.

[Lewis] was literally the first politician in Barbados ever to conceive how free secondary education could be brought about. Let's cast our minds back to the 1940s and 50s. This was a time when the concept of abolishing fee paying in government secondary schools was about as revolutionary as marching into Government House and striking the Governor General on the bottom. Until TT, no one thought free secondary education was either possible or necessary. This was probably another of TT's areas of disagreement with Adams. To TT Lewis alone must be ascribed the original thinking on free secondary education. Here was how he did it. In those days, part of the government's budget included a provision for the secondary grant-aided schools. A minor portion of the total amount it cost the treasury to fund these schools – Harrison College, Foundation, Queen's and so on – was always contributed by fee-paying parents. TT's idea for reform was so simple that none of us could understand why we hadn't thought of it before. If it cost, for argument's sake, $100 to run a school – with the treasury paying $75 of this amount and the fee-paying parents contributing the other $25 – TT said: why not stop taking fees altogether from the parents? Let government absorb the entire cost of the operation. This way you can get totally free education for just that little bit extra.

Author: What did he say to those who would have demanded to know why he was removing an obligation to pay from those who could most afford to do so?

Sir James: TT's response was simple. He said that these citizens were already paying their fair share – through taxes on private property and so on. Moreover, they might even be coaxed into spending the money saved in this way on other socially desirable ends if taxation policies were modified towards these same ends. So, in the end, when I became Minister of Education in 1961, it was easy to institute a policy of free secondary education in the government secondary schools because TT had laid the groundwork. All I did was to instruct the governing bodies of the secondary schools never again to collect fees. If there was any shortfall, the government would be required to make up the difference. And that is how it was done. Really, TT must take all the credit.

From 1962, collection of fees at government-maintained secondary grammar schools ceased. Commentators on educational policy in Barbados during this period have noted that education was finally coming to be regarded as an instrument of social change. Free secondary education had come hard on the heels of the so-called Common Entrance Examination in 1959. As described at the time, this examination would be the "sole determinant of entrance to government secondary schools" and was intended to eliminate preferential treatment based on class, colour and family background. Overall, "educational policy makers were gradually becoming aware of the need to link what schools do to what society requires, particularly in the area of economic development."[12]

Tudor claims that Lewis' views on free secondary education were the product of a man possessed of a strong developmental perspective that trusted the citizens to run with the ball if they were given the first push. He says Lewis used this perspective to show how mutually reinforcing linkages were possible if the country's leaders took the time to inculcate a sense of pride and self-worth in its ordinary citizens.

Here is something he taught me personally. He said: "Look, if the DLP ever gets into power, we must spend money on the people. This will make them more creative. Equally, they're going to feel that they owe more to the island. The more creative you make them, the more conscious they will become of the problems of development. Simple." You see, TT was a democrat who trusted the people to help themselves so long as you gave them the first push up. (Sir James Tudor)

Concluding Years in Opposition

Lewis' remaining years in political exile appear to have been taken up with his interminable passion for the minutiae of public finances reflecting his very clear perception that the proper handling of financial matters was the best criterion of good government. The subject exercised him enormously: the federal customs union, municipal taxes for local government and his old favourite, the revenue equalization surpluses (examined in chapter 9). But by this stage, his writings, penned within two years of his death, had become verbose and ever so slightly bitter. He writes contemptuously, for example, about Grantley Adams and his band of "pigmy politicians" building up large reserves of idle money while "sick men, women and children have decayed two and three to a hospital bed".[13]

Lewis was no doubt a state interventionist in the traditional sense.

Parts of the island like St Lucy, Christ Church and St Philip – the drier parts where there was lower rainfall – saw the worst privation when the [sugar] crop was over. If there was no rainfall, there was no weeding necessary on the estates and the people literally starved because they were dependent on wages to buy staples and couldn't get work. So TT said that if the people couldn't get work weeding the cane fields why not let the government give them work weeding the roads in the wetter areas where this work was needing to be done. The government would have to pay, and it was just a question of shifting them from one area of work into another. This idea was his and Errol Barrow's, and it is the forerunner of the roadside weeding that we see being done today all round the countryside. (Sir James Tudor)

Owing to his thorough command of the principles of public finance, some said that Lewis would have been slated for the job of minister of finance in the victorious incoming DLP government of 1961. However, Barrow would not likely have given Lewis the finance ministry job which by Caribbean tradition goes to the prime minister or premier. Lewis would instead have probably been made a minister without portfolio in the Ministry of Finance. Whether he won a seat or not, Lewis would certainly have been given a cabinet post.

That he missed out on the DLP victory that was just around the corner appears fatally consistent with the picture of a man who possessed a hugely undeveloped sense of political timing. For speaking his mind forthrightly, he had earlier gotten himself fired from his job and found himself without a sustainable income in the period before members of the House started to receive a salary. For a parliamentarian so senior and with such an established track record to have then gone for so long without a 'cabinet' post is as much an indictment of Lewis' poor political sense of timing as it is to his absolute intellectual honesty in speaking his mind with scant regard for the political consequences. This proved the cause of his schism with Adams. It seems that the well-cultivated oratorical skill of equivocation was not among the armoury of political weapons he possessed. Tudor summarily assessed his political value to the DLP thus:

TT was widely regarded as the most knowledgeable person in t
finance, budgeting and so on. In fiscal matters, no one excelled him. However, while he had a powerful intellect, he was essentially an architect, a backroom boy. He would probably never have become a prime minister, but certainly no PM could ever have done without him. (Sir James Tudor)

Writing six years after his death, the DLP would call Lewis the "greatest parliamentarian of his time", and pay the following tribute to their deceased colleague: "In the counterfeit evaluation of our time, he had the skin colour which is deemed sufficient for a man in these parts. Yet he scorned these doubtful aids, and chose to die in honourable poverty, in splendid testimony to himself."[14]

LIFE AFTER THE CENTRAL AGENCY

Lewis died with $35 in his bank account. Having started politics with nothing he ended with nothing. Some of the interviewees claimed this to be a fitting metaphor for his honesty as a political figure. Throughout his career he grappled with financial problems even though he was not given to drinking, gambling or any of the other vices that drain away an individual's income. Between his

A Daughter's Reflections

(Sonya Lawrence)

When Mummy and Daddy were first married they lived in Chelsea Road. I was born at what is now Brigade House on the Garrison Savannah at about one in the morning, yet my father would not come to see his first born daughter until he had taken his early morning swim at the Aquatic Club and gulped down his ritual seawater. He and Mummy later moved into their own home at Clifton Terrace. I remember him there, for my first seven years, as a very popular person because there were always so many people in the house. On the night Diana was born they banished me to my room – but I was able to peep out and see Daddy and the doctor fussing and rushing around and then relaxing in the living room amid the delivery screams from the bedroom.

During this time Cecil Jordan and his wife came to live next to us in Clifton Terrace and this either began or continued the long friendship between Cecil and TT, with Cecil coming to Daddy's aid when he was fired from the Central Agency and offering him a job at Office Equipment Ltd doing the accounts. Cecil always reminisced that the best accounting and business advice he ever got was from TT.

The split between Mummy and Daddy happened in two stages when I was about 7 or 8 years old, but it never registered much on me. Daddy was still travelling through the islands and had come to Dominica on one or two occasions. He would then visit us at home but always stayed in a guest house. Those were the years when we visited him in Barbados for a few weeks during the holidays. He would commandeer one of his friends to meet us when we arrived – either by interisland schooner, the Ladyboats, the Grumman Goose and eventually those awful two-engine planes. Invariably, it was either Colly [Frank Collymore] or Cecil who brought Daddy to meet us at the pier head or airport.

His pride and joy was to take us around visiting his friends like we were curios. We hated it. His purpose in taking us around the neighbourhood was twofold, for he never owned a radio and so these visits were timed to coincide with the BBC news on Rediffusion at 7 pm. There was never any transportation, so we walked on those visits and there was always so much to talk about. He was never uncomfortable in talking with us and he never talked down to us like children. It seemed he talked to us exactly the same way he talked with his friends and told us all the same jokes and cussed whoever was the topic of the day the same way he would to his adult friends.

Lewis with daughters Sonya (left) and Diana in the mid 1950s.

Some of my recollections of those holiday visits are simple but indelibly clear. For instance, he never had transportation and after his illness not even the bicycle. So we always went to town by bus. Whether he was accompanying us or not, he always stood at the bus stop with us and you could be sure that not more than one or two cars would pass before someone stopped for him. He seemed to know everyone. It was worse when he took us to Bridgetown with him. It would take us about an hour just to walk the length of Broad Street. Every step he took . . .   (text box cont'd next page) (cont'd from previous page) . . . someone would stop him for a chat – a political topic or a stupid joke or whatever. Today I can look back on how popular he was, but back then it was so damn annoying.

Sonya and Diana (1993)

When I became old enough to go out on my own with young men known to TT he was like an old sitting hen. He let me know what time I was expected to return and was up and awake and "looking out" when I got back. Then there was usually a row because I was invariably late. Diana said she never had this reaction from him when she lived in Barbados with him, so maybe I was just the bad one. When I finished school in Canada the plan was for me to come to Barbados to live with him and find a job. By the end of the third month I had no job and I could not take the constant differences of points of view and the altercations with him. So we parted amicably and I returned to St Lucia.

He met my husband-to-be and took an instant dislike to him. He didn't even try to hide it and did his utmost to dissuade me. But I was young then and knew better than everyone! To our surprise, when I decided to get married he agreed to come to St Lucia for the wedding to give me away. I was so thrilled. A close friend of his later told me it was I who killed my father by marrying that man.

dismissal in 1949 and his hiring by Jordan and Rogers in 1954, Lewis would have funded himself on the declining balance of his termination settlement from the Central Agency plus whatever he received from the public purse as a legislator. But he would have been considerably underemployed in his place of work. Hoyos recalls that following his electoral defeat in 1956, so keen was Lewis' thirst for politics that when the post of Clerk of the House of Assembly became vacant, he applied for the job but was unsuccessful. His peculiarly critical nose and the legendary care and attention he gave to parliamentary bills and amendments seemed to mark him out as the choice candidate.

The Clerk of the House of Assembly should have logically been TT's job. [Another individual] who was in no way his equal, had been given the job. As it turned out, this man didn't last long in the job. The only person who had voted for Lewis, I found out later, was [conservative] Fred Goddard. The reasons why people voted this way were party political. TT had angered the BLP by going over and joining the Dems [DLP]. (Sir Alexander Hoyos)

Illness and Death

The last known photograph of Lewis alive

Towards the end, Lewis' health grew steadily worse. He was stricken with chronic heart failure. He was instructed to take medication for this condition and had to be careful about what he ate. Hoyos relates that he hardly ate or drank at all. Nonetheless, the sort of wit for which he is celebrated appears to have stayed with him to the end. An example is related in the following anecdote:

> One inquisitive telephone caller, not recognizing TT's voice, asked if he had heard the rumour that TT was dead. "Yes," TT answered, "the poor man is gone. The funeral service is tomorrow. All his close friends are being invited . . ." After the caller had thanked him for the information, TT revealed his identity and the fact that he obviously wasn't yet dead. (Sir Donald Wiles)

Few people can plan their deaths the way they wish. For Lewis, however, when death came, as it did on 31 July 1959, it arrived in a devastating manner for his immediate family.

> . . . Sonya [Lewis' elder daughter] was preparing for her first marriage. TT travelled to St Lucia on the Thursday . . . to the house on Vigie hill where Sonya and Marge were living at the time. On Friday, the day before the wedding, Sonya and Marge went into town to do some shopping. When they returned from Castries, they found TT dead in his bed. The wedding took place the following day under the shadow cast by TT's death. (Constance Younglao)

Part of Lewis' eulogy detailed his final hours:

> On the day of his death, he awoke as usual and after breakfast went for a stroll, and on his return sat down with a copy of the local paper, a copy of *Time* and his ever present companion, a lead pencil. As he was reading and underlining, he slipped away into that other world which is never far from each one of us. He died as he had lived, reading, noting, underlining, preparing to defend.[15]

> Just before TT died, he was showing the strains of ill health and was approached by the funeral director father of the men who now run Two Sons Funeral Home. He said to TT: "If you let me take your measurements now, I'll give you a ten percent discount off the final price." So said, so done. TT agreed and the man took his measurements for the coffin. TT had the last laugh, however, for he died and was buried in St Lucia. After TT died, Sir James (then Cameron) Tudor organized the memorial service at St Mary's Church. But the mood was far from sombre. People were consciously cracking jokes and making fun as if TT himself were there among us. (Sir Donald Wiles)

Life and Death with the Democratic Labour Party

Ironically for a man who had contributed so much to Barbados, Lewis could not even afford to be interred in his native soil. He was instead buried at the seaside cemetery near Castries in St Lucia, near to where his wife and daughters then lived. Family finances would not have permitted the expense of shipping his remains to Barbados.

TT was a man well known and well liked. I went to visit TT often when he was ill in his house in Bay Street. At that time TT was forced to sleep upright in a chair as he was suffering from water on the heart... After his death, our Freemasonic lodge paid for the erection of a headstone to mark TT's grave in St Lucia. (Noel Weatherhead)

NOTES

1. The other two were O.T. Allder and J.C. Tudor.
2. *Barbados Annual Review (1954–55)*, 78.
3. P. Emmanuel, "Shifts in the balance of political power: unions and parties" in *Emancipation III*, 109.
4. *Democratic Labour Party – Ten Years' of Service (1955–65)*, Advocate Commercial Printing, Bridgetown, 1965.
5. R.L. Cheltenham, "Constitutional and political development in Barbados (1946–66)", PhD dissertation, University of Manchester, 1970, 120.
6. Officially, the leader of the PCP was Fred Goddard.
7. *Democratic Labour Party*, 12.
8. Objecting to the idea of total freedom of movement within the Federation, the two spacious mainland British West Indian territories – British Guiana (now Guyana) and British Honduras (now Belize) – rejected federation from the outset. The Bahamas also opted out.
9. The West Indies Federal Labour Party: an alliance of the leading socialist political parties in the British West Indies to which the prime ministers of both Jamaica and Trinidad & Tobago also belonged, though neither bothered to take part in the federal elections, thereby robbing the result of prestige and weight. The federal opposition was made up of the Democratic Labour Party led by Alexander Bustamante of Jamaica.
10. See earlier discussion on Lewis' efforts to promote free secondary education in chapter 5.

11. As measured, for example, in the Human Development Index (a ranking devised by the United Nations Development Programme). This yardstick for measuring quality of life, first used in 1990 to rank all countries in terms of their level of human development (as opposed, simply, to economic attainment) has seen Barbados emerge as one of the highest ranking (in 1991–95 it was actually the top) developing countries in the world.
12. R. Jemmott and D. Carter, "Barbadian Educational Developments (1933–93): An Interpretive Analysis", unpublished, 1994, 18.
13. A.E.S. Lewis, "Taxation and Surpluses", *Barbados Advocate*, 10 April 1958.
14. *Democratic Labour Party*, 18.
15. *Barbados Observer*, 8 August 1959.

CHAPTER ELEVEN

TT Lewis – An Assessment

The man who can most truly be accounted brave is he who best knows the meaning of what is sweet in life and what is terrible, and then goes out undeterred to meet what is to come. (Pericles, Funeral oration to the Athenian dead, 431 BC)

In the end, one must always ask any work of biography the somewhat impertinent question: So what? Did TT Lewis really make that much of a difference? Would the future evolution of Barbadian political landscape have looked all that different if he had never existed? There is also the broader question: what clues and answers do the life and times of Lewis hold for successor generations of Barbadians?

Lewis' obituary appeared in the *Barbados Advocate* on 1 August 1959. In it he is portrayed as a maverick figure who had difficulty getting along with certain establishment figures as well as people in the then ruling BLP, one of the several political parties to which he belonged during his lengthy career in politics. In terse and economical 'obituarese', his notable achievements were described as being a member of a clerks' union and several sports clubs. Hardly an indication of remarkableness. Lewis died at the relatively young age of 54 and would fail to see Barbados become independent. He would never hold a cabinet position. Bereft of real family life, even after marriage, Lewis also lacked material wealth and in his final years, he would struggle to get by. The political career that was his lifeblood expired three years before his own end.

And yet, listening to the voices of those still alive who remember the times in which he lived and his influence upon those times, an altogether different picture emerges. "As a white man, TT's presence and views on behalf of the working class were so untypical that in the social addition he counted for more than just one person." (Sir Hugh Springer)

To be sure, Lewis was a rarity in Barbadian politics. In those times of great social cleavage, he identified himself totally with the progressive movement, and won five successive electoral contests on the basis of an essentially socialist platform. Although vulnerable as an employee to the possibility of victimization at the hands of the white oligarchy which then ran the island, Lewis spoke openly about the iniquities of the system in which he and others lived. Inevitably, he encountered the wrath of the planter and mercantile class. They no doubt thought of him as a renegade and probably said as much among themselves.

John Wickham (1992)

Barbados was and to some extent remains a polarized society. The general populace at the time categorized the split as 'white is bad and black is good'. Therefore, the significance of Lewis is that, in the eyes of the populace, he was very much the exception. For here was a man who showed openly where his sympathies lay. He suffered for his honesty by losing his job. In a small country like Barbados, this action was hugely symbolic. It demonstrated an extraordinary firmness of purpose. It is the sort of example which can always be quoted to contradict someone wanting to make a point about the universally exploitative nature of the white community. There were whites, no doubt, who were kind hearted and who would have liked to try to bridge the gap, but they couldn't or didn't. Here on the other hand was TT, someone who was prepared to be ostracized by the high white community for his beliefs. The rarity of this kind of declaration of faith shows how little things have changed in the social sense. At that time, it would have taken an enormous amount of courage to make the sort of sacrifice that TT made. In a way, only heroes and giants can ever consider sacrificing everything they have for what they believe in. This was TT's great contribution. (John Wickham)

I remember TT. I can see him now: a man of absolute integrity. If there was one man who has suffered for politics and for championing the cause of the poor downtrodden that man was TT Lewis. Truly he paid the price of his commitment. He was a dedicated socialist and cared for the common man even though he himself was not a man of affluence. He could have easily gone over to the other side and as a white could have made it easy on himself. (Sir Frederick Smith)

The fact that Lewis could have chosen to join the establishment and be welcomed with open arms was repeated time and again in the interviews. That he did not take this option was seen by almost all as a distinguishing characteristic of his integrity and firmness of purpose.

Lewis was indeed a rare type of Barbadian white even when compared to others who had attempted to improve the lot of the island's dispossessed. Whites such as Sir John Gay Alleyne appear to have invariably been motivated by a patrician, almost genteel, sense of obligation. Their benefaction was handed down. It appeared intended to atone for shortcomings of fellow whites. But Lewis' origins and disposition could never qualify him as a benevolent aristocrat. "TT used to say: 'Don't bother to blame me for the past 300 years, I may be white but I ain't so old.' " (Tony Hinds)

Tony Hinds in the 1940s (left) and in 1995 (above)

No one since the days of Clennel Wickham (see chapter 4) had endured more in the cause of democracy. While still a relatively young man, and with family responsibilities, he jeopardized his economic security and ultimately his health through his passionate championing of this cause.

Sir Hugh Springer: In those times, when any white man showed any consideration towards black people this was a major milestone. Whites and blacks would live their separate and isolated lives. Many whites in senior positions would never meet or speak to ordinary black people during the ordinary working day. They had no feeling for the conditions of life which operated outside their own environment. I remember one well-placed white man who got to know me and I can't help feeling that he always valued our relationship more than I probably did because it offered him an opportunity to see into the world of the black people living in Barbados.

Author: What sort of role would you see Lewis playing in today's Barbados?

Sir Hugh: You don't have to take the sort of stands today that you had to then. So I guess you probably wouldn't have heard much from TT in today's Barbados.

Sir Hugh Springer in the 1940s (left) and in 1992 (above)

Inevitably, Lewis is remembered differently by different sectors of society. To the black Barbadian of his time he is seen as an unlikely, but curious and admired ally in the struggle against the ruling oligarchy – a man of faith in the struggle for better working conditions in the island. Crucially, he had proven himself a noble champion making secondary education free – a defining characteristic of successful societies in the twentieth century, and the best proven way to boost female education. Poor whites saw him as one of their own: a self-taught fellow white who had untypically and admirably risen to a prominent position in the island's legislature. But someone who had not forgotten his origins either. In fact, to the contrary. Together with many coloureds, for whom he was also a hero, lower income whites see his greatest achievements as twofold. First, the abolition from the statute books of the Occupancy Tax which tended to hit them as an economic group. Secondly, his ability to organize the Bridgetown clerks in an attempt to resist mercantile pressure.

Establishment whites either grudgingly admired his tenacity or viewed him as a traitor – one who sold out to a cause that would further undermine their already crumbling political position within a changing social order. The most generous of them regretted that his talents were not put to better use in the service of their part of the white community.

The fact that he was a white man championing the black underclass was an awkward puzzle to the white establishment. He understood the gradations of Barbadian society and clearly perceived that there was a white working class – store clerks, plantation overseers and bookkeepers – which had no possessions but its labour. Thus his political orientation was the product of his social experience. (Sir James Tudor writing in the *Daily Nation*, 31 July 1989)

For a Barbadian white, Lewis appears a man far ahead of his time. Aside from his ability to show that race need not be an overriding factor in Barbadian politics, he demonstrated that in his personal life it was equally irrelevant. He showed why such a thing as the universal franchise was to be welcomed – not conceded reluctantly; and that the path to upward social mobility for all Barbadians was possible by means of free access to the sort of education from which he had never benefited.

The great Bermuda Triangle of Barbadian politics, or the Black Hole if you will, is the total indifference of present day politicians to the experiences of people still alive who sat in the pre-independence legislature and wrestled with the enormous problems of the day. TT definitely belongs to the pre-1966 era. But even there he was different. The majority of us marched into the future without properly preparing for it. His political outlook prepared Barbados for a future which was not then on the horizon. This is why his ideas appeared so radical and so upsetting to some. He was a futurist and he saw that the future worked. (Sir James Tudor)

The reasons why people either stand out from their social milieu or are subsumed by it have vexed scientists and sociologists for years as they try to unravel and categorize the effects of nature versus nurture. Since people are the complex products of both genes and environmental influences, it seems that no single chain of causality can be attributed exclusively to either factor. In the case of Lewis, it is intriguing to speculate about what may have brought out his outspoken nonconformism, his deep sense of humanism and his desire to reshape colonial Barbados when few or none of his contemporaries of the same class and colour were visibly doing likewise. Was it his origins and early upbringing in the rural parishes and the poorer quarters of Bridgetown that made him that way? Did his view of the way society operated emerge gradually or did he experience something of a "road to Damascus" conversion? Answers to these questions, never entirely reliable even in the presence of dependable information, become ever more elusive when sources of data are patchy or anecdotal. Most of the answers will never be known fully.

But when Lewis did decide to strike out in defence of what he perceived to be right and just, the degree of social ostracism he would have encountered from many local whites was immense:

I always remember TT walking down Broad Street with me when he spotted a big, fat black woman, Ruby I think her name was. Anyway, TT rushes up to her and plants a full-blooded kiss on the lady and says "wha' happenin' man, I en' seen yuh in so long . . ." In those days this was unheard of behaviour and would have certainly been noticed on the street. But that was just like the man. Didn't care who he offended by doing something like this. (Sir Alexander Hoyos)

TT was an individualist and had strong views about things. He had to be a strong man to find himself separated from his white friends because of the stance he took. TT was a heart man, not a party man. He could not be directed by a man or a crowd. In TT's era, it was difficult to see a white man striking out and coming over to blacks, but because he was strong, he could. (Sir Frank Walcott)

Nonetheless, the extent of his migration through one political party after another within the space of a decade and a half is quite staggering. Measured by any political yardstick, such a rapid pilgrimage would appear to demonstrate opportunism and a tendency to move with the political fashion. But contemporaries recall otherwise:

TT couldn't live easily in a democracy that looked for sides. By that I mean that he could not live in a rigid party system for long. He was truly independent in his thoughts. Being strong-willed, temperamental and independent, TT was not one to compromise easily. His tongue was very sharp and he would always tell you what the score was. (Sir Frank Walcott)

> TT moved from party to party, but they all let him down. The reason was that he was a seeker after political truth. He expected politics to have some inner truth and for it to be for the benefit of the mass of the people. For this he sacrificed his job and his marriage and ended up in personal disaster in so many cases. Perhaps he was too eager to find the truth. (Sir Alexander Hoyos)

> This journey from party to party casts no reflection on his character or judgements, because he never shifted from his basic principles of an abiding concern for the poor, the dispossessed and the deprived. (Sir James Tudor writing in the *Daily Nation*, 31 July 1989)

Thus, to see Lewis as a political acrobat would be demeaning. It is true that Lewis never seemed happy within the confines of a political party. In the heat of political battle, he would move through three: the Congress Party, the BLP and the DLP. In this he was not alone. Political contemporaries such as Wynter Crawford and Edwy Talma would move through the same three in their political lives. Yet in Lewis we witness an agonized struggle for notions of the ideal in politics – a struggle reflecting restlessness and a constant searching for some greater political truth that transcended political opportunism. Indeed, some of his political choices could hardly be described as astute. One gets the impression that party obligations and the reciprocal and lively anticipation of favours to come from party membership did not motivate him. None seemed to him to fully represent an honest vehicle for the expression of his own political ideals. It certainly seems that no party possessed enough crusading zeal to sustain his attention. Logically, therefore, one must assume that had he lived, he would sooner or later have left the DLP.

One eminent Barbadian calls Lewis the great neglected statesman of the country. But although certainly neglected, it seems impossible to escape the conclusion that Lewis' uncompromising and often adversarial nature, while adding to his well-deserved reputation for honesty and integrity, detracted greatly from his potential to demonstrate statesmanlike qualities. It was noteworthy that at no time in any of the interviews did anyone observe that Lewis possessed the makings of a great premier.

Despite the vigour and vitality with which Lewis carried himself and his ideas, elements of tragedy stalk his character. From his various political struggles he emerges penniless, in poor health and separate from family. Any claims to common heroism rest squarely but not insignificantly, on the fact that his considerable contribution to political life cost him everything but his integrity.

Lewis was a man thinking far ahead of his times. He took on the power of the vestry and succeeded in abolishing the hated and highly regressive Occupancy Tax. He was forthright in his championship of the cause of free secondary education from which generations of Barbadians, including the author, have subsequently benefited. The level of articulateness with which he was able to set out his ideas bears profound testimony to the notion that intellectual excellence can push its way past humble origins and hard knocks. On this basis, one may even venture to label Lewis a brilliant man.

Yet his true role, whose significance cannot be underestimated in any society governed, as is Barbados, by constitutional democratic principles and the rule of law, is that he provided critical, insightful and forward looking guidance on the important issues of the day. Stripped of nonessential fluff, all assessments of Lewis return to his core role as an improver, a doer and a social critic. A critic in the most authentic and sincere sense of that word.

Like a native champion of truth and openness, he drew attention to his own society's structural and systematic abuses of power. He exposed the false appearances of that society for all to see. He gave expression to rank and file Barbadians' deepest sense of how they felt they ought to be entitled to live. He showed the principles and procedures by which one might set things right. He never failed to be uncritical of those in power (even those among his allies) whose views he considered were misdirected. He was a critical patriot and a man committed to democratic politics that were, for him, never democratic enough.

APPENDIXES

APPENDIX ONE

Barbados: Geographical Location

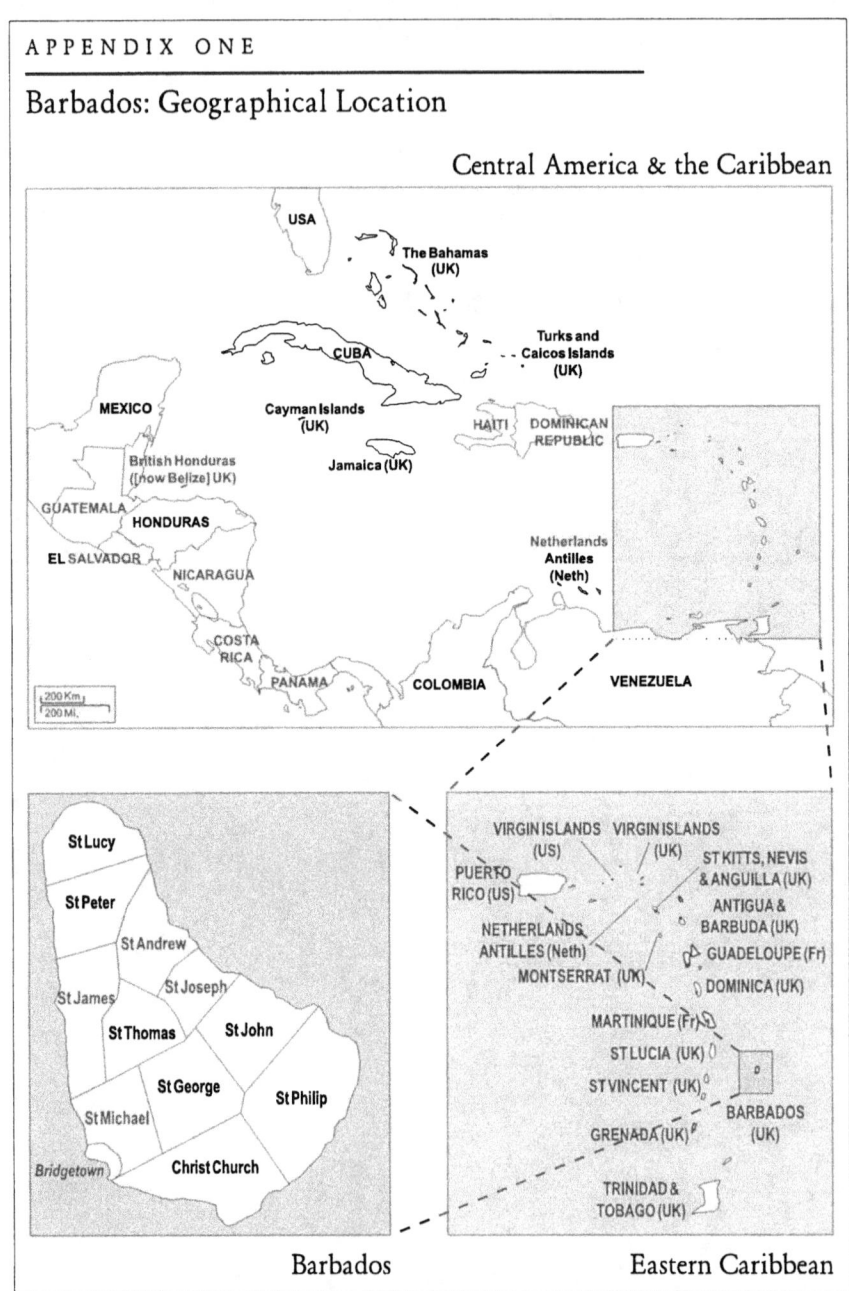

Barbados   Eastern Caribbean

NOTE: In addition to geographical location, this graphic portrays the colonial status of territories in the Caribbean Basin in the 1940s. In the case of colonies, the name of the administering metropolitan power is given in brackets.

Appendixes

APPENDIX TWO

The City of Bridgetown (1948): Tramping Ground of TT Lewis

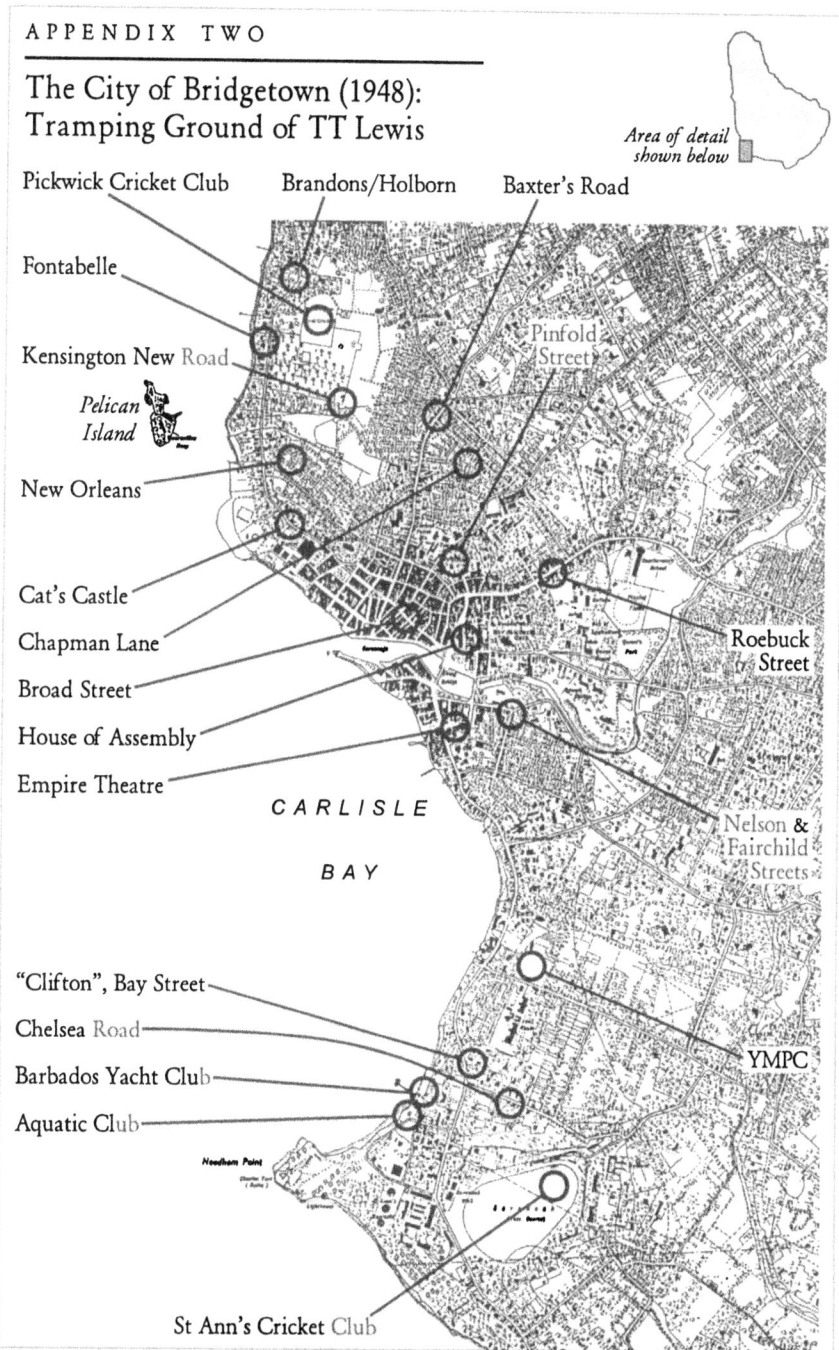

Area of detail shown below

- Pickwick Cricket Club
- Brandons/Holborn
- Baxter's Road
- Fontabelle
- Kensington New Road
- Pelican Island
- New Orleans
- Cat's Castle
- Chapman Lane
- Broad Street
- House of Assembly
- Empire Theatre
- CARLISLE BAY
- Pinfold Street
- Roebuck Street
- Nelson & Fairchild Streets
- "Clifton", Bay Street
- Chelsea Road
- Barbados Yacht Club
- Aquatic Club
- YMPC
- St Ann's Cricket Club

Depicted on this map are the main parts of Bridgetown referenced in this book. Interestingly, Pelican Island is still a separate landmass, prior to its being linked to the mainland during the building of the deep water harbour in 1961. (Section of a town plan of Bridgetown published by the Directorate of Colonial Surveys, UK, 1948)

APPENDIX THREE

Barbadian Constitutional Structure:
Part 1 – The Old Representative System (1640s–1946)

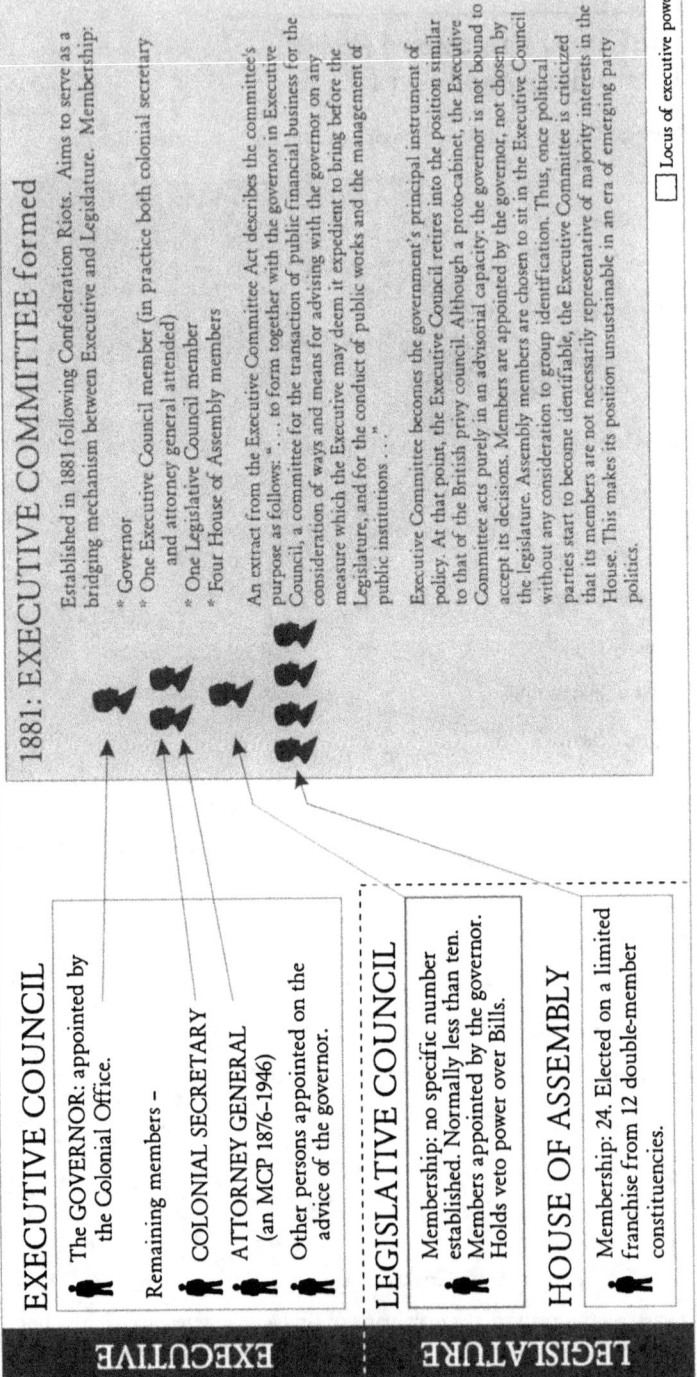

APPENDIX THREE

Barbadian Constitutional Structure:
Part 2 – The Bushe Experiment (1946–1954)

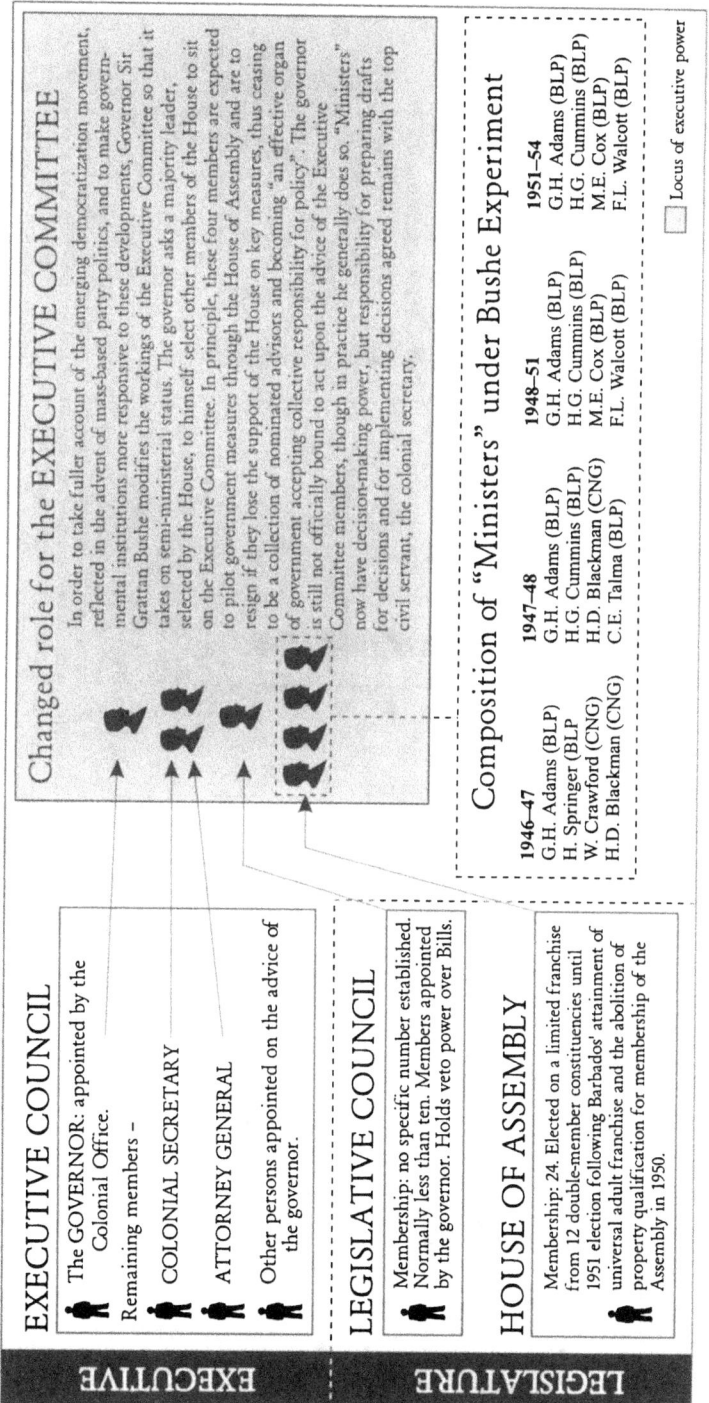

APPENDIX THREE

Barbadian Constitutional Structure:
Part 3 – Ministerial Government Introduced (1954)

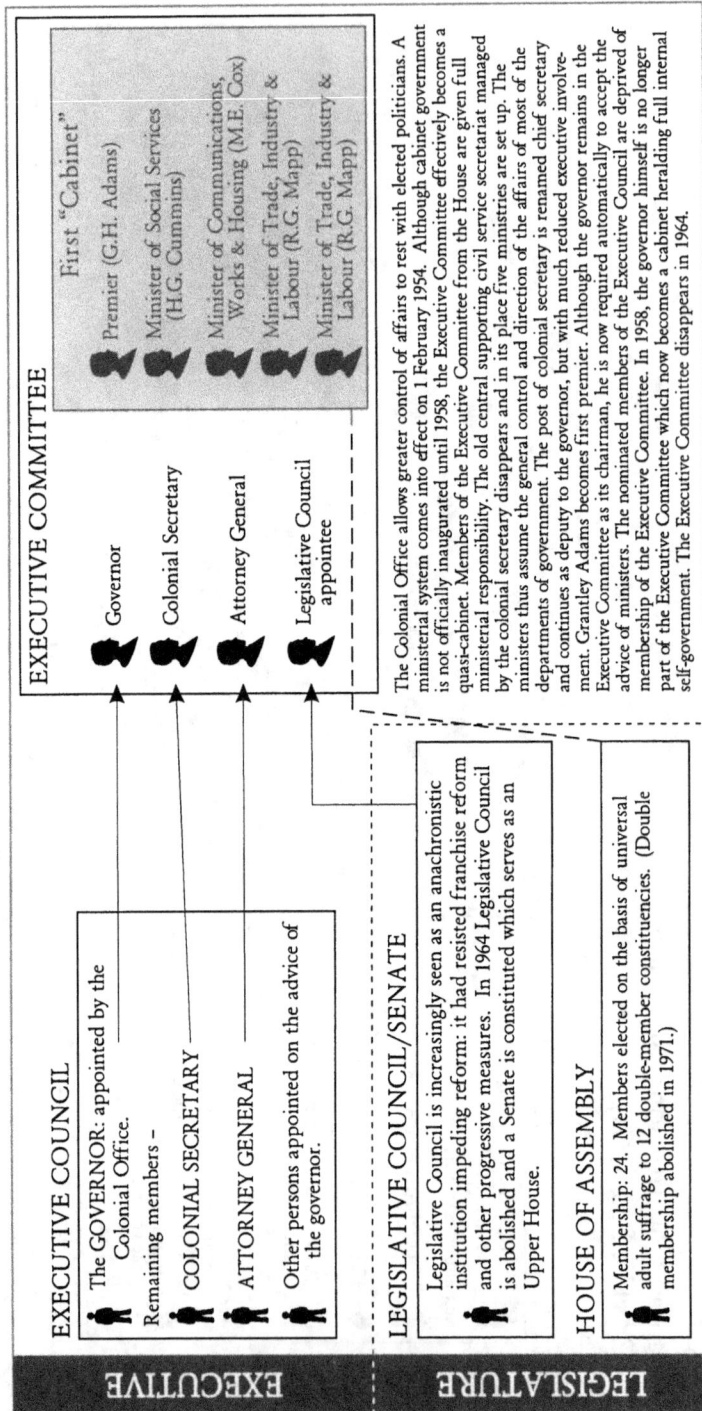

Appendixes

APPENDIX FOUR

Barbados Election Results: 1942

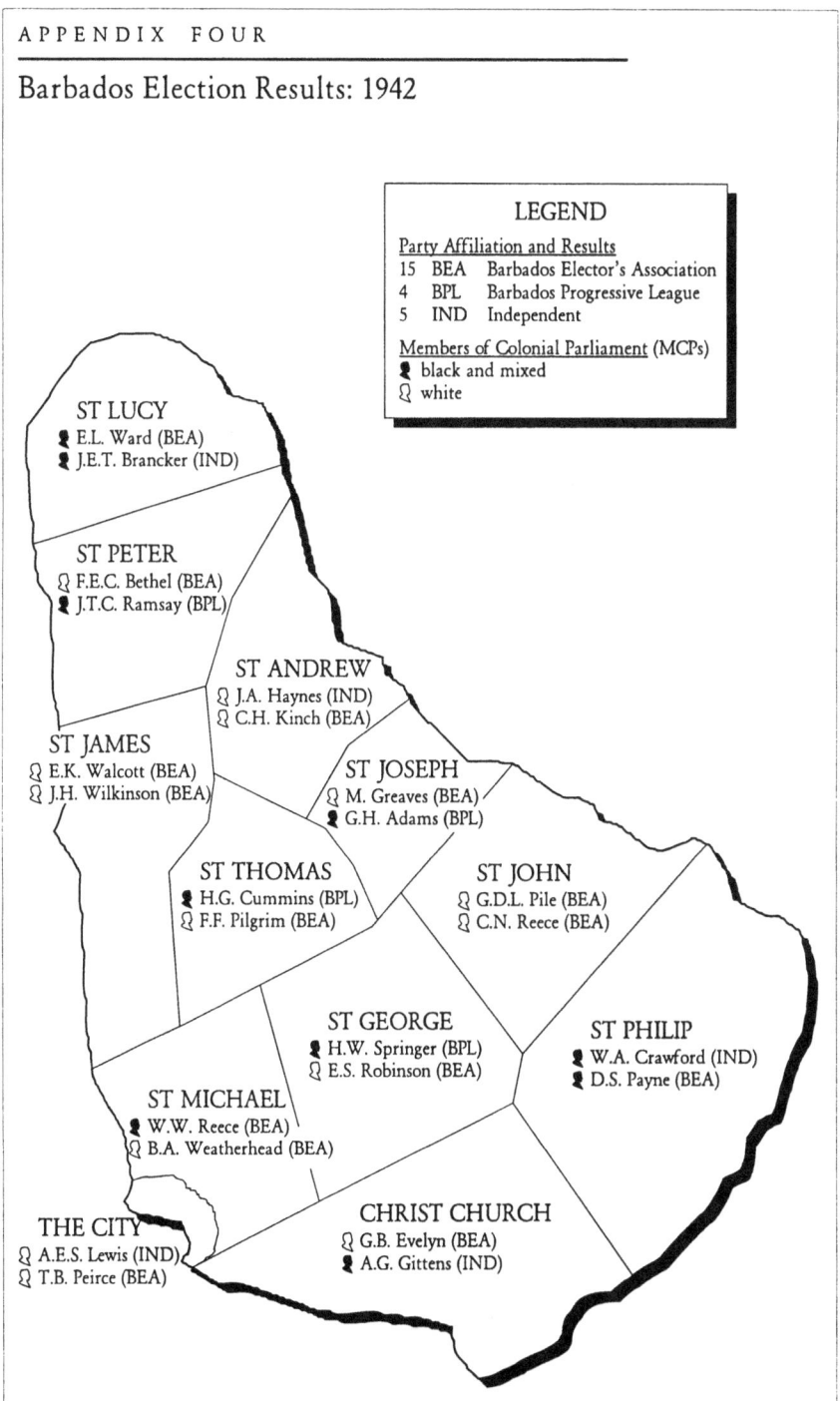

APPENDIX FOUR

Barbados Election Results: 1944

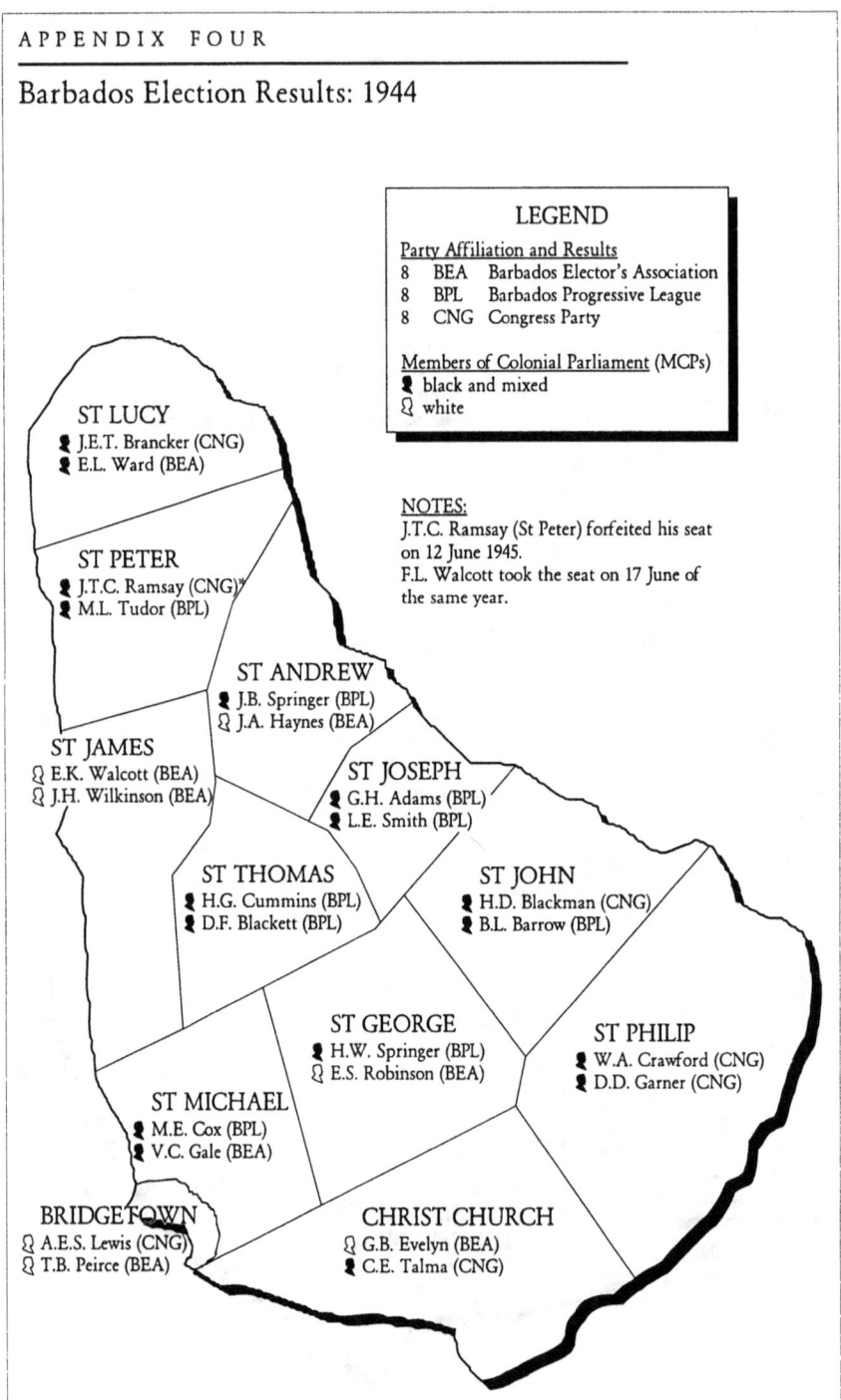

APPENDIX FOUR

Barbados Election Results: 1946

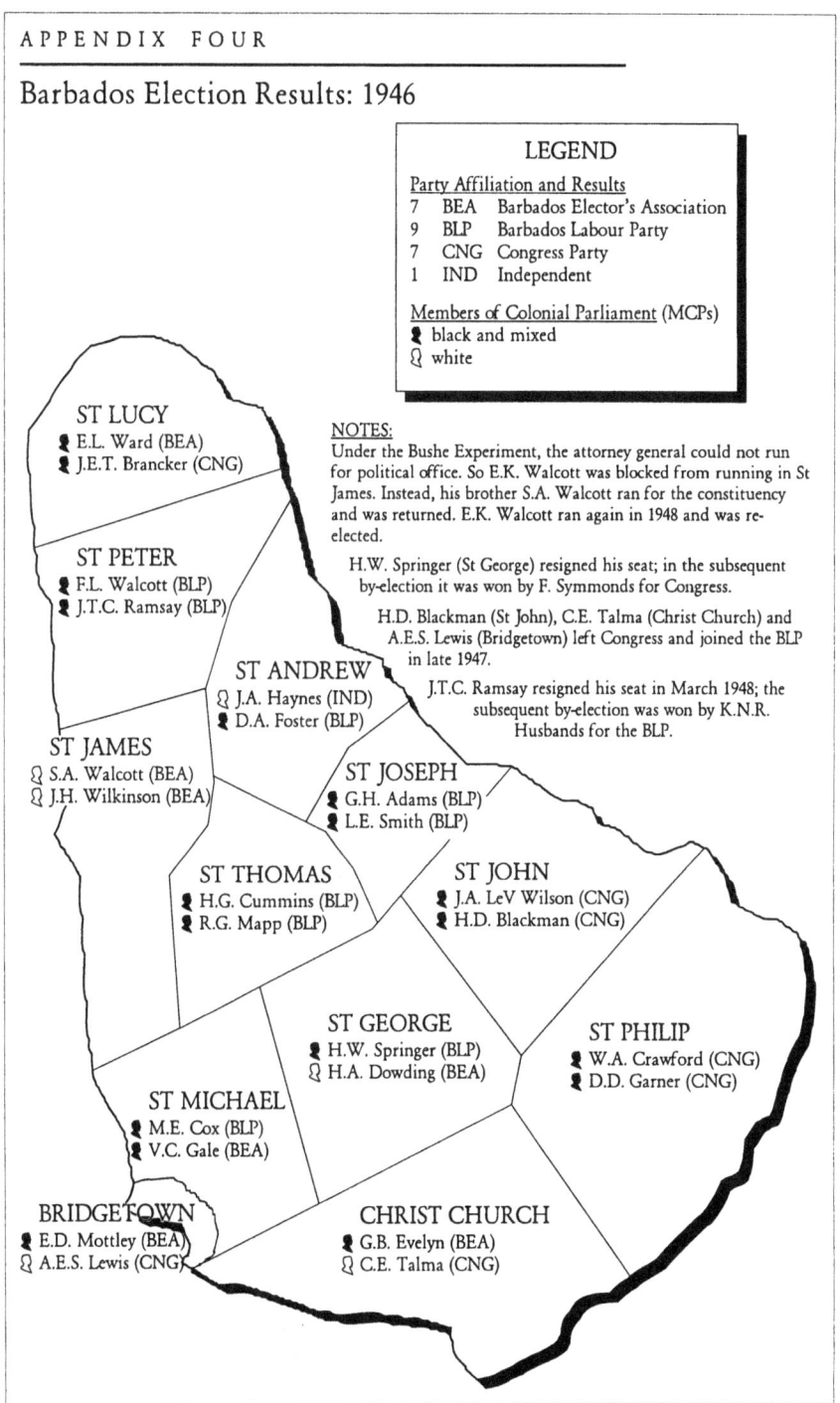

APPENDIX FOUR

Barbados Election Results: 1948

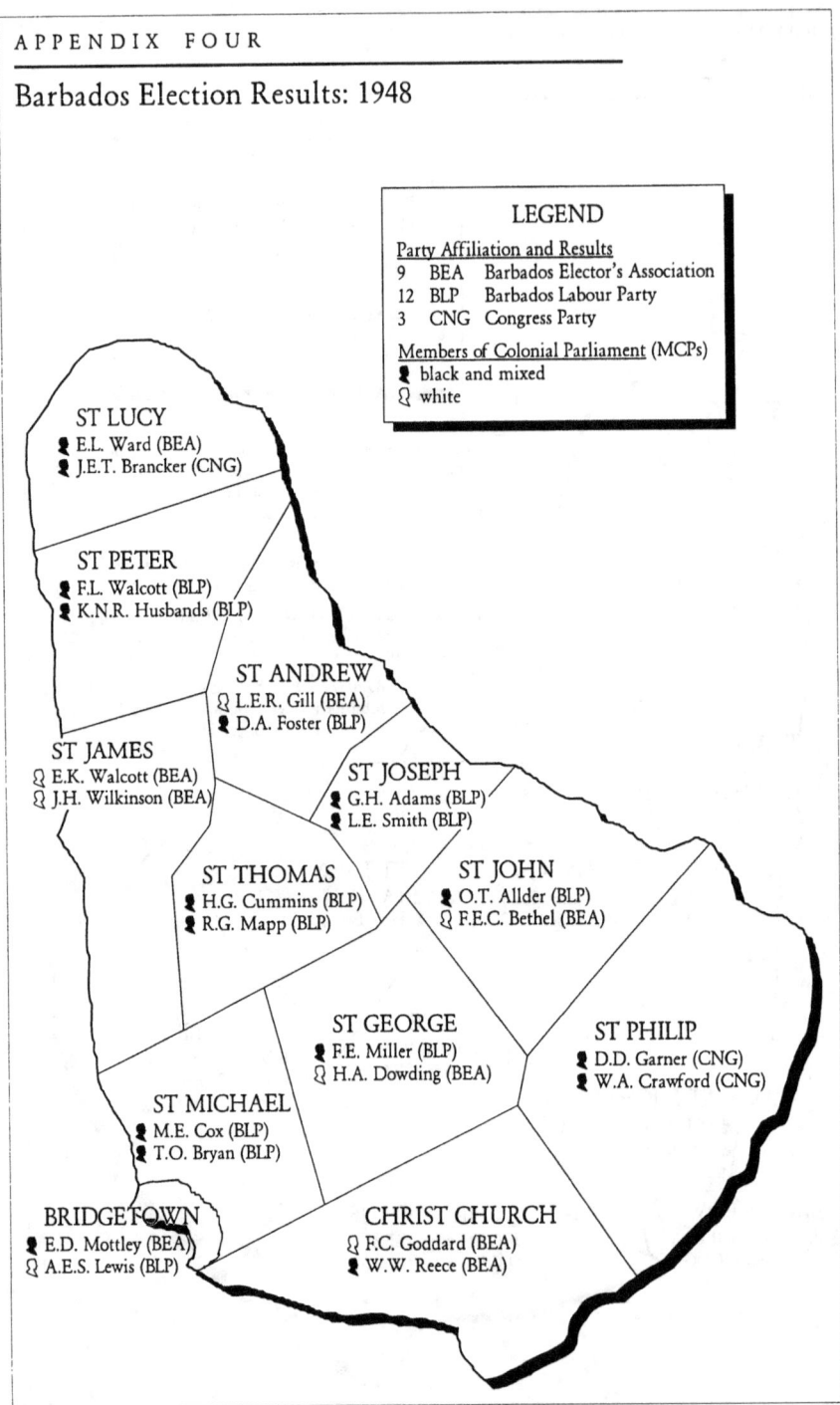

APPENDIX FOUR

Barbados Election Results: 1951

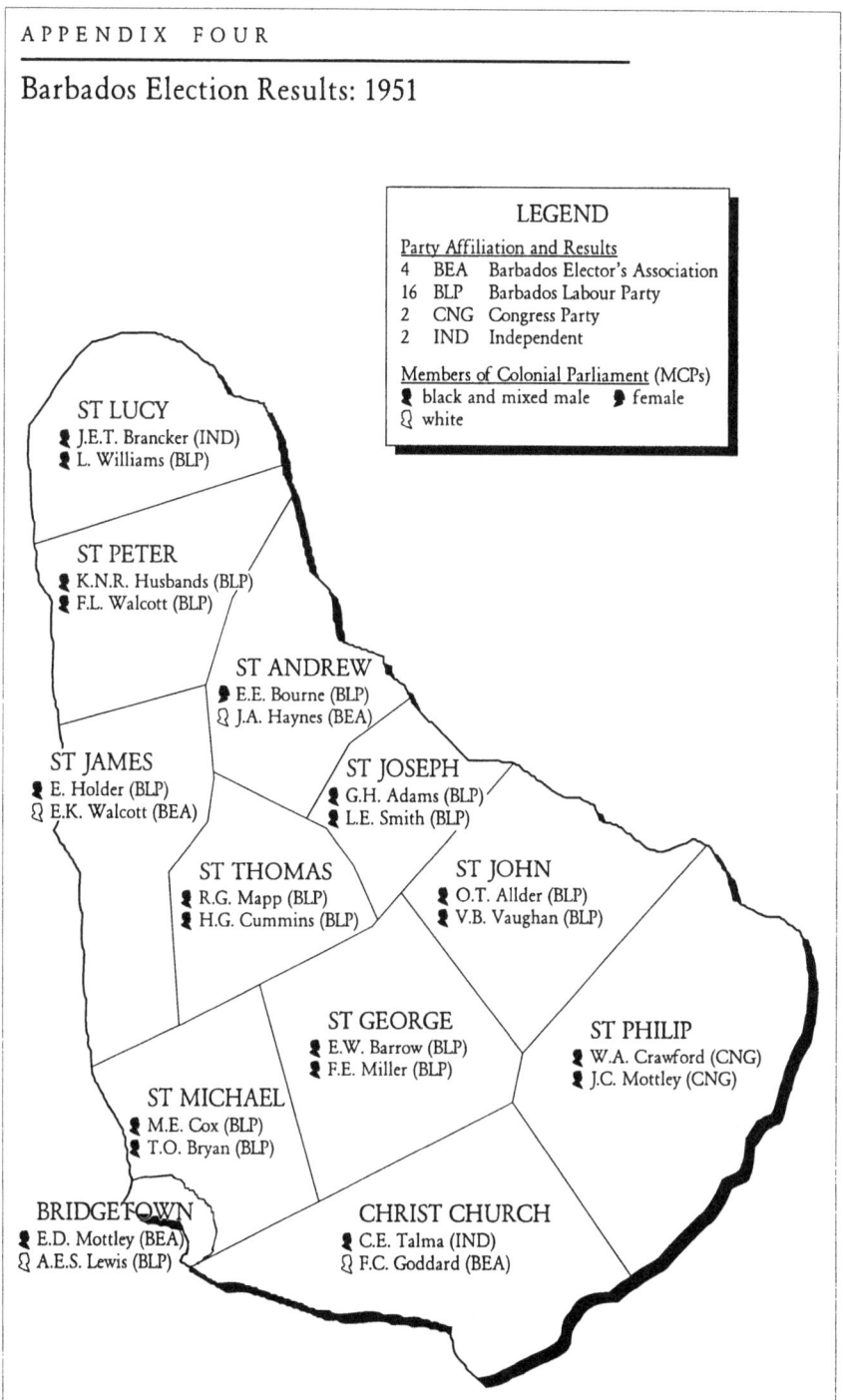

APPENDIX FOUR

Barbados Election Results: 1956

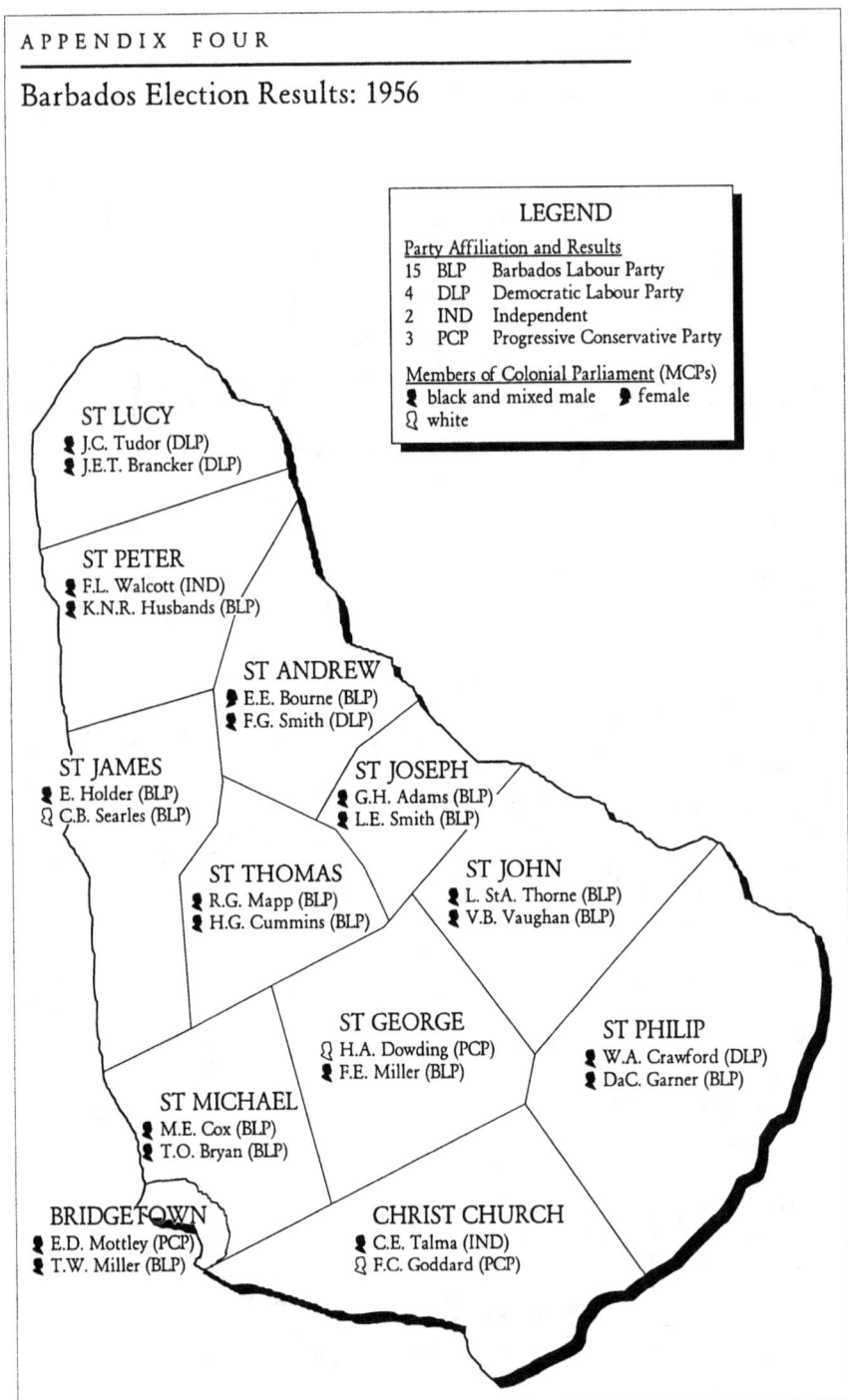

APPENDIX FIVE

The Changed Colour Composition of the House

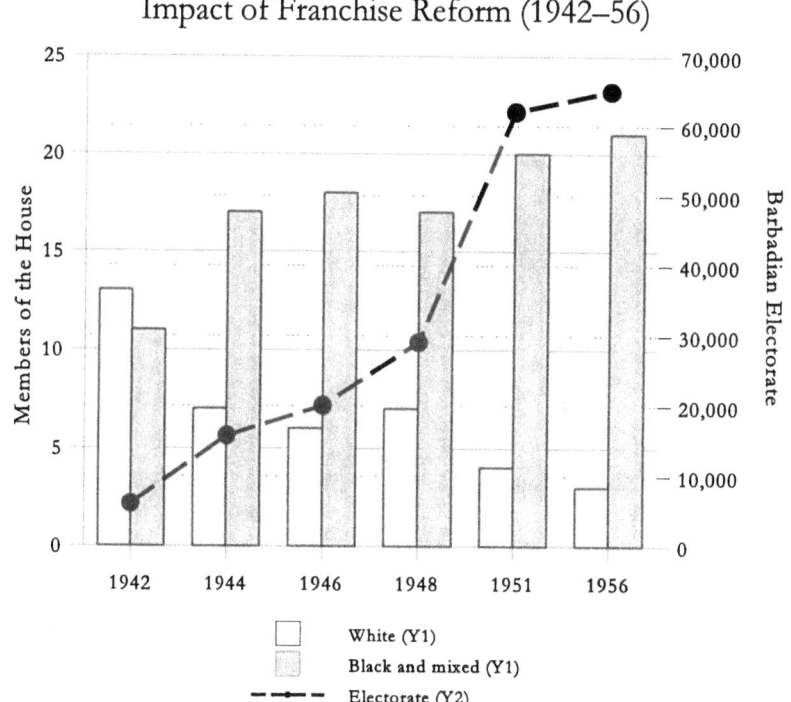

The above graph demonstrates the tremendous erosive effect of the expanded franchise on the grip of white politicians in the Barbados House of Assembly in the period 1942–56. Although not depicted above, one hundred years earlier, in 1841, when the electorate was only 1,100 all members of the House were white. By 1905 the picture had hardly changed at all: in a population of approximately 200,000, only 1,692 citizens were eligible to vote in that year.

By 1911, the figure had risen to 1,986. By the 1940s, however, as the assault on the property qualification gained momentum, the number of nonwhites eligible to vote increased significantly. As a natural consequence, the number of whites elected to the House declined. The process continued beyond the 1951 elections – the first to be held under the one-person-one-vote system. The 1966 elections were the first to produce a House without any white members of parliament.

APPENDIX SIX

Family Names of the Barbadian White Elite in the 1920s

In 1920s Barbados, the planter and commercial classes accounted for the bulk of the island's wealth. If one looks only at the agricultural sector, the list of planter names enumerated below represents about one-half of the total locally owned portion of the Barbadian sugar industry. The estimated percentage breakdown of its ownership components is given in the pie diagram on this page.

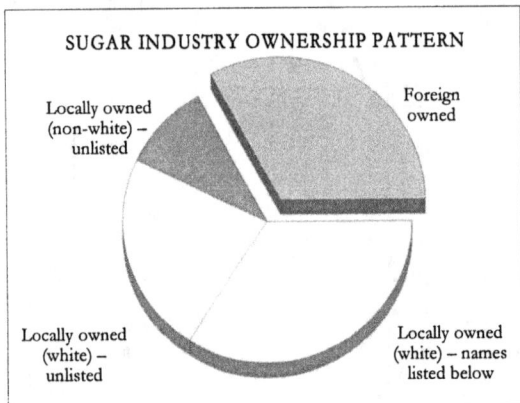

The diagram depicts estimated ownership in the 1920s based on acreage possessed by each of the constituent sectors.

Foreign ownership of the Barbadian sugar industry in the 1920s, though substantial and standing at approximately one-third, was still considerably smaller than in most of the other larger British sugar-producing colonies of the time such as Jamaica, Guyana and Trinidad & Tobago. Of the island's total of approximately 200 estates at the time, some of the more significant foreign holdings were Drax Hall and Kendal – which shared 1,500 acres between them – Pool, Cleland, Farley Hill, Newton and Seawell. The most prominent sugar estates owned by nonwhites were Harrow in St Philip (400 acres), Malvern in St John (300 acres) and Babbs in St Lucy (100 acres). Interestingly, about 30 mills existed in the 1920s – about half of which would still have been wind powered at that time.

PROMINENT WHITE FAMILIES AND THEIR MAJOR PROPERTY INTERESTS:

Alleyne: Plantations – 3 in St Lucy: Bromefield, Bourbon and Epworth.
Austin: Commerce – Gardiner Austin. Member of "Big Six".
Bryden: Commerce – A.S. Bryden.
Challenor: Commerce – R&G Challenor. Member of "Big Six".

Appendixes

Challenor: Plantations – 3 in St Joseph: Blackmans, Fisherpond and Easy Hall. Part owner of Andrews Factory.

Chandler: Plantations – in St John (Todds, Henley), in St Lucy (Alleyndale) and in St Peter (Portland).

Cox: Plantations – 3 in St Joseph (Castle Grant, Retreat and Redland). Part owner of Andrews Factory.

DaCosta: Commerce – DaCosta & Co. Member of "Big Six".

Evelyn: Plantations – several in Christ Church (including Kingsland, Adams Castle and Wotton). Kingsland Factory.

Hawkins: Plantations – four in St Philip (Foursquare and Grove) and Christ Church (Lower Greys and Hannays). Foursquare Factory.

Haynes: Plantations – three branches of the family held at least 10 estates in various parishes including Clifton Hall, Bath and Bush Hall (St John).

Leacock: Commerce – Mussons. Member of "Big Six".

Mahon: Plantations – 4 in St Thomas (Vaucluse, Lion Castle, Farmers and Dunscombe). Vaucluse Factory.

Manning: Plantations – 3 in St Lucy (Spring Hall), St James (Westmoreland) and St Thomas (Applewhaites). Spring Hall Factory.

Manning: Commerce – Manning & Co. Member of "Big Six".

Massiah: Plantations – 3 in St James (Springfield, Taitts and Sion Hill).

Pile: Plantations – four estates in St George (including Bulkley, Boarded Hall, Stepney and Carmichael). Bulkley Factory.

Robinson: Plantations – 1 estate in St George (Constant).

Sealy: Plantations – three branches of the family. Several estates throughout the island including The Valley in St George.

Skeete: Plantations – 4 estates with acreage in four parishes St Philip (Edgecumbe), Christ Church (Bentley), St George (Frenchs) and St John (Byde Mill).

Smith: Plantations – 5 in St Philip (Thicket, Sandford, Mapps, Three Houses and Fortescue). Three Houses Factory.

Ward: Plantations – 3 in Christ Church (Cane Vale, Maxwell and Warners).

Wilkinson: Plantations – Carrington Estates Ltd. Lancaster estate in St James.

Wilkinson: Commerce – Wilkinson & Haynes. Member of "Big Six".

Williams: Plantations – Joes River estate in St Joseph (including Frizers and Mellowes).

ACKNOWLEDGEMENT: The information in this appendix was prepared with the kind assistance of Ronnie Hughes.

SOURCE: E. Goulburn Sinckler, *The Barbados Handbook*, London, Duckworth & Co. (1913). See part III: "Sugar works in Barbados", pp. 81–102.

BIBLIOGRAPHY

Periodicals

Barbados Advocate
Barbados Annual Review
Barbados Observer
The Beacon
Daily Nation
The Economist

Hansard
Herald
Outlook
Sunday Sun
The Torch

Printed and Unpublished Sources

The Adams Collection, Barbados Department of Archives, (Reference Z17/4/10).
Greaves, G.C. "At the cross roads – a survey of big cricket in the West Indies 1924–36" (undated pamphlet).
Lewis, A.E.S. Letters and Memoranda.
Minute Book of the BLP Executive for 1952. Bridgetown, 1952.
Rules of the Barbados Clerks' Union, undated.
West Indies Royal Commission: Proceedings of the Investigation in Barbados. Bridgetown, 1939.

Books and Articles

Alleyne, C. "Later clubs". In *100 Years of Organized Cricket in Barbados, 1892–1992*. Bridgetown.
The Applicant, The Grand Lodge of Scotland, Edinburgh, [undated].
Arendt, H. *The Origins of Totalitarianism*. New York, 1958.
Atwell, N.G.D., ed. *Yearbook of Freemasonry in Barbados and the Eastern Caribbean*. Volume I. Bridgetown, 1985.
Carr, E.H. *What is History?* London, 1961.
Cheltenham, R.H. "Constitutional and political development in Barbados 1946–66", PhD dissertation, University of Manchester, 1970.
Cozier, E.L. *Caribbean Newspaperman: The Life and Times of Jimmy Cozier*. Bridgetown, 1987.

Bibliography

Democratic Labour Party. *Democratic Labour Party – Ten Years' of Service (1955–65)*. Bridgetown, 1965.

Editorial Committee of Research Lodge Amity. *Yearbook of Freemasonry in Barbados and the Eastern Caribbean* (Volume II). 1987 (no publication details).

Emmanuel, P. "Shifts in the political balance of power: trade unions and political parties". In *Emancipation III: Aspects of the Post-Slavery Experience of Barbados*. Barbados, 1988.

Hoyos, F.A. *Barbados: A History from Amerindians to Independence*. London, 1978.

Hoyos, F.A. *Grantley Adams and the Social Revolution*. London, 1974 (1988).

Hoyos, F.A. *The Quiet Revolutionary*. London, 1984.

Hoyos, F.A. *The Rise of West Indian Democracy: The Life and Times of Sir Grantley Adams*. Barbados, 1963.

Hunte, K. "Twenty-five years of education in an independent Barbados: a critical review and the future agenda", Memorial lecture in honour of Rudolph Greenidge, Barbados, 1991.

Hutchinson, L.C. *Behind the Mace: An Introduction to the Barbados House of Assembly*. Barbados, 1951.

Jemmott, R., and D. Carter "Barbadian Educational Developments (1933–93): An Interpretive Analysis", unpublished, 1994.

Karch, C. "From the plantocracy to BS & T: crisis and transformation of the Barbadian socioeconomy, 1865–1937". In *Emancipation IV – A Series of Lectures to Commemorate the 150th Anniversary of Emancipation*, edited by W. Marshall. Jamaica, 1993.

Knight, S. *The Brotherhood – The Secret World of the Freemasons*. London, 1985.

Lewis, G.K. *The Growth of the Modern West Indies*. New York, 1968.

Lowy, M. *The Politics of Combined and Uneven Development*. London, 1981.

Mandel, E. *Revolutionary Marxism Today*, London, 1979.

Mark, F. *The History of the Barbados Workers' Union*. Barbados, undated [but probably 1966].

Emancipation III: Aspects of the Post-Slavery Experience in Barbados. Barbados, 1988.

Marshall, W., ed, *Emancipation IV – A Series of Lectures to Commemorate the 150th Anniversary of Emancipation*. Jamaica, 1993.

Newton, E. "Education policy and human resources development in Barbados – a case study". Unpublished study prepared for UNESCO/UWI Workshop on Methodologies used in Educational Policy Analysis as Related to Human Resources, Planning and Management in the Caribbean. Barbados, 1991.

Phillips, A. "The Parliament of Barbados, 1639–1989". In *Journal of the Barbados Museum and Historical Society*, No. 4, 1990.

Popper, K. *The Open Society and its Enemies*. New York, 1945 (reprint 1966).

Richardson, B. *Panama Money in Barbados (1900–1920)*. Knoxville, 1985.

Ross, P.M. (Ed), *The Victoria Lodge: One Hundred Years of Masonic Work (1887–1987)*. Bridgetown, 1987.

Sandiford, K. "100 years of organized cricket in Barbados, 1892–1992". In *100 Years of Organized Cricket in Barbados, 1892–1992*. Bridgetown, 1992.

Schapiro, L. *Totalitarianism*. London, 1972.

Sinckler, E. Goulburn. *The Barbados Handbook*. London, 1913.

Stoute, E. "The Poor Whites of Barbados" (Part IV). The *Bajan* (February 1972).

INDEX

Adams, Grantley, xxi, 36, 58, 88, 89, 90, 97, 99, 102, 107-108, 124ff, 173; break with Barrow, 168-169; break with Lewis, 160-166; and controlled capitalism, 158; on censorship, 74-75; on franchise reform, 70, 73; on labour movement, 124; and Lewis demonstration, 137-142, 146; on Liberal Association, 60; photos of, 102, 138, 140, 142, 144, 154, 163; rivalry with Crawford, 88-89, 100-101; and speech at UN, 124, 135n 142; on sugar industry, 86n; on war effort, 79

Adult suffrage *See* Franchise reform

Airy Hill, birthplace of TT Lewis, 2-3

Allder, Owen T., xvi, 14, 90, 181n; on Lewis, 64, 69; on Lewis demonstration, 139; on revenue equalization, 159

Alleyne, Charles, 41n

Alleyne, John Gay, 185

Alleyne, Warren, 85n

Aquatic Club, 24, 27-28

Arendt, Hannah, 86n

Armstrong, Geoffrey, 21n

Atwell, N.G.D. "Gotch", xvi; on Lewis, 53, 54n

Barbados: class structure in, 117-121; constitutional structure, 194-196; cricket in, 29-32; economy and sugar in, 5, 22n, 67; elections during 1942–56; *see also* Elections; freemasonry in, 46-54; legislature, 6-7; militia in, 42n; monetary system of, 6; political development in, 6, 7, 21, 57-110; race relations in, xxv-xxvi, 13, 19-21, 34, 37, 47-50, 58, 117-121; society at turn of century, 4-5; theatre in, 27-29; war effort in, 65-66, 75-80

Barbados Advocate, 66, 90, 91, 183

Barbados Battalion of the South Caribbean Force, 76-77

Barbados Clerks' Union (BCU), xvi, xvii, xviii, 13, 106, 110-121, 130-131, 139, 183; failure of, 117; victimization of members, 115-116; *see also* Clerks

Barbados Elector's Association (BEA), 60-64, 84n, 88, 91, 98, 108, 124, 152, 171

Barbados Labour Party (BLP), xvi, xxi, 58, 59, 63, 84n, 87, 101, 107, 108, 122ff, 146, 149-166, 168-170

Barbados Liberal Association, 59-60, 84n

Barbados National Party (BNP), 60, 61

Barbados Progressive League (BPL), 59, 61, 66, 70, 71, 78, 84n, 87, 89, 90, 91, 99

Barbados Volunteer Force (BVF), xxiv, 33-35, 49, 75-77

Barbados Workers' Union (BWU), xviii, xix, 11, 13, 58, 60, 66, 89, 110, 117, 118, 130-131, 136, 137, 143, 145, 146, 157

Barrow, Errol, 18, 27, 58, 76, 89, 156, 157, 160, 161, 162, 166, 171ff; break with Adams, 168-169

Beacon, 131, 136

Beckles, Hilary, 148n

209

Index

Beckles, Seymour, xvi; on Lewis demonstration, 137

Bethel Hall, 25, 36

Black intelligentsia, 8, 25, 36

Blackman, H.D., 102, 107

Blacks, economic conditions of, 7, 8, 10-11, 67-69; migration among, 8; social position of, 5, 6

Bookkeepers, 10-14

Bourne, J.E.T. "Jonny", xvi; on Lewis, 35, 53, 106

Brancker, Theodore, xvi, 18, 36, 85n, 107, 166

Bridgetown constituency, 67-69, 97; map of, 193

Broome, Joe: on growth of party politics, 91-92

Bryan, T.O. "Orrie", 137, 138; photos of, 101, 154

Bryan, W.H. & Co., 16

Burke, Hammond, xvi, 31, 110, 114, 122; on Lewis demonstration, 140; on Lewis' dismissal from Central Agency, 133

Burke, Irwin, xvii, 112, 118

Bushe, Grattan, 58; political reforms of, 88, 99-100, 152, 155, 195

Carr, E.H., xxiv

Cash boys, 17

Cecil, Robert, xvii, 17

Censorship, in Barbados, 74-75

Central Agency Ltd., 17, 19, 38, 41, 52, 126-135, 136, 165; and Lewis settlement, 143-147

Challenge Cup, 29

Chandler, J.W., xvii; on Airy Hill, 3

Cheltenham, R.L., 109n, 158, 166n, 167n, 181n

Christine, Andrew, xvii; on Lewis' dismissal from Central Agency, 133

Class, in Barbadian history, 19-21, 117-120

Clerks, status of, 9, 11, 12, 13, 17, 75; *see also* Barbados Clerks' Union

Collymore, Ellice, xvii; on TT Lewis, 2, 17, 43, 53

Collymore, Frank, 15, 26-28, 43, 81, 178

Coloureds, 4, 5, 14, 28

Confederation Riots, 69

Congress Party, xxi, 87-110, 124, 157, 158

Constitutional structure: Bushe Experiment (1946–1954), 195; ministerial government (1954–), 196; Old Representative System (1652–1946), 194

Contract Act (1840), 7

Cox, Mencea, 137, 153; photos of, 154, 163

Cozier, E.L. "Jimmy", xvii; 64; on the BEA, 62-63, 84n; on Lewis 25, 41n, 53, 82, 86n, 138n, 167n; on Lewis' split with the BLP, 165

Crawford, Wynter, xvii, xxi, 85n; rivalry with Adams, 87-88, 100-101, 102, 107, 124, 146, 188

Cricket: in Barbados, 28-29; clubs, 29-32; Lewis' involvement in, 28-32

Cummins, Dr H.G., 138, 144, 153, 163; photo of, 154

Daniel, Rudolph, xvii; on freemasonry, 45, 47-48, 49; on Lewis, 34-35

Deane Commission, 57

Democratic Labour Party (DLP), xvi, xvii, xxiii, 18, 84n, 87, 161, 162, 165, 166, 168-181

Democratic League, 57, 59-60, 65, 84n, 92

Dowding, Herbert, xvii; on the BEA, 61, 63; on TT Lewis, 73, 165

Drax Hall plantation, 1, 2, 12, 19, 21n, 22n

Edghill, Evelyn "Bunghee", xvii, 10-11

Education: free secondary, 69, 92-96, 155, 174-176; Mitchinson report on, 93; of whites, 92-93

Education Commission (1875), 93

Elections: in 1942, 64-74, 84n; in 1944, 87-92; in 1946, 98-102; in 1948, 124-126; in 1951, 156-158; in 1956, 170-172

Index

Election results: in diagram form – (1942), 71; (1944), 90; (1946), 100; (1948), 125; (1951), 158; (1956), 171; in map form – (1942), 197; (1944), 198; (1946), 199; (1948), 200; (1951), 201; (1956), 202

Election process: in Barbados, 65

Emmanuel, Patrick, 58, 84n, 85n, 181n

Empire Cricket Club, 29, 49

Empire Theatre, 27

Evelyn, George Birt, 74

Faria, Norman, 167n

Federal elections (1958), 18, 172-173, 181n

Foster, D.A.: photo of, 154

Foster, Elsie, xvii, 14

Foster, Mike, xvii, 28

Franchise reform, xxi, 3, 65, 69-74, 84n, 89, 90, 155, 156, 158

Freemasonry: in Barbados, 46-54; discussion on, 43-46

Gale, Trevor, xviii, 15; on Lewis, 25, 66, 80, 81

Gittens, Stanton: on Lewis, 30

Goddard, Fred, 179, 181n

Greaves, George C., 41n

Herald, 81

Hinds, Tony, xviii; on Lewis, 30, 66, 185

Holder, Gladstone, xviii; on Lewis demonstration, 138-139

Hoyos, Alexander, xviii, xxiv, 156; on the 1946 election, 102; on the BCU, 112-113, 115; on the BEA, 62; and the BLP manifesto, 156-157; on Frank Collymore, 26-27; on labour conditions in the 1940s, 111; on Lewis, 16, 23n, 37, 64, 66, 103, 108n, 109n, 124; on Lewis demonstration, 138, 142, 148n; on the Liberal Association, 59-60; on the occupancy tax, 103; on split with BLP, 163-164

Hughes, Ronnie, xviii, 119, 205; on the class structure within white community, 118; on the Lewis demonstration 115; on Lewis as traitor to whites, 123; on Lewis' views on investment in South Africa, 159; on poor whites, 11

Hunte, Keith, on elections in Barbados, 65, 109n, 120n

Husbands, K.N.R.: first black Speaker of the House, 125; photo of, 154

Hutchinson, Cecil, xviii, on Lewis, 68

Jagan, Cheddi, 27

Jemmott, R. and Carter, D., 109n, 182n

Jordan, Cecil, 147, 178, 179

Karch, Cecilia, 22n

Kensington New Road, 4, 14-15, 24, 26, 66, 68

Kensington Oval, 29

King, A.R.E. "Bob", xviii, 123

Knight, Stephen, 52, 56n

Labour: and the Contract Act (1840), 7; conditions in the 1940s, 111-112; conflict in, 88-89; growth of, 91; Lewis as agitator for, 122; and Lewis demonstration, 136-148

Lansbury, George, 79, 85n

Laski, Harold, as influence on Lewis, 81

Lawrence, Sonya *See* Lewis, Sonya

Lewis, Diana (TT's daughter), 39, 178-179

Lewis, Emily Ethel Elise (TT's mother), 1, 15, 18, 26, 40

Lewis, Eyre (TT's brother), 3, 14, 15, 16, 40

Lewis, G.K., xxvi, 148n, 167n

Lewis, Henry "Harry" (TT's father), 1-4, 12, 13, 15, 21n

Lewis, Marjorie (TT's wife), 37-41, 178, 180; TT's letters to, 125, 128-129, 134, 141, 144, 147

211

Index

Lewis, Sonya (TT's daughter), xviii, 38, 41, 178-179, 180

Lewis, TT, xxii-xxiv; assessment of, 156, 183-189; birth of, 1-3; and the BCU 110-121; and the BEA, 60-64; and the Barbados Liberal Association, 59-60; and the BLP, 149-166, break with BLP, 160-166, 168; and the BVF, 33-35; and censorship, 74-75; with Central Agency, 126-135; and Central Agency settlement, 143-146; and Congress Party, 87-110; and cricket, 27-32; death of, 180-181; and the DLP, 168-181; demonstration, 136-148; as deputy speaker of the House, 153-156; dismissal from Central Agency, 128-136; education, 18-19; employment, 15, and free secondary education; *see also* Education; final years, 177-181; formative years, 24-41; and franchise reform, 69-74; health of, 170-171; involvement in freemasonry, 43-54; and labour, 122-123; and literary societies, 36-37; and marriage, 37-42; and nurses, 40, 42n; and occupancy tax, 103-106, 154-155; in opposition, 176-177; philosophical influences, 80-83; relationship with family, 15-18, 26, 40; and remuneration for government members, 149-151; and theatre, 27-28; traitor to whites, 123-124, 186-187; and war effort, 75-79; and West Indies Federation, 172-173

Lightermen, 67, 140

Literary societies: in Barbados, 36-37

Long, Frank, 135n

Lowy, M., 86n

Mandel, Ernst, 86n

Mapp, Ronald, xviii, 157, 162, 163

Mark, Francis, 120n

Marriott-Mayhew Commission (1932), 94

Marshall, G. Vernon, xviii, 92, 142

Marxist analysis: limitations of, 19-20, 119-120

McCarthyism in Barbados, 161

Medford, Shirland "Hawk", xviii, 129

Miller, Freddie, 154, 172; and Lewis demonstration, 141, 143

Miller, "Tommy", 171

Mitchinson report on education, 93

Montego Bay conference (1947), 152, 172

Mottley, E. D., 63, 171; and free secondary education, 95-96; and vestry system, 96-98, 101, 102, 105-106

Moyne Commission (1938), 67-68, 86n, 94

Nazism, 75, 77, 78

Newton, Earle, 109n

Occupancy tax, 69, 92, 103-106, 153, 155, 186

O'Neal, Charles Duncan: as founder of Democratic League, 57, 59, 65, 84n, 92

Outlook, 81

Overseers: as members of a class, 9-14, 23

Overseers' Association, 10, 13

Panama money, 8, 22n

Party politics: development of, 91

Perryman, Marjorie *See* Lewis, Marjorie

Phillips, Anthony, 84n

Pickwick Cricket Club, 29, 30, 31, 49

Plantations: social hierarchy of, 12-14

Plumps, 65

Political development: Barbados, 7, 57-84, 91

Pool plantation, 2, 12, 19

Popper, Karl, 85n

Prescod, Samuel Jackman, 68, 70

Primrose League, 75

Progressive Conservative Party (PCP), xvii, 60, 61, 84n, 98, 171

Race relations *See* Barbados

Ramsay, J.T.C., 70

Redlegs, 9, 121

Reece, W.W.: photo of, 154

Representation of the People Act (1901), 3

Research process of author, xxii-xxvii

Index

Revenue Equalization Debate, 158-160, 176
Richardson, Bonham, 22n
Riots: in Barbados, xxi, 21, 32-35, 66, 69, 152
Roberts, Aubrey, xviii; on Lewis, 52
Robinson, E.S.: on franchise reform, 72
Rogers, H.N. "Turk", xviii, 147, 148, 179
Ross, P.M., 55n, 56n
Russell, Bertrand: as influence on Lewis, 80

Sandiford, Keith, 29, 41n
Schapiro, Leonard, 86n
Second World War, 74-80
Sergeant, Dudley, 154
Shaw, George Bernard: as influence on Lewis, 80
Sinckler, G. Goulburn, 205
Small, Lawrence, xviii, 111; on Lewis demonstration, 141-142; on Lewis' dismissal from Central Agency, 134
Smith, Christie, xviii, 113, 116; on Lewis, 39, 97; on Lewis demonstration, 142; on Lewis' dismissal from Central Agency, 132-133; on Mottley and Occupancy Tax, 106
Smith, Frederick, xix, 162, 169; on Lewis, 184
Smith, L.E. "Boychild": photo of, 154
Smitten, Kathleen, xix, 25-26
Snipers, 112, 113
South Africa: and apartheid, 58; and the revenue equalization debate, 159
Soviet Union (and the Red Army), 76, 77, 78
Spartan Cricket Club, 20, 29, 30, 49
Springer, Hugh, xix, 102, 108; on cricket, 30; on franchise reform, 72; on Lewis, 130, 184, 185; on literary societies, 36; on the Soviet war effort, 78
St Anne's Cricket Club, 31, 49
St John, Vincent, 112
St Mary's school, 18
Stoute, Edward: on poor whites, 121n

Talma, Edwy, 18, 107, 173, 188; on Occupancy Tax, 106; photo of, 163
Theatre, 26-28
Thomas, Charlie, 101, 112
Thomas, Lisle, 154
Tolstoy, Leo, xxiv
Torch, The, 160
Trade Union Act, 66
Trotsky, Leon: as influence on Lewis, 80-81
Tudor, James Cameron, xix, 18, 22n, 162, 173, 180, 181n; and the 1951 election, 157; on the BPL, 89; on E.K. Walcott, 152; on free secondary education, 175, 176; on Lewis, 51, 53, 83, 97, 107, 153, 176, 177, 186; on Lewis' dismissal from Central Agency, 134; on the Liberal Association, 59; in opposition, 176-177; on revenue equalization, 159; split with BLP, 164-165
Twelfth seat issue, 108, 124

Vanguard, The, 74
Vaughan, Hilton, 36, 59-60, 68
Vestries Act (1911), 104, 153
Vestry system, 96-98, 104-105
Victoria Lodge *See* Freemasonry
Voting: system in Barbados, 7-8; registration list for, 22n

Walcott, E.K., 63, 133, 141, 145, 151-153; on remuneration for government members, 149-150
Walcott, Frank, xix, 89, 113, 132, 137, 138, 153, 154, 156, 161, 166; on the BCU, 113-115; on Lewis, 187; on Lewis demonstration, 139; and split with the BLP, 166
Wanderers Cricket Club, 29, 30, 31
Ward, E.L.: photo of, 154
Warner, J. Jabez: as freemason, 48
Weatherhead, Noel, xix, 181
West Indian National Congress Party *See* Congress Party
West Indies Federation, 172-173

213

Index

Whites: attitudes of, 7; control of land by, 6; education of, 92-93; erosion of power of, 58; low income, 4, 5, 119; planter class, 22n, 204-205; social stratification among, 9-14, 30, 32, 118-121

Wickham, Clennel, xix, 81, 181; on Barbadian white elite, 7

Wickham, John, xix; on conservatives, 63-64; on Lewis, 184; on occupancy tax, 103

Wiles, Donald, xix, 40; death of, 180, and free secondary education, 175; on Lewis, 24, 153

Wilkinson, J.H.: photo of, 154

Williams, Lorenzo, 161, 162

World War II, *See* Second World War

Young Men's Christian Association (YMCA), 36, 111

Young Men's Progressive Club (YMPC), 30, 32, 35

Younglao, Constance (*neé* Perryman), xix; on Lewis, 16, 37, 38, 180

www.ingramcontent.com/pod-product-compliance
Lightning Source LLC
Chambersburg PA
CBHW051521230426
43668CB00012B/1686